Wired For Sound

by Sammy Jones

With special thanks to

Marshall Amplification

Cover art & illustration by Luke McDonnell

With thanks to Jon Ellery, Jeff Oates, David Langfield, Pete Winkelman, Jane Russell, Nikki Bloomer, Duncan Jackson, Ben Raza, David Jackson

A big 'thank you' to everyone who has trawled through their photo archives or shared their memories, and to all the musicians, promoters and fans who contributed

Every effort has been made to identify photographers
If we missed anyone, we apologise

Additional images: MK Citizen, MK Gazette, MK Mirror archives

Freaky Publishing

wiredforsoundmk@gmail.com

First published in November 2020

Printed by BCQ, Buckingham

Milton Keynes
Wired For Sound

I remember seeing Showaddywaddy in Bletchley shortly before I turned five years old and, although I didn't realise it at the time, that must have been the start of my love affair with music.

I probably owe those teddy boy types in their coats of many colours a few words of thanks.

In my pre-teen years I was a regular visitor to the local branch of Woolworths buying up packs of TDK tapes, ready to record the week's Top 40 chart countdown.

But it was a short time later, when I discovered a quartet of rockers hidden under the cover of make-up and was struck by their songs including Cold Gin and Strutter, that everything changed for me.

Rock 'n' roll had gained a new disciple, and I was hooked.

Bands like Kiss and Guns N' Roses were my proper gateway into music, and it was a voyage of no return.

My exposure to new bands came from the music magazines I read from cover to cover, and as a teenager with a voracious appetite for sounds, I would tape the Radio 1 Rock Show (still using those TDK tapes), record late night music programmes and take in as many live shows as I

could. Living in Milton Keynes, music venues The Pitz and The Countapoint became hugely important, and allowed me to further explore thrash, metal and punk.

The Pitz was a haven for bands working the national circuit, and quickly became a second home.

I would watch an AOR band one night and a death metal mob the next, and I loved it all.

I don't remember when I decided that I wanted to be a music journalist, but I do know that I didn't 'just' want to be one of the audience at a gig.

I wanted to know the story behind the song, and I wanted to know what made the band tick.

I wanted to be involved. I signed up to every mailing list on every merchandise stall, and promotional postcards would be delivered by the postman (imagine that!) sharing the latest single release news and tour dates.

At school, I used any opportunity to shoehorn music into coursework – and once completed a sociology project on censorship in the industry, interviewing Napalm Death. Obviously.

I started a fanzine and used to head through the school gates early every morning to use the one word processor in our classroom to type up my ramblings.

Life as a music journalist would let me dig beneath the surface of the bands I loved and it meant I'd get a great record collection too.

I banged on the doors of every local newspaper (there were a few then), begging for work experience and the chance to get my words into print.

I was soon providing snippets to papers in and around Milton Keynes, Bedford and Northampton, and later graduated to working for many of the national rock music titles.

It is a career that is seldom as glamorous as you might think, but I've had some amazing times, and my memory bank is overflowing with cool stuff.

Along the way I've made lifelong friendships that were fostered through a shared love of music, and have been privileged to interview those who were heroes to the teenage me - including Kiss and Guns N' Roses.

I spent nearly two decades as the music editor for a newspaper in Milton Keynes.

That job gave me access to those who were there at the dawn of rock 'n' roll, and the new artists making waves today, and it was clear that Milton Keynes had a musical past to be proud of.

Recording it seemed obvious.

Wired For Sound explores the history of some of our homegrown musicians, and delves into the past of those who moved here and made the new town a haven for music-makers and fans.

Wired For Sound also looks at the venues, new and old, and talks with some of the giants of music who have plugged in and wowed in Milton Keynes. It has been a while in the making, and certainly isn't exhaustive, but hopefully these pages will shake awake some of the memories from the past, and keep the history alive.

Sammy Jones

Contents

Marshall Amplification

His name has been on more stages than any rock idol and his products have powered bands for decades. This is the true story of a real rock icon.

Behind every great guitarist, you will find a great Marshall Amp. Rock music's finest musicians swear by them. Jimi Hendrix was wowed by the Marshall brand, along with Pete Townshend, Jeff Beck, Jimmy Page, and Slash, and so many more.

Jim Marshall's name takes centre stage all over the world, from the buzz of the small clubs to the roar of the stadia.

But his early years showed no glimmer of the impact he would have on the world of music.

Jim Marshall spent much of his childhood in a hospital bed, before taking up tap-dancing and singing.

His work ethic showed itself early on, and as a teenager he would regularly labour for 16-hours a day.

It was hard work that paid off, and the business he founded, Marshall Amplification, would become world famous.

Jim was born in London, on July 29, 1923, to Beatrice and Jim Marshall.

The first of seven children, Jim's early years were far from great.

He suffered with tubercular bones, and from the age of five was in plaster cast, spending seven long years in hospital. But his uncle, a teacher, taught Jim basic skills.

"When I came out of hospital, I couldn't go to school right away, and didn't end up going until I was nearly 14.

"When I did, because of my age, I was placed in the top class, and I hadn't got a clue what they were talking about!"

Jim's father managed a fish and chip shop in Southall, West London, and Jim pleaded to be allowed to give up his school studies to work at the shop.

Eventually, his father gave in.

Jim recalled: "He said 'Alright', but only if I agreed to learn tap dancing too, because he thought that would help to strengthen my legs. And he was right."

As the only boy in a class full of girls, his tutor wondered quite what to do with him. But she had heard Jim sing, and decided he would do the 'Fred Astaire thing' - he

A star is born: On his mother's knee, and left, Jim behind the drum kit

would sing and dance.

At a performance for parents, Jim's talent was discovered. A grandfather of one of the girls in the troupe was in the audience and was quite struck by the boy Marshall. He also happened to be the leader of an orchestra.

An audition was arranged, which Jim never forgot: "When I had finished auditioning, I heard 'Marshall!' and thought 'Oh God, what did I do wrong?'

"So I walked across the stage a bit sheepishly and he asked, 'What are you afraid of son?'

"I said I didn't know if I had performed all right, or made any mistakes.

"'No,' he said, 'You can start regularly with me from Monday.'

"From then on, I was singing at five or six engagements a week. I was 14 years old."

Witnessing his father's financial struggle was the motivation needed for Jim to make a success of himself.

"There were times when my father was out of work for 18 months or so, and I decided I was definitely not going to be stuck like that," he said.

"As I had no formal education I thought the only thing I could try and do would be to work a lot more hours, and I did – I existed on four hours sleep a night.

"I used to go in to work at 4 o'clock in the morning, filling milk bottles.

"At 8 o'clock I was in a jam factory, and at night-time I was singing with the band."

Eventually, Jim swapped the Big Band sound in favour of a jazz collective.

"It was more money," he says simply.

During the war Jim worked in engineering, but when the conflict ended, he returned to his love of music and turned professional.

It wasn't only his singing voice that separated him from the pack though, and he soon became a more than proficient drummer too.

So good in fact, that he was badgered into giving lessons.

It was a decision he thought he would regret, but actually, he found he loved sharing his skills.

When one pupil wanted to learn rock 'n' roll drumming, Jim duly obliged. That pupil was Micky Waller, and he took his newfound knowledge to good places: "He became the drummer with Little Richard, then Rod Stewart, Jeff Beck…"

In 1953, Jim opened a drum school in Southall, and, as with everything else he turned his hand to, he set about the task with absolute dedication – teaching 64 pupils for an hour every week.

His recently launched retail business was flourishing by this point too, and it was drum kits that occupied most of the

J & T. MARSHALL
MUSICAL INSTRUMENTS LTD.

Talking shop: Jim (left) outside his first store with Screaming Lord Sutch (second left)

floor space. They proved particularly alluring to one youngster, whose name was John Mitchell: "I'd just finished teaching and was walking back to the shop which my son was looking after at the time," said Jim.

"I could hear this racket going on and saw this kid sitting behind the drum kit I had put in the shop window the same morning, a brand new one, and he was knocking hell out of it.

"Anyway, the boy slid off the kit and walked out the shop," Jim recalled.

"A few days later he came in and said 'Mum says I have to apologise and if I caused any damage she said she's going to pay for it.'

"I told him to forget about it, although I had to replace the hoof and all the skins and it cost me quite a bit of money.

"He said 'You need a Saturday boy, don't you?' He became the shop boy and finally asked me to teach him properly...

he went on to be the drummer for Jimi Hendrix - Mitch Mitchell!"

Regular clients at the store included Pete Townshend, renowned session player Big Jim Sullivan, and Ritchie Blackmore.

"They said if I would stock guitars and amplifiers too, they would buy from me instead of going elsewhere."

Jim tried new lines and the stock shifted with haste. He had found his place in the market.

But the seeds of Marshall Amplification still hadn't been sown. That would happen soon after, and change everything.

"The same type of people were coming back to me and saying 'The amplifiers aren't built for our type of music. Will you have a go at it, Jim?'"

At the time, the West End was still a market thriving on orchestral and jazz musicians.

Rock 'n' roll wasn't looked upon with favour, and purveyors of the 'noise' were

treated with a certain amount of disdain.

Jim took on the challenge and looked to Ken Bran, at the time working as his shop repair man, to produce a rock 'n' roll beast of an amp. It has been said that some of the very first amps used valves taken from old Spitfire plane dashboards!

The sixth prototype was the one that hit the shop floor.

The cabinet-less chassis was an instant hit, shifting an incredible 23 units in the first day.

Today, you will find that first creation displayed in the Marshall museum at the company's Bletchley headquarters.

That first amp sold in 1962, and within four years the Marshall sound had become the 'noise' of choice.

The brand has given definition, oomph and sheer power to musicians all over the world.

Unsurprisingly, Jim formed lasting friendships with many of the musicians who favoured his products.

But who left Jim with the fondest memories?

"It has to be Hendrix. He was my biggest ambassador worldwide," Jim told me, "Jimi had been playing at Ronnie Scott's in London's West End, and the group on stage before him had used Marshall. Jimi said: 'I'd like to get some of this amplification. It sounds a lot better than what I'm using,' adding, 'I want to meet this character who has the same name as me.'

"So he was brought to see me at the shop, this tall lanky American, and he says to me: 'I'm gonna be the greatest,' and I thought 'Oh Christ – another American wanting something for nothing!

"But, almost in the next breath, he said: 'I don't want anything given to me. I'll pay the retail price.'

"That was very unusual, because all of the top groups would come in and say, 'I want this and this and this...what discount do I get?'

"Hendrix bought four complete stage set-ups to have in different parts of the world, so that he wouldn't have to transport the goods in.

"He said he wanted support for repairs or whatever, wherever he was in the world," Jim recalled.

"I thought I was going to need a technician on the road with him all the time.

"As it turned out, I think his roadie spent six weeks at the factory learning basic repairs, and we were never called out once!"

When Jim was unable to renew the lease on his London premises, he was told to look for a new working home in Corby.

But Jim recalled Stony Stratford from his days on the road touring with the band, and made tracks to the area.

On the beat: Jim in his first shop

With Zakk Wylde

Collecting his OBE

Jim with the first amplifier, Number One

Receiving the Freedom of the Borough (left)

He eventually found Bletchley, and stumbled upon one remaining unit available for rent that was perfect for his expanding empire.

A couple of weeks later and Marshall was settling into its first Bletchley premises, on the Lyon Road, before moving to First Avenue.

Nearly half a century on, and Marshall remains rooted in the area, now on Denbigh Road, with a staff force of 160.

It is the coolest brand for miles around.

Jim received an OBE in 2004: "When Jim told us, we all laughed because when we asked dad as young kids what OBE stood for, he immediately replied 'Old Big 'Ead,'" recalled Jim's brother Al.

"To think his son would become one would never have crossed his mind, but he and mum would have been so proud!"

A self-confessed workaholic, Jim was still putting in 10-hour days when he was 80 years old.

A holiday? Jim didn't 'do' those: "I took a holiday in 1948," he answered when asked about getting away from it all.

And how did the man who helped power rock 'n' roll spend what little spare time he had?

He used to make bird boxes for his friends.

Somewhere, feathered-types will be benefitting from Jim's craftsmanship, nesting in the best homes around!

Jim's contribution to the industry is immeasurable, but he didn't just give volume to music makers. Incredibly generous, he was a member of the exclusive and oldest show business charity, the Grand Order Of Water Rats. He also gave back to his adopted area, donating vast sums of money to charity in Milton Keynes.

There is a reason why the main hall of The Stables music venue is called The Jim Marshall Auditorium, of course.

Kerry King: 'Jim Marshall was the ultimate rock star'

And in 2003, he presented Macmillan Cancer Care and Willen Hospice with a gift totalling £1 million.

It might have been his biggest charitable donation, but there had been numerous others: "It's the best thing I can do, and I enjoy seeing people's faces. It makes you feel good," he said of that giving nature.

"I came from a very poor family, we had hard times and I don't forget my roots..."

Jim passed away at Willen Hospice on April 5, 2012, aged 88.

Musicians - from bedroom players to those who occupy the world stages - were vocal in their tributes, and the biggest rock music festival in the country, Download at Donington Park, honoured him by dedicating the main stage to 'The Father of Loud.'

"The music industry lost an innovator and a legend with the sad passing of Jim Marshall," promoter Andy Copping said.

"We had to remember him in some way and having the main stage dedicated to his name seemed the perfect tribute."

Later the same year, on September 22, 2012, musicians and fans gathered at Wembley Arena to plug in the amps and give Jim the most fitting tribute possible - by playing loud!

Artists playing their respects included members of Iron Maiden, Whitesnake, Slayer, The Cult, Slipknot, Judas Priest and Chickenfoot. A stellar line-up for a man who helped change the face of music.

"Beyond doubt, Jim Marshall and the team have shaped the sound of rock music for eternity," said Iron Maiden drummer and long-time friend Nicko McBrain, and it was a fact echoed by Slayer guitarist Kerry King.

"If I stand in front of my rig, if my nuts ain't shaking then I ain't satisfied...and the only stuff that can do that is my Marshall!" he said.

"To me Jim Marshall was the ultimate rock star because he and his team made us all sound better."

Marshall Amplification - Take their word for it

"Jim was the basis of the style of so many musicians.

I went to his shop before he started making the amplifiers and I wanted to buy a PA.

It was quite expensive and I didn't have the money. I wanted to get a hire purchase agreement, and he said 'No, no, no – you will end up paying three times as much for the thing, and that will only be going into a profit for the bank and won't be doing you, or the manufacturers any good. I've got a little black book here - pay me 10 shillings a week,' he said.

'Come in and give it to me on a Saturday morning, and if you can't, don't stay away - don't let me down. Come in anyway, and say 'I didn't have any gigs this week, I'm broke,' and I will try and find you some gigs, because we get a lot of promoters in here as well.'

When I used to live in the area, we used to go and lunch together quite a lot.

He did a good lunch, did Jim. A very liquid lunch! I brought that story up some 30 years later when I was having lunch with him and I said 'What you did was unbelievable, Jim, and I know you did the same for a lot of others too... did anybody not pay you?'

'I've still got that book, actually,' he said, '...and not one person failed to pay the whole amount.

Everybody paid up eventually.'

He was absolutely fantastic. Without Marshall, where would we all be now?"
Ian Gillan, Deep Purple

"Growing up as a kid, all the guys I ever knew – Jimi Hendrix, Eddie Van Halen, Jimmy Page, Randy Rhoads and any of the countless bands that you would see, all had a Marshall backline.

It was always a Marshall that was behind the guy who was playing.

There is a reason why people use them. It's because they work."
Zakk Wylde, Black Label Society/Ozzy Osbourne Band

"I love Marshall and I always have, and I have been using them since I was 19 years old.

To me, they are the premier amplifier in the world, without a doubt.

One of the reasons is that I have a myriad of different kinds of guitar and no matter which one I plug into the Marshall head, they all sound brilliant.

Marshall is the quintessential British amplifier that crept its way over to America with the likes of Pagey, Hendrix, Clapton and everyone else that was using them.

They are just a great company."
Richie Sambora, ex-Bon Jovi

"I love the company, and Jim was a very down-to-earth gentleman.

The fact that he was not some long-haired rock 'n' roll guy, together with the passion of sincerity that he had, was rock 'n' roll.

He was one of the most important guys."
Slash, Guns N' Roses

"We've used Marshall's for centuries. They are very loud. If Jeff Beck is playing through one, it is the sweetest thing on the planet, and if me or Rick are playing through one, then Jesus Christ they hurt!

The main thing about Marshall is that it's a fabulous British success story, and everyone around the world wants one. There is just something about them."
Francis Rossi, Status Quo

"Every time we plug in and make people smile, we owe him debt beyond counting!"
Joe Perry, Aerosmith

"We used to go to his Uxbridge shop and used to play at a place along the road called Burton's Ballroom - it was a Burton's clothes shop with a ballroom over the top. There were quite a few of those.

Because he was an engineer he used to be able to make a part for you in the same afternoon, otherwise you'd be sending off to America or somewhere.

At the same time as Marshall there were Vox and Fender. Jim was a big friend of Leo Fender and they used to gig in America, with Jim on drums...and Les Paul, they were the legends and they were all friends.

We took Jim's first amplifier to try out, very successfully as it happened, and

carried on from there."
Brian Poole, The Tremeloes

"If you listen to original rock 'n' roll, it was exciting, but it wasn't loud...when Jim came along with his Marshall Amps, quite frankly the whole thing changed.

We had some real rubbish before Jim produced the amps. Real crap!

Jim made an enormous contribution to rock 'n roll, I can't say enough about that. His amps are *the* amps.

Everybody in the business owes him so much, because he made rock 'n' roll loud, and apart from making the best amplifiers in the world, he was a genuine guy, a gentleman, a lovely man."
Joe Brown

A rock 'n' roll icon meets his fans: Jim with former Bon Jovi guitarist Richie Sambora (top) and below (left) with Slash from Guns N' Roses and (right) with Joe Brown

Turning up the volume: Marshall Amplification managing director Jon Ellery

Jim Marshall was a visionary, and an astute businessman.

He took an idea and turned the product into the brand of choice for music makers the world over.

As the brand approaches its 60th anniversary, the Marshall Amplifier is synonymous with rock 'n' roll.

Jim is no longer with us, but he made sure that the man charged with seeing the company through turbulent times and into a new era, would safeguard the brand.

Jon Ellery has spent more than 25 years in the Marshall fold; he started as an IT manager and learned from the man at the top as he progressed through the ranks; as a junior director, a board member director and eventually as managing director.

"I worked very closely with Jim on a number of things, and learned his understanding of what he wanted from the company, why he started the company and what drove him as an individual.

"It was always one thing – his love of music. That was his passion.

"You could never disassociate Jim Marshall, the person, from Marshall the

> **"I want to make Milton Keynes an intrinsic hub for music"**

company, it was intrinsic. I have always said I will continue the company in Jim's name, it will always be about Jim and what he wanted to create."

Jon has successfully taken Marshall Amplification into the 21st century. His stewardship has allowed the company to sail choppy industry waters with ease, and he has steered the company into calmer times.

"The biggest thing I learned from Jim was making sure the company is in a good financial, position.

"We are not beholden to anybody, so if there are changes in fortunes in the industry, which can happen, we can quickly react and make sure the company remains stable.

"Jim always wanted to know what was going on, and if there was a problem, he needed to know about it. He needed to know of new products. He was a believer that you can only deal with the information you are given, and he was never frightened to get stuck in.

"In the early days he would roll his sleeves up and go on production, and show people how things should be done.

Working in partnership: Jon with MK Dons Chairman Pete Winkelman

"Jim always liked to be in the factory first too – at 6 o'clock in the morning, irrespective of if he had been working until 10pm at night!"

Jim's wisdom still helps shape the company today.

"He used to say 'Never employ someone who thinks they know everything, because they will never learn,' and as a company we listen to the artist and what they want - we never assume what they want. I can't think of anything we've done that Jim wouldn't be proud to see his name on."

In 2016 the Marshall Records label was launched. It's a perfect fit for the brand.

"We are selling everything you need to create music, listen to music and enjoy music. That's what Jim was all about – when he started he was a tap dancer, he ran a music shop, he sold musical equipment..."

A short stroll from the Marshall HQ takes you to the Marshall Arena, where music fans can get their live music fix. It is the first step in a new vision for Jim's successor. The first large scale concert at the 4000 capacity venue was hosted in November 2018 when Black Eyed Peas wrapped up their UK tour there.

"I want to make Milton Keynes an intrinsic hub for music. I want bands to think of MK as being on the same circuit as London, Birmingham, Manchester and Leeds, which is one of the reasons we did the arena. Milton Keynes now has the Marshall Arena, Stadium MK and The Bowl. It's a hub for any event.

"For some bizarre reason MK has been overlooked. I don't know why, and I think it's the duty of everybody, and every business in Milton Keynes, to promote it. The best way we can do that is by bringing music here.

"We're going to cause some trouble!"

Linford Manor studio

"I could see this guy asleep under a tree. As I got closer, I realised it was Jay Kay, who'd had a hell of a night before!"

The present Manor house at Great Linford is a jewel in the crown of the park in which it elegantly stands, and a jewel in the new city of Milton Keynes which has grown up around it.

Great Linford's earlier medieval Manor house was purchased from Sir Richard Napier by Sir William Pritchard in the late seventeenth century.

Sir William – who held the position of Lord Mayor of London in 1682 – had the original Manor demolished and the present one erected on the opposite side of the street. Work was finished in 1690.

When he died, Sir William was returned to Great Linford from his city residence, and his remains interred in St Andrews Church, a mere moment away from the house for which he clearly had quite an affection.

The house passed to relatives, and remained with the Uthwatt family for centuries.

Its full history is for another book, but it is an evocative, engaging and handsome home.

Milton Keynes Development Corporation bought the Manor from Stella Uthwatt in 1972.

In May 1981, following large renovation works at a suitably large cost, the Manor was announced to the town as Great Linford Arts Centre, a place for all.

And so it would seem to be; in 1982 a sculpture exhibition commanded use of the house and grounds and featured works by renowned sculptors including Henry Moore and Barbara Hepworth.

Art and craft courses, performance events, and a shop and bar all helped to make the area a hub for creativity.

But in 1984, less than three years after it was opened to become the focal point of arts in the town, its closure was announced, with Milton Keynes Development Corporation ceasing financial support.

The curtain fell on March 31, 1984.

'Good food at sensible prices'
- 1982 advertisements

Lord Campbell of Eskan, president of the trustees and leader of MK Development Corporation told the Citizen newspaper he was heartbroken.

"The centre is a newborn babe and hasn't had time to grow. I feel desperately sad and I am deeply disappointed."

Lord Campbell called the Manor 'staggeringly beautiful' and said the closure was 'a tragedy,' but the £60,000 cash injection needed annually was simply too much.

"The corporation bought what is certainly the most distinguished house in Milton Keynes and made it a very successful arts centre. But they are unpalatable costs and it would be folly to go on building up debts."

In an earlier publicity brochure for the venture, he said: "We are aiming to make something special at Great Linford, a creative centre to which people will really want to come."

While that didn't prove to be the case at that time, his words were truer than he could have imagined; music would get the Manor out of the doldrums soon enough.

Pete Winkelman is the passionate football fan with a business brain as sharp as the best of them, and he achieved the almost impossible when he brought top-flight football to Milton Keynes.

But Pete's past was less about the game of two halves and significantly more about the vinyl and its two sides, as he had established a lengthy career in the music industry before football won him over.

Having worked at an executive level with record labels including EMI, Sony and Time Warner, Pete, who had also established rock music magazine Raw in the late 1980s, and his wife Berni arrived at Great Linford Manor in 1993.

They had two young children and plenty of Winkelman ambition for the 17th century house...

The Manor had already proven itself as a stunning recording facility, thanks to the vision of another music industry operator, the late Harry Maloney, who had taken over the building following the closure of the arts centre.

Harry invited London-based singer Jim Price to move to Milton Keynes to help set the studio up.

"I thought it sounded sexy," Jim recalled,

"A week later I was nailing down squeaky floorboards in the guitar room...

"Once the room was complete, he needed it to be run-in, so I recorded some songs with Richard Digby Smith producing. I used to spend days in the big live room. It had a full size Yamaha grand piano in it. Awesome sound..."

Under Harry's guise, the Manor became one of the first residential studios in the country to invest in digital equipment, and the bands started coming.

John Lydon's post Sex Pistols concern PiL, Del Amitri, and rockers Thunder were among the many who came through the doors.

Harry, whose other musical endeavours included managing Manfred Mann's Earth Band, drove the recording venture between 1986 and 1992, until the Manor became a casualty of the recession and was put into administration.

At the same time, Pete was seeking a new studio. He already had Music Station facilities in London and Birmingham.

"We wanted to move those into the 'musically better' studio of Linford Manor where the plan was to continue in the same vein as in the previous few years – making records, signing bands, and licensing them to major labels. We arrived in Milton Keynes in 1993, and the first thing we held here was the official bash for Metallica's gig at the National Bowl," Pete said, "It was a great do, we had MTV come along, and a police escort to take the groups to the venue. It really was razzamatazz with some big industry types in attendance...

"That was my introduction to Milton Keynes and the Manor, and I loved it.

"For someone like me who had been very, very honed in the music business and didn't even know who my neighbours were in London, it was a chance to get involved in the city," Pete said.

"Slowly over 1994 and 1995, we started to become like a commercial company.

"The first big hit we had from a third party client was Babylon Zoo with Spaceman.

"It was an absolutely fantastic track, and he was an incredibly talented, mad artist who probably couldn't focus that creativity into just his music and so sadly never really had the career he could have had.

"But the track is still a monumental first No.1 for the studio...

"We were very fortunate, we had some great equipment, including our vintage Neve desk.

"Our ears are analogue, we are in an analogue world. I loved the sounds.

"One of the best sessions was Jay Kay and Jamiroquai, who chose the Manor to record their third album Travelling Without Moving, in 1996.

> **"The first thing we held here was the official bash for Metallica's gig at The National Bowl"**

Manor moments: The Manor has been home to a Lord Mayor, an arts centre and a recording studio

ALL ABOARD FOR THE MAGIC LANTERN SHOW!

By DICK RIND

MUPPET creator Jim Henson, magician Paul Daniels and comedian Kenny Everett are all fans of Doug and Anita Lear's Magic Lantern Narrowboat Theatre.

And in June, after five years of travelling the canals in Britain with their touring show, the Lear family is to settle in Milton Keynes.

Their narrowboats will be moored in the grounds of Great Linford Manor and will form an integral part of the arts complex. The theatre is a throwback to Victorian days – a kind of floating Tardis. The couple use dissolving views, animated pictures and include demonstrations of a hand cranked cinematograph.

All the equipment is original and dates from between 1800 and 1909. The picture show is accompanied by live music on the harmonium, piano harp or American organ.

'Backstage' looks like a jumble of cymbals, whistles, keyboards, slides and ornate, ancient projectors — but Doug and Anita know where everything is.

The couple, who have two sons Elwyn (8) and Merlyn (3), started their wandering round the canals of Britain in 1976 and since then have done more than 3,000 shows.

They have had invitations to do performances in Madrid, Paris, New York and Stockholm, and plan to do more outside shows when they have made their base in Milton Keynes.

For three years Little Venice in London has been their main port of call but they have grown disillusioned with the city, and are also up against strong competition from the theatres in the West End.

Their shows cater for all ages — from three to 93 their brochure suggests — and include Mechanical Movement which is their first show, featuring Storm at Sea, Artificial Fireworks, The Four Seasons, Circus Clowns and the film The Lumière Programme.

Natural Magic is a more recent show with strange effects, the Projection Microscope, Natural Phenomena, The Incredible Polariscope and Journey they call the Moon and two Metéore films.

The Super Short Show is compiled specially for children and lasts or just over an hour.

Apart from the children's show, most performances are at 8 pm and coffee or squash and biscuits are included in the admission price. One seat in eight is free to encourage block bookings, and normally 29 seats are available.

Both Anita and Doug hold degrees and are Lecturers in Design.

"This was very much the beginning of cinema," Doug said. "There seems to be an impression that cinema just suddenly sprang up, but in fact it evolved over more than 100 years.

"For the people of the early 1800s the Magic Lantern Theatre was a very important form of entertainment. In 1844 our show would have cost 1/6d, the equivalent of a week's wages."

Many celebrities have called in to the Magic Lantern Theatre to soak up the Victorian drawing room atmosphere and the show has featured on programmes like Blue Peter and Nationwide and Collecting Now (BBC 2).

BASE: The Great Linford Manor Arts Centre.

Pete and Berni with Jim Marshall

Pete said: "At the time Jay was a semi-famous pop star and had a model girlfriend, so we had a photographer from the Daily Star newspaper down here hiding in the bushes, which gave us our first little taste of being somewhere that had media attention – it was great fun.

"One morning, I came downstairs, and when I looked out over the park I could see this guy, asleep under a tree.

"I was horrified – I thought 'We've got the press here, we've got a top pop band here and now people are sleeping rough in the park.' I could just see the headlines!

"But how was I going to go and move this person?

"I was really wracked with what to do and wandered outside to go and talk to the guy, and as I got closer, I realised it was Jay Kay, who'd had a hell of a night before!

"Jay could rock and roll with the best of them. I tell that story because normally when we had groups in they would get drunk one night and you wouldn't see them for three days.

"But that evening Jay was doing the video for Virtual Insanity, which went on to win an MTV Award.

"The point is that to be a success, you might have to party hard sometimes, but you can never let it deflect you from the work that you've got to do, and Jay's success wasn't a fluke. He was absolutely focused and knew what he wanted to create.

"The single Virtual Insanity was actually

> **"Whenever I hear a particular Skunk Anansie track, 'Boom' and I'm back in the studio"**

written towards the end of the session. We were in the front office, the loo is next door and we could hear Jay in there singing what would later turn out to be that track, before going in to the band and stopping the session.

"He said 'I've got this idea, I love it. I want to do this new track now.'

"Jay's talent was working very hard and knowing when he was on a creative curve and making sure that he was able to get that across to his band."

Unlike the vast majority of residential studios where the recording space would be tucked away in an outbuilding, the Manor studio was centred within the house itself, in the ballroom.

It meant that the music making was closer than in any other studio environments, and that if you were lucky enough to be in the house when a session was midflow you could really hear art being created.

Skunk Anansie arrived as unknown hopefuls, but left an indelible mark on Pete.

He said: "We didn't know who they were when they first came here, but they were a good rock band and Skin was a good singer.

"There was one particular track when Skin was doing her performance and I remember wandering down to the control room, which you didn't really go in very often – it was the group's space - but I found myself walking in there. Berni had

Skunk Anansie

come from another part of the house and arrived there.

"The assistant had left the producer to it, but he came back...and the drummer came down from the top of the house.

"Suddenly we realised that nearly everybody in the house was in the control room listening to Skin because her performance was just so remarkable – it had a magnetism to it.

"We've had other fantastically magic moments. I remember going to a big meeting about the MK Dons stadium plot.

"My gang and I had gone off to see how we were doing with the planning policy, which actually got adopted. It was a step in the right direction and we came back to the Manor in a fantastic mood.

"Anastacia was there at the time doing tour rehearsals and we all went into the ballroom and she gave us a half hour long performance.

"When music is so special, it captures moments and memories.

"Whenever I hear a particular Skunk Anansie track, 'Boom,' and I'm back in the studio. I listen to Jay Kay and 'Bam,' I am back watching him under that tree!

"But for all the great moments, there were some really difficult moments as well, because you are involved with, and living around, people's lives.

"Most of the time it is a creative hotbed, but some of the time it is a political nightmare – you've got the singer falling out with the guitarist and the producer stuck in the middle of it.

"Or you have the pressure of someone who has been successful trimming back and trying to make the next record just as successful.

"You've got the flush of innocence and naivety in people making their first record, and sometimes you can influence things too; I remember when Feeder were here, and I drove up to the Manor in my car, a black jaguar, and it ends up in the song Buck Rogers...great little things that make the situation special.

"One of the funniest things that ever happened – although it was absolutely terrifying at the time, was when a band, who should remain nameless, were having their end of recording celebrations.

"It was the middle of the night and I was awakened by what sounded like a car driving through a window. It really was horrifying.

"I come running down the stairs, thinking that someone has driven into the side of the house. It was that bad.

"In the kitchen I find the singer from the band sitting cross-legged on the floor, crying. The kitchen table is over on its side and a whole bar worth of drink – bottles of whisky, bottles of gin, bottles of vodka, has gone with it.

"The guy couldn't even apologise for anything. He wore this look on his face that said 'This is the end of the world.'

"It turned out that the table had been set up as a bar, he was going to be the barman, and then someone had sat on the corner of the table and the whole lot had gone. "It was a very funny moment, but I don't think the band ever got over that!"

The Manor was revered for its equipment, vibe and clever use of space, and not only by the rock 'n' roll fraternity.

Classical ace Nigel Kennedy visited the Manor too.

He mixed an album there early in 1999.

"What a character Nigel was. He made us strip down everything in the ballroom and leave it bare, all the bits that you make the booths with, everything.

"He would play his violin for at least an hour every day, and we would sometimes come down and stand outside the ballroom, just to hear him doing his scales.

"You are talking about someone who has such a mastery of an instrument that you can't believe.

"After two or three weeks of him being around, I asked 'Why do you practice

> **"The kitchen table is on its side and a whole bar worth of drink has gone with it"**

every single day? Can you not afford to take one day off?'

"He said: 'Pete, if I didn't do much practice now, I would be a good violin player. If I do a bit of practice, then I will be a great violin player.

"'But if I practice every day at this level, and keep the nerves in my muscle groups working quickly enough, then I can be a world-class violin player. And if I don't do this now, even for a few days, then it can take me weeks to get back to the speed.

"'You have to be at the maximum response rate in your mind, nerves and muscles to be a world-class violin player...and I want to be a world-class violin player.'

"It's a bit like the Jay Kay thing – it's about getting nothing from nothing, and if you want to be really special at something, then you have to go the extra mile."

The Charlatans also made use of the Manor house in 1999, laying down Us and Us Only.

Later in the year it debuted at No.2 in the album charts.

With the ballroom now bereft of music and the studio facility reduced to

Pete and Berni Winkelman, 2019

John Lydon (Frontman)
Public Image Limited (PiL)
Recording: Happy? (1987)

"I liked its haunted house vibe very much.
The strangest thing about it was the birds kept smashing their heads into the window panes. Those little birds can be pretty suicidal when they are in mating motion!
The Manor had a strange atmosphere on the staircase and in certain rooms and definitely in the actual recording area.
You would always feel like you were being watched, which I tend to enjoy.
If I can grab anyone's attention I'm happy – dead or alive!
I'm not the kind of person who is easily spooked, in fact I'll pile straight into it.
I don't fear the dead, it's the living that I worry about!

"I'll never forget the concrete cows"

There was a gardener who was growing some very odd things out the back – all manner of beautiful plants and vegetables.
He was doing something really great. We had our pushbikes with us too, and then found nowhere to go!
But it's so typical of me, I've always got pushbikes all over the place and never use them.
I'll never forget the concrete cows in the field. Absolutely, I went to see them.
They are laughable and all that, but it actually gives a town a personality if you think about it.
I quite admire it."

wonderful memories, inevitably the studio equipment has departed for pastures new.

Pete: "One of the pieces of equipment that we were most proud of, was a thing we called Babbey Road – the original monitor rig for the Abbey Road Neve Console, from 1974.

"It was used on a lot of the records here – PJ Harvey, Feeder and all of the more recent stuff we did.

"I spoke with Big Mick Hughes, who is Metallica's audio engineer, and he mentioned Babbey to Metallica frontman James Hetfield who was interested in it.

"We sent him some pictures, told him all about it and the next thing you know, the console is being sent to San Francisco for his studio.

"It's lovely that a unique piece of our equipment has gone to somebody who is one of the world's greatest rock 'n' roll musicians from the last few decades.

"Every major artist has a piece of Neve equipment, just like they have a piece of Marshall equipment."

In 2020, Linford Manor has come full circle, and is once again a family home.

Gone are the bands and the noise and the fun and the occasional fury.

But Pete doesn't just have memories from the era. There are a wealth of albums sitting on stockists shelves all saying 'Recorded at Great Linford Manor.'

"The most exciting part about being at the Manor was being around that creativity," he says.

"It was always inspirational, and the hard thing now is not hearing the noise.

"I love having the house to myself, simply because we had so very many people here for so many years, and it was very invasive, although at the time you go through it, you don't notice.

"It is only when you sit back that you think 'How did I do that?'

"We have a nicer lifestyle now, but I do miss that noise...

"In a residential studio, the whole thing is about making the record.

"It is so focused, and 24 hours a day, every day.

"Real life goes out the window, as do normal hours and you get cabin fever...but boy did we have a laugh!"

Andy Cairns (Frontman/Guitarist)
Therapy?
Recordings: Infernal Love (1995, drums),
Suicide Pact - You First (1999), So Much for
the Ten Year Plan (2000, extra tracks)

"Suicide Pact is one of our favourite albums.
It was our first album for an indie subsidiary
of Universal, called Ark 21.
They basically said 'You can do what you
want,' and we had PJ Harvey's producer
Head for the record.
We were so full of ideas at that time and
there was just something about Great
Linford Manor.
I had never been to boarding school, and by
this time I was in my 30s, but we were like
four kids at boarding school!
Normally with a producer, they like to
record by midnight, then have a little nip
of brandy and go off with a Werner Herzog
movie, get up early the next day, and go for
a game of squash. But Head was very rock
'n' roll and if we had an idea for something

at 1am or 2am, he would start recording.
While we were there we filmed a movie too,
it was a horror comedy called The Speedo
Menace, about a serial killer who only wore
speedos, played by me, chasing the rest of
the band.
A friend of ours, who was a merchandise
guy, was a New York detective on the trail of
The Speedo Menace and the rest of the band
members. It's all filmed in and around Great
Linford, the town and the graveyard.
We are massive football fans, and there were
models of football grounds and stuff around
while we were recording.
We would go and record a couple of tracks,
and then come into the communal room and
on the pool table would be a model of what I
presume is now Stadium MK.
I was so made up for Pete when MK Dons
beat Manchester United!
Whenever my wife sees Pete on the news
she can't believe it's the same guy – because
he used to be running around in his shorts
talking about Motörhead!"

Therapy?: 'There was just something about Great Linford Manor'

28

PJ Harvey in the studio at the Manor: The album 'Stories from the City, Stories from the Sea' won the Mercury Music Award in 2001

Danny Bowes (Frontman)
Thunder
Recording: Backstreet Symphony (1990)

"By the time we began recording the album we had done a few shows playing the material, so we were primed and ready to go. It was pretty exciting.

It was a very nice summer, 1989, and we were there from July to September.

Our method was always to work until we lost objectivity, so we would work from about 11am in the morning through to dinner time, have something to eat, go back and review what we'd done for the day, and then down tools and enjoy ourselves.

We would get a lot done during the day, but the evenings were usually for listening and mucking about!

Some of the guys in the band had been to Great Linford before. Ben (Matthews, guitarist) was an engineer before he was in the band and made an album

> **"Someone said making a Thunder album was a bit like a party where an album broke out"**

there with a Japanese band called Red Warriors, which went to Number Two in the Japanese charts - I think that was part of the reason we went there to do the original demos, which we recorded in the Almshouses across the park.

When we did the album, in the best spirit of complete over-the-topness we did it in both studios at the same time.

It was quite interesting, and there was quite a lot of digging that needed doing in order to connect things.

It cost a fortune, but it did work. We lived there, played cricket on the back lawns, and had our dinner in the gardens.

We had a very, very nice time.

We liked to enjoy ourselves, but always made sure we worked as efficiently as we could. That meant you could have a little relax every now and again and know that you'd earned it.

Someone said at the time that making a Thunder album was a bit like a party where an album broke out..."

Jack Endino (Producer)
Bruce Dickinson Band
Recording: Skunkworks (1996)

"I had worked at Rockfield Studio in Wales before, so the idea of a residential studio outside of London was attractive to me.

Linford had a good Studer tape machine and a Neve board, and the mic list looked good, so I was fine with it.

The Neve desk was a lovely classic, still with an EMI logo on it. I was the last one to use it before Pete had it completely refurbished. The day after we finished, there was a crew of techs in there taking it apart!

Bruce is a great singer, he could do anything he put his mind to.

The Skunkworks album we made has some good tunes on it, and I got Bruce to try some things with his voice he hadn't done before. He was a delight to work with, very focused and professional.

But the whole thing was an experiment. For his next couple of albums, Bruce had ex-Maiden guitarist Adrian Smith join his band, and Bruce's records started sounding more like Maiden than Maiden themselves did at that point.

And then they both rejoined Maiden a few years later!

Aside from visiting the Marshall Amplification factory once, I didn't see any of the town. What I did do every morning was go walking for a couple of hours, as I'd be awake hours before the band.

There's a bike path that goes right past the Manor, obviously an old railroad bed, and it follows an old canal. Lovely countryside."

The Wildhearts

Backyard Babies

Biffy Clyro

The Almighty

Sylvia Massy (Producer)
Skunk Anansie
Recording: Paranoid & Sunburnt (1995)

"I had heard about the band through my manager. He sent some material to me and I really loved Skin's voice. I thought they were a real hybrid of soul with hard rock that I hadn't really heard before. Skin is very unusual and I immediately wanted to be a part of the project.

I require a very particular type of equipment to record on, and at the time there were very few studios in the UK that had it, the Neve AD series, which is dated around 1972.

I had worked on the equipment in L.A and really liked it. That was a requirement for me to get a particular type of sound for Skunk Anansie, and while researching studios I saw this beautiful old house.

Not only did it have a vintage style AD Neve, it also had an EMI Neve, which meant it had a fantastic pedigree.

I wanted to experience the real England away from the city too, so it was very attractive for many reasons.

Recording in an old manor house?

It's a fantasy. For an American, it's living the dream.

It is very important to have an environment that induces creativity and the Manor was one of those places.

We recorded in a big ballroom. It was very old and a lot of care had been taken to keep the original architectural features of the building, so it was a really special place to work in.

It has really high ceilings, was really good for acoustics, and really versatile.

We built a tent inside of the main ballroom so we could have some isolation and try different things.

When we recorded the song Weak the lighting was brought down really low, and there weren't many people around, which was on purpose - we tried to make Skin as comfortable as possible.

She gave an unbelievable performance that was so real. There were tears!

I think everyone in the room was crying, and you can really hear the emotion in her voice.

There were some really special moments during that session, but it was exhausting too. There is so much emotion put into music that it can be hard not to feel what the singer is feeling.

Skin is so dynamic that it was both exhausting and fantastic at the same time.

Pete Winkelman changed my life while I was at the Manor. I had gone there specifically to work on that console and while there, in an off-hand way I said, 'Pete, if you ever find one of these for sale, let me know.'

Two days later he said 'Sylvia, I've found a console for you in London.'

We went to visit the AD series Neve together. I bought it and still have it today.

Buying that console changed my life and has been a source of income for me from that moment until now."

Aaron Aedy (Guitarist)
Paradise Lost
Recording: Draconian Times (1995)

"I remember the local pub, basically next door, was really friendly and had good beer, and that Pete Winkelman was a complete star, a really, really nice guy with some great stories.

I see he still has the same enthusiasm for life when I see him on Sky Sports News. Good for him! The EMI Neve mixing desk was a gem there, it is a shame that set up isn't still around, it sounded phenomenal."

Ace (Guitarist)
Skunk Anansie
Recordings: Paranoid & Sunburnt (1995)
Stoosh (1996), Still Hungry (solo album 2003)

"The band formed in March and we were in the studio by September.
It was that fast, like a dream.

I'd had 10 years of recording with other bands, but that was the first proper record I had done in a proper studio that had been paid for by the record company.

It was the coolest building – an old-fashioned 17th-century place, and we thought 'Wow, what a majestic place to record an album in.'

It was the aesthetics of it that we liked, because some studios are just rooms, aren't they?

We were able to record when we wanted to, but we kept it to normal hours, so at the end of the day we could chill out – eat food, watch television, listen to music over the studio monitors, and play pool, that kind of thing.

It did feel a little bit insular because we were used to being out on the town, socialising all the time, but when we were there we were doing so much stuff and having so much fun that it was really nice to be in our own little bubble.

We went back to the Manor when we worked on the second album, Stoosh, and it took us six weeks again.

As a band, we were more popular then, but the recording was the same.

I went back again when I was doing my solo album and it was like being lost in time. You feel like you were there just yesterday!

Pete Winkelman was a very uplifting person. He was a lot of fun and he did us a lot of favours.

He's a great person to be around and very inspiring, and the Manor was amazing.

Such a great vibe and great history."

'Enjoy a drink in the convivial surroundings of the cellar bar, where the Lord Mayor of London used to store his fine wines and ales' (below)

Ben Johnston (Drummer) Biffy Clyro Recordings: Blackened Sky (2002), The Vertigo of Bliss (2003)

"It was a really big deal for us going to the Manor, especially with it being such a grand place, and I think we were massively overwhelmed by the whole thing.

We didn't even know places like that existed.

We were really, really proud of what we made – it was a wonderful sounding room and we worked really fast.

Our producer Chris Sheldon really liked it there too.

I think it was partly down to Chris and the management that we went there.

We were quite green at that point and didn't really know what studios were around.

A lot of bands go into the studio with half-arsed ideas and end up having to write in there.

You are spending money all the time,

> **"It was a really big deal for us going to the Manor ...we were massively overwhelmed"**

just being in a studio.

We were on an independent label that certainly didn't like spending money at all.

We went back to do the second album with 16 tracks completely done, knowing that nothing needed to change and knowing exactly what we were going to do.

This time we recorded all the guitar, bass and drums in one day.

We were young lads at that point too, and full of energy.

We had gotten better at recording and better at playing, and I guess that because we had been there before, we felt a lot more relaxed at Great Linford Manor.

The surroundings are also important and Linford Manor was ideal for us.

We don't really go out drinking and if we are going to party we keep it insular.

I think we only left the grounds once! We went through loads of roundabouts and ended up at a shopping centre..."

Biffy Clyro (Ben Johnston, left): 'Linford Manor was ideal for us'

In early 2002, OK! magazine's cover featured Victoria and David Beckham.

At the time, David was the England football captain, and son Brooklyn was a toddler.

And then, just as now, the media had an insatiable appetite for the couple.

This particular photoshoot was hosted at Great Linford Manor, during Victoria's bid for solo chart success.

Adam Wakeman was the keyboard player during the shoot.

"It was hilarious. She was really good fun to work with and I had these false comedy teeth that I put in without her knowing.

"When they were taking the photos, I smiled which revealed these awful teeth. She cracked up laughing as did the other guys.

"The downside was when my mum went out and bought the magazine and there were no pictures of me with my real teeth, so all her friends thought I had terrible teeth for real.

"She didn't speak to me for about a week!"

Above: Great Linford Manor makes the cover of OK! Magazine, and right, Adam's toothy gag

Grant Nicholas (Frontman/Guitarist)
Feeder
Recording: Echo Park (2001), Comfort In Sound (2002)

"The first time we went there we recorded Echo Park with producer Gil Norton, who has worked with everyone from The Pixies to the Foo Fighters and Echo and the Bunnymen.

We liked the atmosphere. It was always very relaxed which was bizarre really.

Pete and the whole family had a lot of patience, because they were hearing these bands make a complete racket all day, but they seemed to enjoy the whole process of having bands there. It had a really good drum room and was a comfortable studio, with a really good vibe.

I don't think I ever spoke about it, but I am still convinced one of the rooms is haunted. We all had to share rooms, but I had a little bit of space away from the others so I could write lyrics, and managed to blag the room next to Gil, who was in the producer's suite.

It was quite a small, single room, and every time I was in there it felt like there was someone with me.

It wasn't like I completely freaked out, and I still slept in there. I just felt like there was someone else around. It definitely had something going on.

We used to work really late sometimes, Gil was a hard worker and not the sort of producer to finish at 9pm.

He would work right through.

We had a couple of quite drunken times – I remember Gil was quite partial to Jameson Whiskey as well, so it all got out of control then. They were the fun nights.

We used to be in the pub across the way all the time too, The Nags Head. It was a bit too near the studio - a little bit dangerous.

Later, we came back and did a lot of Comfort In Sound there, and learned a lot from Gil and the way he worked in the studio. Some of it was difficult for me, but I realise now some of the small things I didn't think were important, actually make a big difference.

We were just finishing up the album and everything was going really well when I said 'Gil, I've written this song.'

'We don't need another slow song,' he said, but I convinced him. That track was Just The Way I'm Feeling, which ended up being one of our biggest hits, so I was quite pleased I'd pushed it!

Echo Park and Comfort In Sound were both platinum albums for us – Comfort In Sound has gone double platinum now, so both albums we did at the Manor were really successful.

When I was working on Echo Park I was in this Beatles-y Sergeant Pepper headspace and wanted the album to have some sort of cool intro, so our engineer Matt and I walked around hearing our feet on the gravel and it's that which opens up the album – it was recorded right in front of the house during a fete (the Waterside Festival).

Every time I hear it I have a flashback to that time."

Feeder (Grant Nicholas, centre): "It always felt like there was someone with me"

Blinding Studios

"You could hear the sound of sirens, the crackle of burning wood and the firefighters shouting commands."

Blinding Studios was, for a time, a hub of activity in Newport Pagnell. Tucked away in the old Taylors Mustard yard behind the High Street, it was convenient, out of sight, and the perfect place for bands to make a lot of noise and not interfere with anyone.

The three rehearsal rooms welcomed many new city bands through their doors, and business was brisk.

The fully-equipped soundproofed rooms opened in May 1997, and the studio followed in August of the same year.

Lee Carter spent some time heading up the studio before tragedy struck and silenced the sounds for good

"In 1998 I met a local lad through my day job. He told me he was in a band and I should go and check them out live. The band was Lupa. They played with

a passion and I began going to The Pitz venue regularly to watch them and catch other local bands."

Lee also began visiting Blinding Studios where Lupa rehearsed.

"I would help out, have a little listen and make the tea. Around the same time I met Sammy Jones and Paul Rivers, and started to have the belief that I could do something to aid local music.

I could see there were quite a few young bands in and around Milton Keynes.

There was sometimes a bit of rivalry, but it was a good, healthy, friendly rivalry, and there was a good vibe within the scene."

In 1999 MK band Fono announced they were upping sticks and moving Stateside.

The band had been responsible for Blinding and there was no option but to close the doors.

Lee said: "I remember thinking 'Where will my mates practice?' Then I had the idea of taking Blinding on.

Over a JD and Coke (or 10) with Andy and Del from Fono we sorted the details and I took over the running of the studios before the end of the year.

I managed to rally a few of the guys from the bands I knew, and we gave the place a bit of a spruce up.

I invested in some new PA equipment and re-opened early in 2000.

It went a bit mad with customers, and not too long after opening we had 40 bands and artists coming to write, rehearse, record music and chill out every week.

They were great times - getting to meet so many talented, nice people and being able to support them.

When the studio shut up for the night, or after the curtain had come down on gigs, everyone would head up to Bar Central where the vibe was awesome, everyone knew everyone else and it was always a good night. It was a great scene.

I drove around the country with Headfly and Graveltrap and always had a great time.

But the studio wasn't to last; on New Year's Eve in 2002 I was due to host a party at the studio to say 'thanks' to the bands for enabling me to keep the place running.

Headfly were due to play a gig that night and had gone down to load up their gear for the show.

They called and said they couldn't get in because the fire brigade was there - the studio was on fire.

When I took that call, my heart sank and I made my way there as fast as I could.

The High Street had been closed and as I neared Union Street, you could hear the sound of sirens, the crackle of burning wood and the firefighters shouting commands. Standing out against the night sky was the orange glow of fire and the flashes of blue lights. The fire wasn't actually in my premises, but the adjacent building.

I felt hopeless; I called everyone to let them know the party was now being held at my flat. We had the get-together as planned, albeit dampened by the events of the evening.

I went there the following day to assess the damage, and the studio building itself seemed to have escaped the fire, but it did take a hit of a few thousand gallons of water. You could smell the cold, damp charcoal in the air in every room of the studios.

I got the electric back on, cleaned the place up as much as I could and re-opened for a second time in March 2003. But not for long.

The fire brigade report stated the cause of fire was arson. Because of that arson attack, the roof on one of the oldest buildings in Taylor's Yard had collapsed.

Once the roof had gone, my neighbours could also hear everything in the studio, and environmental health were called in to see how the situation could be remedied.

There was nothing more I could do - I had been told the building wouldn't be repaired or rebuilt.

The rehearsal rooms closed for good in April.

When Blinding was open it was one of the best times of my life - the friendships I still have all these years later are testament to that time."

Devastation: The aftermath of the fire

Blinding & the blues

"As well as being cold and damp in the winter, it was excruciatingly hot in the summer... but we loved the place."

Pearl Handled Revolver (PHR) bring together raw, visceral blues with psychedelic rock, and they've stage-shared with aces like The Black Crowes and Wilko Johnson.

But before fronting PHR, Lee Vernon learned his craft as the frontman in Blunderherd, alongside Simon Rinaldo, Gawain Simons, Neil Revitt and Malcolm Lett.

The rhythmic bluesy mob were popular players on the new city scene.

Rehearsals were originally held at the rear of The Two Brewers pub in Olney.

"I remember sitting with a beer to watch them play for the first time and thinking 'I want to be a part of it,' so I joined and brought my songs with me," said Lee.

"Just as I was settling in though, I had to leave - my three-year course in fine art began in 1990, a magical time to be in Manchester for music and art.

"I was rehearsing at The Boardwalk alongside Oasis, Inspiral Carpets and The Roses. I knew I would be home eventually and that I'd need to get back with the band when I did return, in '93.

"Thankfully, the boys were still jamming, only now we had all grown as musicians.

"And so, it seemed, had the local music scene."

When they went looking for a new rehearsal space, Blunderherd rocked up at Blinding Music in Newport Pagnell.

"It sounded perfect - three rooms, two in-house PAs, and a chill-out room.

"It proved to be the making of us, and many other bands. One thing I'd learned from my time in Manchester was the importance of contact with other bands. "With the rehearsal space becoming a social hub, we became a tight unit.

"I realise how 'rose-tinted' I could be about our time at Blinding Music, but in reality it was a bit of a dive!" Lee recalled.

"As well as being cold and damp in the winter, it was excruciatingly hot and damp in the summer. The moisture would condense on the ceiling and fall like rain on us as we limped on, at times even oxygen deprived.

"Then we would congregate out the back on the steps of the old factory to smoke, talk and exchange ideas with other bands. We loved the place and it worked well for us.

"We all had a sense of camaraderie for our own little 'club' - we suffered for our art together in our 'semi-squat' studio, which I think gave us all a sense of purpose and validated our obsession.

"As a 'club' we were all stronger and self-sufficient. Many of the 350 gigs we performed as Blunderherd came via a contact gleaned from another band, a gig swap or by word of mouth, and they were nearly always connected to our rehearsals at Blinding."

When the curtain came down on Blunderherd, a temporary incarnation followed; Origin Red delivered a rock, dub and dance fusion.

"...but it wasn't really us," Lee admits, "After two or three gigs we went our separate ways, but I would stay close writing partner and friends with Simon Rinaldo."

Lee wouldn't sing professionally again for another eight years: "My stepson at that time (Luke McDonnell of Ocasan) was applying for university and needed a demo to impress the panel and secure a place. I called Simon, who by that time had a small home studio set up, and arranged for us all to play on some songs I had written. The demo had some merit as Luke gained a place at Bath University, and we really liked the results ourselves."

That studio session was the catalyst that started the Pearl Handled Revolver story: "The plan was hatched between me and Simon to find the rest of the line-up for an avant-garde, alternative blues group. One that would make the most of my gravel tones and Simon's complementary 'dirty' Hammond sound. Luckily we found them in Chris Thatcher (drums) and Andy Paris (guitar) and we never looked back.

The name? Pearl Handled Revolver was lifted from a previously unaired scene from the Monty Python team.

"The line went something along the lines of '… it's the pearl handled revolver for me Sergeant.'

"The name perfectly described the juxtaposition between the dark undertones of our lyrics and the fizzing vitality of our music, especially live. It just felt right."

The blues beasts celebrated their 10th anniversary in 2018.

Their catalogue so far includes four studio albums, two live albums and four EPs.

Pearl Handled Revolver and (facing page) Blunderherd

Senior producer Roy Leonard.

On the air in MK

The longest running radio station in MK has battled closure on more than one occasion. It is now housed in a former toilet block, and flush with success.

W hen Milton Keynes was in its early infancy, it was finding its way and breaking new ground the whole time.

One example was the partnership between the MK Development Corporation (MKDC) and British Telecom which gave the new city its own television channel.

Co-Ax Cable Communications Ltd delivered Channel 40 which offered residents the chance to create their own film of their hometown.

"But it was sadly before its time," recalled Mike Barry, a former Milton Keynes Mayor, who was the man behind the venture.

"Programming was scarce and repeated several times a week. It was decided the experiment was not going to be a success, and would cease.

"Fortunately, it was pointed out that all the facilities including studios and equipment could be used for a local cable radio station, and CRMK – Cable Radio

Milton Keynes – was conceived."

The name? That was an easy nod to the way it would transmit – through those cables which were a part of the UK's first-ever analogue cable network.

It was 1978 when the station established itself, and it began broadcasting a year later. The cable radio network allowed 17,000 homes in the city to access the station.

Three members of staff and a station manager were recruited and funded by the MKDC to oversee the day-to-day running of the station, with volunteers taking over in the evening.

But when Chiltern Radio hit the airwaves, also covering Milton Keynes, and the station's limited advertising budget ran dry, things weren't looking so bright.

However the passion of the volunteers was enough to convince Co-Ax to let them continue running the station.

Until this point, its home had been Fishermead, but with the cash injections all

Peartree Bridge: Home to CRMK in the early 1980s

dried up, a new base was needed.

The station relocated to a mobile home in Peartree Bridge.

"The station moved there in the early '80s and enjoyed many happy years," Mike recalled.

But more change was coming: "Chiltern Radio were looking at the possibility of a new radio station in MK, Horizon Radio, and approached Co-Ax to see if they would be willing to put in a joint bid," Mike said.

Horizon Radio won the franchise bid and moved into Crownhill, taking CRMK with them.

The plan was for the CRMK crew to take on the evening stints at Horizon, but in the end just three members were given shows. Several presenters went on to further their careers in commercial radio and at the BBC.

When Heart Radio bought out Horizon Radio, CRMK moved to Central Milton Keynes and when the pennies ran out again, the station was put into limbo.

"Perhaps our greatest achievement was doing the Guinness Book of Records broadcast from The Point in December of 1986," says Mike.

"We started the marathon at 4pm on the Friday and finished at 9pm the following Tuesday."

"...Community radio in Milton Keynes will continue for many years to come..."

Thirteen production teams and 214 guests enabled Mike to reach the 100-hour mark of continuous broadcasting.

"Regrettably, although the Guinness Book of Records said they would recognise the attempt, and the validation certificates were sent, they were moving offices at the time and the paperwork was lost. But we know we did it!" Mike promises.

"It would be inadvisable to try and mention all those people who kept the station going over the years. Individuals who committed time, expertise and a loyalty towards the community station that meant it was able to survive for so long."

But the story doesn't end there.

The station is back, and somewhat flushed with success – home is now a converted old toilet block by a cemetery in Newport Pagnell.

The flash in the pan idea turned an ivy-covered shell into a state-of-the art internet radio station, and seeing as how technology has progressed, music-shows can find listening ears worldwide, of course.

Mike Barry is thrilled that the station he gifted the city is back, and brighter.

"I know that with the new volunteers and premises, community radio in Milton Keynes will continue for many years to come..."

Shane Quentin holds the title of the DJ who has been with CRMK for the longest time.

His Garden of Earthly Delights show has been offering CRMK listeners the quirky, the alt, the off the wall and the downright obscure since 1991.

"The early presenters were very specialist in what they played. There were Irish, Christian, soundtracks and every genre of music show which were all presented with a passion and a commitment by knowledgeable and enthusiastic men and women.

"The later generation of presenters were just as keen but the show subjects changed to more contemporary sounds like house and electronic dance music.

I have never tired of the burning passion to play new music I have discovered, or the excitement of having live bands in session.

It isn't something I could ever find boring. It's in my DNA!

When I was a teenager I enjoyed playing weird and unusual records I had found in one of my father's second-hand shops to my friends, and the passion tipped over into playing DJ sets in now defunct pubs like The Starting Gate and other CMK venues.

I still have a letter written by the programme controller in 1994 warning me that 'If I ever play ANY record with the C-word in ever again, I will be taken

Shane Quentin: 'I will never spin a U2 or Adele record'

off air – FOR GOOD!'

Luckily it never happened and anyway, that programme controller is long gone.

We also had a presenter called Harry Perryman who was a lovely chap.

He did a '40s music show into his nineties. He was in the middle of his show one evening when he collapsed with a heart attack and died.

As I've been with CRMK the longest of all the DJs still with us, I suppose I should be a little more behaved than I am, but I still have the cheeky fire to push the boundaries of musical experimentation.

I'm afraid I will never spin a U2 or Adele record on my show!"

Bog standard: The Newport Pagnell home of CRMK

Breakfast chat: Trevor with Helen Legh

A new Horizon

Under his leadership Horizon Radio bagged two Sony Awards.
The city fell in love with Trevor Marshall, and he fell in love with the city.

" Simple Minds first brought me to Milton Keynes and I never realised that seven years later I would return and never leave.

Like many others, I did wonder 'What the hell is this place?' when I first came up on the train to go to The Bowl and see one of the finest stadium bands in the world.

My return visit was in a rusty Vauxhall Astra.

It was jammed with my life's belongings, which wasn't much, to move into a house I shared with Swanny, a car salesman who worked at Perrys in Bletchley.

That was the start of my love for MK. I had served my apprenticeship at Chiltern Radio in Dunstable, and with a spring in my step and my first contract in my back pocket - to present an evening show on Horizon Radio - I couldn't get out of Dunstable quick enough and over to the magnetic pull of the new city.

The evening show was meant to be a cutting edge dance show.

There was only one problem with that - I was more into the Hothouse Flowers

than the hotbed of dance action new to the scene. But I fudged my way through it.

One occasion highlighted I wasn't alone in being out of my musical depth: The boss, Clive Dickens, who trusted me to deliver this new show to the new city, handed me a new 12 inch vinyl record and said 'You have to play this tonight,' which I dutifully did.

Two minutes into the tune there was more swearing than a night at the Clocktower in Emerson Valley!

The phone was ringing off the hook and when I answered there was more swearing.

It was Clive asking me what the f**k I was doing.

I am good friends with him now. In fact he is a director of the radio station where I currently work, but it was a few years later that I got the nerve to tell him he should have listened to more than two minutes of that 12 inch he gave me!

In 1993 I went from the evening show to presenting the drivetime show, moved in to my own flat in Bancroft Park and was privileged to be part of a forward-thinking city and radio group.

Horizon was as much a part of the city as the shopping centre, the Citizen newspaper and The Golden Flamingo nightclub - I have many fond memories of the party nights we held there.

I was in my early 20s and enjoying life. A few of us loved working at Horizon so much that we would just hang out there. Horizon Radio is where I met Helen Legh, who was desperate to get on the radio, and those were the days where you could hang around and eventually get on air.

Helen and I went on to present the breakfast show together for many years and enjoyed becoming part of the fabric of the city.

She was a real talent and a treat to work with.

We were very different people, but did have two things in common; a love for radio and Milton Keynes.

I am proud and humble to have been a small part of MK's brief history.

I have not been on the air in MK for a long time, but there are still many people that remember Horizon and the breakfast shows I presented with Helen, Cueball, Ros, Wes and Jim in the Black Thunder for 13 years.

It was extremely hard to leave.

I did try once and soon came back for a further five-year stint - Coventry was not for me.

"The phone was ringing off the hook. It was Clive asking me what the f* *k I was doing"

There were many proud moments; being part of the city status bid in 2000 when we campaigned on air that MK was the world's best new city, which I truly believe.

And I had the time of my life performing in pantomimes at the new Milton Keynes Theatre, starting in 1999.

I had to pinch myself when I was in a rehearsal studio with Linda Robson, Paul Nicholas, and Paul Barber from Only Fools and Horses, three fine actors in big TV shows at the time, getting ready for Peter Pan, the theatre's inaugural panto.

The proudest moment of all was being the programme controller of Horizon that led an amazing team to win two Sony Radio Academy Awards for the Radio Station of the Year.

Milton Keynes has given me so much and still does.

We live here with my beautiful family and I am proud to be the voice of the MK Dons, after a call from chairman Pete Winkelman in 2003 asking me if I would be the matchday announcer when the Dons arrived.

That was a good phone call.

Over the last 13 years I have been a part of the groundbreaking Jack FM family in Oxford, which has been a lot of fun.

I hope one day to be back on the air in Milton Keynes.

Never say never!"

MKFM 'The beat of MK'

When Chris Gregg was offered the chance to head up Horizon Radio, he wasn't exactly thrilled at the prospect, but the negativity didn't last long.

" I'd heard about the concrete cows and roundabouts of Milton Keynes - it felt like I was being offered the chance to move to a depressing, post-industrial wasteland," he remembers.

But Chris agreed to visit the station and take a look around the town with former Breakfast show host Trevor Marshall.

"His enthusiasm for Milton Keynes was infectious. He drove me around the leafy, green reality of the town and in the space of an afternoon I was converted to the Church of Milton Keynes, and enthusiastically signed my contract.

"When I joined Horizon Radio it was a station that had won prestigious Sony Awards and had some of the best audience figures in the commercial radio industry - not just because it didn't have any commercial competition, but because the audience could hear the station was part of the community and passionate about Milton Keynes."

Presenters included breakfast show hosts Cueball and Ros, Mikey Faulkner heading up the weekend call, and the double-header team of Emma Caldwell and Wes

Venn taking care of drive time. Jim Hellier kept a visual presence for the station, eating up road miles around town in the Black Thunder.

A converted warehouse unit in Crownhill was home.

"When I arrived, the BBC had a local breakfast show for Milton Keynes on Three Counties Radio, and cable radio station CRMK was broadcasting with an online service from a small office at the Horizon Radio base, which had its own entrance at the back of the building.

"Their presenters would sometimes emerge from the mysterious door in the corner of our office to collect their mail, confusing new members of the team who thought they lived in a cupboard!"

In 2008, Horizon Radio turned eighteen and had a birthday bash befitting of the special anniversary.

"At the time it felt like Horizon Radio would be around forever..."

But Horizon's owners GCap Media were taken over by a new chief executive, and stations, including Horizon, were re-branded in an effort to make the business sustainable: "...but it came too late to make much of a difference before GCap became the target of a takeover bid from Global Radio."

Eventually, shareholders accepted a bid and Horizon Radio had a new owner.

In September 2008 it was announced that the Horizon name would disappear.

Heart Radio had arrived. Across the new city bus stop posters invited listeners to 'Give it some Heart.' Remember those?

The first year of Heart operation produced record audience figures, but relaxed regulations soon saw shared programming across regions.

The former Horizon Radio station was merged with the Chiltern and Northants 96 stations and a new broadcast centre opened in Milton Keynes.

With a surplus of DJs, all the Milton Keynes presenters were made redundant. It was the end of an era.

Seeing a gap in the market for a truly local service, Chris began taking advice and hatched a plan.

"I put my redundancy money from Global Radio into the project and began working out the next steps..."

With lots of hard graft and support, MKFM was born. But it was still in name only.

"I was working in Oxford as an airborne travel news presenter at the time and doing a split shift on breakfast and, during the day time, I built the MKFM website in the office at the airport."

A Facebook post generated nearly 100 people who wanted to volunteer for the new station - as presenters, engineers, reporters and the street team.

The station, Chris assured, would have the same professionalism as other radio stations, but serve the community.

"We celebrated the launch of MKFM's first test transmissions on 107FM at 1.07am live in Oceana nightclub and launched our first programme at 1.07pm on June 5, 2011, with a live performance of Empire State of Mind by singer Sophie Clark on a stage next to the transmission pod."

A trial broadcast offered up some tasty moments - including a live broadcast by rapper Chipmunk, and a partnership with

The final Horizon FM team

the Foo Fighters concert at The National Bowl.

The station also revealed its very own mascot, Samantha the Panther.

New funding meant stability and renewed enthusiasm and the station continued to grow in stature.

A motion raised at a Milton Keynes Council meeting early in 2012, calling for the council to give its backing to the new station, won unanimous support.

As a result, the council leader wrote to Ofcom asking them to speed up the process of advertising a community radio licence for Milton Keynes.

Ofcom visited for an inspection of the transmission system, and the aerial was hastily moved from the top of Xscape to the top of the lamppost next to the pod, utilizing a cherry picker to get the job done under the cover of darkness!

When the engineer came to visit, he couldn't believe the whole station was operated from a tiny pod.

'Ok, so where's the rest of the radio station?' he asked.

The transmitter was on the floor under the desk and there was barely room for three people in the pod!

"It felt like I was being offered the chance to move to a depressing, post-industrial wasteland"

49

On air: Chris Gregg (top left), launching the studios at intu (above) and current MKFM CEO Darren Dorrington (bottom right)

News that the Herts, Beds and Bucks DAB multiplex was to launch early in 2013 saw a chance for MKFM to launch itself as a full time service almost immediately.

For a business that had operated on a tight budget, the £50K annual transmission costs were scarily big, but seizing the moment, Chris and the team went for it.

All was going swimmingly well, until the end of the year when news was received that Ofcom had changed their timetable for advertising community radio licences.

Just as the station was preparing to apply for its FM licence, it faced a delay of another year.

Milton Keynes MP Iain Stewart called a debate in Parliament asking Ofcom to review their community radio policy, pointing out that Milton Keynes was the largest urban area in the UK without a dedicated local radio service, since BBC Three Counties had now closed their local breakfast programme.

For 30 minutes, MKFM was the subject of a parliamentary debate which saw Ofcom change their timetable again - the station would be able to apply for a licence on December 15, 2014.

A larger board of directors was recruited and Chris spent several months writing the mammoth application.

Then the team could do no more than sit back, with fingers, and everything else, crossed.

When the call came through giving the green light to the licence, it meant all systems go - and work started on the studios that were housed at intu.

Keen to keep costs down, Chris donated his own dining table for the board room!

MKFM launched full time on 106.3FM in September 2015.

The station has already proven to be a training ground for national careers - One former presenter is now a BBC Radio 4 producer, while another is flying high at Capital FM.

In 2020 Darren Dorrington is CEO at MKFM, and the station has vacated its space at intu Milton Keynes.

It now operates from another bustling hub in the new town, with a state of the art studio at Stadium MK.

Needless to say, it continues to be the beat of MK.

Sir John Dankworth & Dame Cleo Laine

John was warm, witty, incredibly intelligent and completely down to earth.
He was made up of the best bits of the ordinary and the extraordinary.

John always spoke so colourfully of his past as a young man discovering jazz and the world of possibilities away from his home in London, and of that fateful meeting which led to an unbeatable partnership, onstage and off.

John came from a musical family. His mother was a more than competent singer, his uncle a pianist as adept at playing the organ in church as he was at sound-tracking silent movies. Music quickly embedded itself in the young John, and his aunt proved a great inspiration.

"She played the cornet in the Salvation Army Band, the French horn in the local orchestra, and was a musical renaissance. "It was basically a classical family. I had been taught the piano and the violin, but I couldn't get anywhere with it.

"When my parents gave up on me I got interested in jazz.

"That horrified them – it was like being interested in heavy metal in those days, your parents wouldn't exactly welcome it. "But they could see that I was consumed by it.

"Some of the lyrics in those days of the blues were probably as bawdy in their own way as rap is these days. They were a lot milder, but the shock was the same.

"They said that if I must get involved with this horrible music I had better learn to play properly, and sent me off to the Royal Academy of Music.

"Nowadays, you have to be a genius to get in, but in those days it was wartime and they were delighted to get anyone in there – people weren't racing to go and get bombed in Central London!"

John focused his attentions on learning the clarinet, spending two years working on his playability, until post-war when he

*John at home with wife Cleo, and (right) topping the
Melody Maker polls*

was called to serve in the army.

John simply joined the army band
and his passion continued to flourish,
although he had no job to go to when
he left the forces.

Then he learned of a ship about to
set sail for America that was in need of
a band.

John auditioned, along with a young
Ronnie Scott. They got the job and set
sail, starting a journey that would change
their lives, and 'strike chords' with millions
of people all over the world.

"I had gone from a country barely out
of the war and arrived in New
York. It was like being in cloud
cuckoo land," John said.

"I had never been abroad
in my life before and all of a
sudden I found myself in this
mad Broadway atmosphere
with yellow cabs and
hamburgers. They were unknown in this
country at that time. It was like a dream.

"It used to take us five days to get there,
then we had two days in New York and
back we came.

"We did that for six months, listening
to all of our musical gods at the time and
experiencing that life."

> **"I got so fed up
> winning those
> polls that I
> deliberately tried
> to lose them"**

By 1949, John was making friends and
influencing people with his flair. Melody
Maker magazine declared him Musician of
the Year.

It was the start of an annual
tradition.

"I got so fed up winning
those polls that I deliberately
tried to lose them to someone
else," he said.

John began working for big
band leader Ted Heath, who
suggested that John start his own band and
gave him a night at the famous London
Palladium.

"We soon became rivals on the big band
scene and played musical leapfrog for
about 10 years.

"It was a period of extraordinary
success."

*Sir John with Dudley Moore (left), and (above left)
with Michael Parkinson and his wife Mary*

53

Sir John with Duke Ellington

Sir John & Dame Cleo with Roy Castle and Bill Oddie

"I said 'Do you think she's got something?' The trumpet player said 'I think she's got everything'"

Touring with his own troupe of 20 people, John had to lend an ear to the personal problems they had, as well as the sounds they were making professionally.

"I was only 25 years and having to be a father figure to people older than myself, advising them what to do with their marriages and their drink and drugs problems..."

Seeing the trauma of others helped John to avoid the pitfalls.

John, Ronnie Scott and other keen musicians settled in London, where they established Club Eleven.

"There were 10 musicians and another guy that used to look after the books and sat on the door," John said, explaining the name.

"Then I decided to get several musicians out of it, form a band and go on tour – I called it the Johnny Dankworth Seven and we worked it for three years.

"We had a vocalist, a remarkable guy called Frank Holder, but felt we needed a girl singer as well.

"We couldn't find anyone that suited us. "We more or less gave it up, but then my agent phoned and said there was a woman in the office with her manager who thought she deserved an audition.

"She sang Stormy Weather I think. The pianist and I both sat up – we couldn't believe our ears. She was really very good.

"We were a co-operative band who shared all decisions and so she was invited to return and audition before the band entire.

"In the interval when she wasn't there I said to the other guys, 'Do you think she's got something?' and the trumpet player said 'I think she's got everything.'"

So Cleo Laine was in the band, and in John's life, though the two wouldn't begin a relationship for a couple of years, after Cleo was divorced from her first husband. They married in 1958.

"But we haven't got a singular vision – personality and musically we are poles apart and we have lots of arguments. It is healthy to do that," John said.

"We are very close to each other and the fact our music is so interwoven helps to steady you a bit.

"Cleo is extraordinary, and she sings in a way the New York Times says is still one of the great voices of the world.

"When I listen to some of the early records that absolutely floored us in 1951 I think they are good, but she's singing a hell of a lot better now," he said in 2005.

"If anyone's had a lot of good fortune in their lives it's certainly us, but we pride ourselves that we had a little bit of talent to go with it as well…"

In 2002, London's Royal Albert Hall was the venue for their Golden Music Jubilee Concert.

Stars and friends paying tribute included Bruce Forsyth, Acker Bilk, Julian Lloyd Webber and The Beatles' producer Sir George Martin. A standing ovation wrapped up the night.

"They are something of a rarity at The Albert Hall so that was lovely," John said.

In 2006, John was given a knighthood and became Sir John in the New Year Honours list, following on from his wife who had been made a Dame in 1997.

They were one of a select few partnerships to both hold titles of their own. But then few partnerships were so fruitful; John was a musical genius with a breathtaking catalogue of compositions, including many film scores.

A revered composer, his work sneaked into the homes of millions on a weekly basis too; for it was John who delivered theme tunes for The Avengers and Tomorrow's World.

He also acted as musical director for British visits by Nat King Cole and Ella Fitzgerald, and was MD for his wife, whose voice wowed on Broadway and in the West End.

Cleo duetted on an album with Ray Charles (Porgy & Bess) and appeared with Frank Sinatra for a week-long season of shows at The Royal Albert Hall.

The lady with the ace scat singing ability is also the only female to have been nominated for a Grammy in the jazz, popular and classical music categories.

"It creates an interesting situation that she can now also be called Lady Cleo – but says she will probably stick to Dame just to show who is boss," John said when his knighthood was announced.

"I thought that the whole system of knighthoods had gone so far into the pop or rock or classical genres that I didn't think I would be on the list.

"When it happened I was surprised and pleased because I'm in a specialist music minority. Apart from any personal aggrandisement it gives, it is so hard for jazz to get noticed in the media these days."

John and Cleo's relationship, both on stage and off, was exceptional.

The secret of such an enduring partnership wasn't anything to do with unity, trust or support though.

It really was much simpler than that, John had told me with a big twinkle in his eye: "People ask about the secret of our marriage and the truth is you must have two bathrooms.

"Whatever other luxury you can't afford or don't have, you've got to have two bathrooms, because one bathroom can be the cause of strife, splits, quarrels and homicides!"

> **"One bathroom can be the cause of strife, splits, quarrels and homicides!"**

'Europe's best alto player'

Rod Argent enjoyed a wonderful friendship with John that inevitably saw them collaborate on many occasions.

The founding member of The Zombies recalls their very special relationship.

"John was an extraordinary man - an original. I first really chatted to him one evening in 1980. The two of us hit it off immediately and began a 30-year friendship.

Everything he did musically was driven by uncynical enthusiasm and he had the true open–mindedness that seem to mark the great musical figures.

Love and admiration of Duke Ellington's music was one of the first things we found we had in common.

He had also seen at first hand the seismic revolution in jazz that occurred at the hands of Charlie Parker, Gillespie and Monk at the famous 52nd Street New York clubs in the late 40s.

I loved to hear him talk about this – and about the time that he met and played with Parker in Paris.

Parker asked if there was anyone who could lend him an alto.

John had his with him and handed it over to the great man. After a few choruses, Parker gestured to John to play; loved what he heard and then began swapping eight-bar, then four-bar, then two-bar phrases with him before handing him back his instrument.

After that, Parker would always refer to John as 'Europe's best alto player.'

John had an extraordinary facility to write 'on the hoof' with all sorts of distractions going on around him.

There was one album of Cleo's for instance, on which he wanted to record one of my songs.

I ended up playing on all the tracks and late one evening, with lots of noise in the control room, watched him scribble out a string arrangement in about 15 minutes, which he then got me to play on the synthesiser.

I remember one evening about two days before Christmas 1982, answering the phone. 'Hi Rod – John here. I wondered if you'd like to make an album with me. I'd like to do it on clarinet. We could each write half...'

'John – yes – I'd love to.'

'Good - I've already booked the studio time for the week after Christmas – that'll give us time to write the material.'

I remember saying, 'John, we've got family staying here, to celebrate something called Christmas!'

Somehow, though, we managed to get the music together, and recorded the album 'Metro,' with Jon Hiseman, Paul Hart and John Mole also on the record.

I was to experience John's penchant for last-minute arrangement over the years, as I was asked to be involved in quite a few of the 'John and Cleo's Christmas' concerts at The Stables.

John would call in the late summer, promising, 'This year, everything will be written and planned well in advance,' and every year a week before the shows, another call would notify of a rehearsal the day or two before the first show.

Masses of music would be presented and each of us given mad choreography to perform as the show progressed. And we were expected to memorise everything!

Always, though, there was a fantastic amount of humour and I always enjoyed the mayhem and spontaneous nature of the performance.

John brought a huge presence to those Christmas shows and the essential humour and charm, which in fact were the overwhelming characteristics of the man, always shone through.

I feel really privileged to have known John and to have been able to have counted him as a friend.

He's left a big space behind him in the world and I still miss him."

"He was a lovely man, a gentleman, and had the kindest presence.
Irrespective of his music, there was still so much more to him. He had generosity of spirit and was utterly courteous."
Lord Robert Winston

"I always knew he was a great man and very popular, but was knocked sideways at the reaction when he died and the enormity of it.
It was more than the music.
It was the way he could touch people's lives just by being kind, that was almost as important as the music he gave."
Jacqui Dankworth, John's daughter

"We did a show with Johnny and he said 'I've done an arrangement for Ain't No Pleasing You. I hope you don't mind?'
We were honoured. He was great, and so broadminded with his music as well.
All these so called purists ain't musicians.
He was a proper musician."
Chas Hodges, Chas & Dave

"John was a totally natural, instinctive musician. My father was a very critical person and came from the classical side. When he heard the piece I did with John, Fair Oak Fusion, he said 'I tell you what, he's a really good musician.'
Coming from my father that was something quite special."
Julian Lloyd Webber

"I've always been very confident live, but breaking it down with a jazz band when I worked with John was very different.
It was great to do that and see why people like jazz.
When you are in the moment with it, it almost feels like impromptu freestyling. John Dankworth's legacy definitely lives on."
Craig David

"When I first met John in 1976 he was totally charming.
Charm is cheap, of course, and it took me some time to discover that this warm, congenial, humorous persona went right through him like the lettering in a stick of Brighton rock.
We are all beneficiaries of the breadth of his vision and the depth of his talent and the musical world is a poorer place without him."
Hilary Davan Wetton, founder of Milton Keynes City Orchestra

"I had the privilege of working and collaborating with Sir John on a number of occasions.
He was one of the great composers and jazz performers of the 20th century.
He was always encouraging and set a great example of good taste and good manners to everyone he met.
An important part of Britain's musical knowledge."
Jools Holland, pianist and band leader

Sir John Dankworth and Dame Cleo Laine perform at the Royal Festival Hall, London Jazz Festival 2009

Dame Cleo with Ray Charles

59

Superstar: Dame Cleo with daughter Jacqui

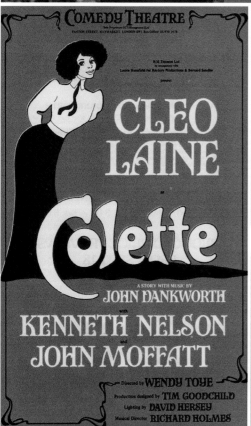

Matt Armour

"He had a profound love of traditional folk music and anyone wanting to join in was made wholly welcome."

Born in St. Andrews and raised in Fife, Matt Armour's music embraced the life of the Scottish fishing villages that surrounded him.

When he left the area he took the sounds, and the very essence of those communities with him.

Matt found himself stranded as a penniless student in Paris during the late 1950s and began playing the guitar out of necessity.

"I was flat broke so a fellow student showed me how to play three chords and I went out busking," he recalled in 1973.

"The kids use pop music as background music, but with folk it is the lyrics that are important, not the tune, so you have to listen to them."

Eventually Matt found his way to Stony Stratford where he settled.

It was a long way from Scotland but with a similar sense of community.

Still enthused by folk, he wrote, performed, promoted and encouraged others to celebrate the genre and kept a regular column in the local newspaper, spreading the word to music lovers across the city.

Matt led the way, nurturing folk sessions at The Stables, in Whittlebury, in Stony Stratford at the Vaults Bar, and at the Song Loft, which launched in 1976.

He was a leading part of the annual StonyLive! festival too and ran musical troupes The Gaberlunzies and The Elastic Band.

His own compositions were revered and his tireless support for the genre meant that he was respected by one and all.

Matt passed away on February 9, 2009. He was 73 years old.

His legacy continues with The Song Loft, the club he founded more than 40 years ago, which offers new talents a platform alongside scene leaders – everyone from The Tannahill Weavers to Isla St Clair and the late Johnny Silvo have played under the Loft's name.

The club is still active in Stony Stratford, and at The Vaults Bar, Matt's image still adorns the pub sign, courtesy of artist Derek Daniells.

"You could judge Matt by the quality of his friends"

"My mother knew Matt before me and they met through their love of music. Although I may have met him as a child, my first clear memory is when I sang at Whittlebury Folk Club.

I would have been in my early 20s at the time and remember going to his sister's house.

Together with his nieces we put on a puppet show which was great fun.

After I finished on the Generation Game I had my first child, Elliott, and decided I wanted to go back to my roots.

I had been missing gigs and singing because of the television work I had been doing and it was Matt who really helped me get back into the scene.

He had various contacts and before I knew it I was very busy.

He was a huge help.

He was pivotal in so many people's careers and helped keep the genre and songs alive with integrity.

Matt was a larger than life character, a wonderful, all encompassing man and his passion for music was wholehearted and beyond reproach.

He had a profound love of traditional folk music and anyone wanting to join in was made wholly welcome.

You could judge Matt by the amount and quality of his friends.

He was an exceptional sort of bloke and I was honoured to call him a friend."

Isla St Clair

"Matt's songs were musically and lyrically anchored in the Fife fishing villages where he grew up, and he used intimate or family settings to reflect on wider timeless issues to paint lyrical pictures of the ordinary man struggling against the world around him or the elements.

By contrast I was just a cartoonist, writing about little human fads and foibles. Matt taught me to write what came naturally and what I knew about.

I knew music was fun, but Matt taught me that to be good at it I had to practice my craft; and because he had confidence in my abilities I developed confidence in them myself.

One particular song I wrote called 'A pint at the Bull on Sunday lunchtime' provided the perfect context to thank him for his support.

Matt was a major influence on my life and my music, for which I shall always be grateful. I think of him often and will think of him always."
Dave Summers

"In the early '70s, when the folk song revival was at its height, Matt opened a folk club in the Fox & Hounds at Whittlebury.

The small village pub attracted folk enthusiasts from miles around, by virtue of Matt booking top names and encouraging a wonderful, almost family atmosphere.

Chorus singing was renowned and although all folk music was welcome, the community singing lifted spirits and everyone went home happy.

The club had a who's who of folk artists – The Jon Campbell Folk Group, Ewan MacColl, Peggy Seeger, Isla St Clair, Jake Thackray, Bob Davenport, Barbara Dickson, Bert Jansch and more.

Matt booked many guests from his native Scotland and the North, introducing their songs to eager Southern folkies.

Matt's love of folk music, his songwriting and enthusiasm has left a lasting influence in the South Northants area."
Jeff Wesley

Matt captured at The Vaults Bar by Derek Daniells (top) and collecting his lifetime achievement award at the MK Citizen GO! Awards (right)

WAP
presents Folk at the Stables
with
HAMISH IMLACH
MITHRAS : SUE MALLESON
MATT ARMOUR
SATURDAY, 24th JANUARY
at 7.45 pm
Tickets 75p. from the Stables, Wavendon
WOBURN SANDS 582522

"He was larger than life, a true friend and a wonderful mentor.
It is no exaggeration to say he changed my life and gently but firmly put me on a musical road with him that lasted over 30 years.
Of course he was also a songwriter of prodigious talent, many of his songs recorded by well established artists.
Matt was a bull of a man in the nicest sense; indestructible, indefatigable and with a surprising gentleness that those of us who were lucky enough to call him a friend appreciated when times were tough.
He was always there for you, with you and willing to listen.
Matt was and still is my friend.
I miss him every day - always will
I was privileged to know him, he leaves a mighty legacy of music in Milton Keynes and in the heart of each of his friends."
Malcolm Gladstone

"My husband played guitar in the Gaberlunzies, and having folk danced since I was a toddler, I readily fell into the role of caller, MC-ing barn dances for PTA events, birthdays, festivals and wedding receptions.
As the Gaberlunzies we played events far and wide and had a monthly residency at The Stables where Matt organised the folk nights.
This meant singing to a discerning audience every four weeks as support group for professional folk singers and groups. Matt was our anchor man, introducing the songs and telling the jokes."
Sue Malleson

Terry Lightfoot

Terry's story is one of unbridled enthusiasm for sounds and it's an enthusiasm that still shines brightly today through his family.

Terry was at the forefront of the British jazz scene and in the 1960s was a familiar face on the small screen, with regular appearances on the super-successful Morecambe & Wise Show.

He toured with Louis Armstrong, and was supported by a couple of unknown groups called The Beatles and The Who.

Terry also took the title of Britain's youngest bandleader.

His musical ability took him far and wide and allowed him to rub shoulders with world leaders.

Born in 1935 in Potters Bar, his ears were first tipped to jazz and swing thanks to Glenn Miller's wartime broadcasts and his parents' record collection, which featured artists like Benny Goodman and Artie Shaw.

He enjoyed a brief stint as a boy crooner and took piano and cornet lessons, but

interest soon waned and a passion for jazz was realised aged 14 during his time at Enfield Grammar School. He listened to a friend's collection of Louis Armstrong and Jelly Roll Morton 78s and was enamored by what he heard.

Terry's first clarinet cost the handsome sum of nine pounds and was paid for by his parents. It allowed him to fill the last vacancy in a trad jazz band formed by his schoolmates. He taught himself to play.

Post-school, Terry started working as a reporter on local newspaper, The Barnet Press. But that job didn't last for long and rather than writing the stories, Terry would soon find himself the subject of editorials.

In 1951 Terry led The Wood Green Stompers, who supported leading music figures including Chris Barber, Humphrey Lyttelton and George Melly when they played the Fishmongers Arms in North

The Terry Lightfoot Band

London. They stomped for the final time in 1953 and Terry was called into the RAF for his two years of National Service.

Later he would form the first collective to take his name, Terry Lightfoot's Jazzmen, a semi-professional band operating at London clubs.

Their first major concert appearance happened at London's Royal Festival Hall in early 1956 and was favourably reviewed in the New Musical Express by Benny Green.

That same year he met Louis Armstrong.

The band turned full-time professional and laid down their debut album in 1957, with a 17-year-old Ginger Baker at the drums.

In the same year Terry's band took to the stage at London's Royal Albert Hall again, performing on the first ever British all-night carnival of jazz.

They toured too – with skiffle ace Lonnie Donegan and country star Slim Whitman.

Kenny Ball was in the band too, but left in 1958 to piece together his own famous Jazzmen.

The band rode the crest of a wave during the so-called 'trad boom', and chart

He toured with Louis Armstrong and was supported by The Beatles and The Who

success came with numbers King Kong, True Love, and from the film It's Trad Dad! Tavern in the Town.

When a young Des O'Connor was given his first television series in 1963, Terry's band were the resident music-makers.

American tours followed and as one of the first British ensembles to cross the pond they didn't follow the trend but rather helped start it.

A brief break from music-making followed, but in 1968 Terry was called back to his love, re-forming his own band with Ian Hunter-Randall on trumpet - beginning an association that would last for the best part of 25 years.

The decade that followed saw a successful venture into cabaret clubs, working alongside comic faces including Les Dawson, Frank Carson and Cannon & Ball, but the band never forgot fans serving abroad - from the military bases of Cyprus and Gibraltar, to Oman and Central America.

In 1978, with wife Iris, Terry became the proprietor of The Three Horseshoes pub in Harpenden, which benefitted by having an esteemed player at the helm.

A 'quiet drink' at the establishment was sometimes livened up by musical friends - Acker Bilk, Don Lusher, George Melly, Chris Barber and Humphrey Lyttelton were among the many who played - and the famous faces continued bar side too, with Eric Morecambe and Frank Ifield among those supping the wet stuff during Terry's time at the pumps.

The landlord and landlady left The Three Horseshoes in 1983, and put the sole emphasis on music-making once more.

In 1985, an appearance in the star-studded film Plenty was bagged, a big screen delivery starring Meryl Streep, Sting, John Gielgud and Charles Dance.

Terry celebrated three decades as a band leader in 1987 by releasing the album As Time Goes By and the following year took to the stage of the prestigious Royal Albert Hall with superstar James Last.

Terry's band was subsequently booked for more Albert Hall dates with Last, returning in 1990, 1991 and 1992.

Lightfoot's 1990 album Stardust made such an impression with Radio 2 they awarded the disc 'Album Of The Week' status - the first time a British jazz band had ever been given the honour.

As the years continued so did Terry's

Terry with daughter Melinda (above) and with Louis Armstrong (right)

musical prowess - he fronted the Acker Bilk Paramount Jazz band for a national tour while Acker recovered from illness and in 2000 received the coveted gold badge of merit from the British Academy of Songwriters for services to music.

From 2004 Terry could be found touring the UK with shows including The Special Magic of Louis Armstrong and Hit Me With A Hot Note.

His unbridled passion for sound rubbed off - daughter Melinda followed the musical path as a singer and accompanied him as featured vocalist.

"One of my earliest memories of Dad, not when he was playing, but something that sticks out for me, is as a young child coming downstairs in the morning.

"Some of the musicians would be sleeping in the lounge and Mum would be cooking a big fry up in the kitchen for them all!

"Dad and the guys would then head off to the next gig - there were gigs most days back then. I first realised how important a musician Dad was when I was old enough, maybe 11 or 12 years old, to take on board some of the greats he had played with - Louis Armstrong, Kid Ory - and how much he was admired as a bandleader and clarinettist.

He was the ultimate professional and his stage presence was incredible."

Memories of a man who had coloured the jazz world for more than half a century are plentiful, but for Melinda, the most special of all happened in Milton Keynes at The Stables in 2011, when Melinda's sons Joe and Ollie joined their Mum and Granddad at musical play.

"To sing with my dad and his band and be accompanied by both my sons can only be described as magical," Melinda recalled. "The look on Dad's face to see his daughter and grandsons by his side said it all!"

Terry passed away in 2013, aged 77.

Clem Curtis

*"Our first North American tour was at the time of racial tensions.
Clem was very calm and collected."*

Clem Curtis was the singer who found fame with soul group The Foundations, and for many years Olney was his home.

Clem came to the UK from Trinidad aged 15 and worked various jobs while also packing a punch in the boxing ring.

His mother was a jazz singer, but Clem didn't find music early – he was in his late 20s when he joined London-based collective The Ramong Sound as a backing singer.

For a time Arthur Brown, who later found fame with his own group The Crazy World of Arthur Brown, was in the ranks, and he and Curtis would share vocal duties covering material by Sam & Dave.

By the start of 1967 Brown had departed and the band had gone through name changes, eventually sticking with The Foundations.

Clem now found himself fronting the band.

Recalling the role change he said: "I was so afraid of it, because I had never sang like that before."

Clem was the lead singer with the band on their chart-topping 1967 hit Baby Now That I've Found You (billed as the first official chart hit by a 'British multi-racial band'), and Back on My Feet Again.

The Foundations toured widely, including stateside stints with artists Tim Buckley, Solomon Burke and The Byrds.

Clem left the band before the release of its most famous number Build Me Up Buttercup, but went on to enjoy solo success for his singing, and acting roles followed too, including spots in the West End.

He was a regular performer in Milton Keynes, often showing out at Olney Wine Bar and building dates at The Stables into his touring itinerary.

Clem passed away in March 2017.

"Clem would always be at rehearsals or photo sessions before the rest of the band, whether that was a throwback to a strict discipline from his boxing days I don't know," recalled guitarist Alan Warner, one of the founder members of The Foundations.

"Anyone who was late would certainly feel the sharp end of his tongue. "Better that than his fists, I suppose.

"Our first North American tour was at the time of racial tensions and riots and a lot of dates were pulled beforehand because of this.

"Clem was very calm and collected.

"I will always remember him for those qualities more than anything else, although another thing I found was his eagerness to learn from other singers such as Arthur Brown and Rod Stewart.

"Yes, Rod Stewart did actually turn up to one of our rehearsals with a view to maybe even joining the band at one stage before we became famous.

"Our first big breakthrough came when we were asked to back the American soul singer Edwin Starr for a tour of the UK.

"Obviously Clem wasn't included on the tour but he would turn up every night anyway and try to learn as much from Edwin's performances as possible.

"Although Clem left The Foundations a year later, I have fond memories of the short time he was with us."

"Rod Stewart turned up to one rehearsal with a view to maybe joining the band"

Adam Ficek

"We were outside the gates when our manager called to say Pete was in Paris with Kate Moss. That was the end of our relationship with Oasis."

One former Bletchley boy swapped relative obscurity for the drum stool with a notorious band of players during the noughties.

Adam Ficek was the cog that kept Babyshambles turning smoothly at the height of their fame, when Pete Doherty was a familiar feature in the tabloids.

Adam now splits his time between music making, and supporting other musicians in his role as a psychotherapist.

"Growing up in MK it was always difficult to find a source for alternative music. In the early '90s, The Pitz or Madcap in Wolverton was where it was at generally.

"Because of the scarcity of live stuff, I made sure I went to every show at The Pitz and remember having my ears damaged by the likes of Curve, The Boo Radleys, Back to the Planet, Mega City Four and even Blur.

"When Britpop crept into the eye of popular culture, being in a band was suddenly the choice of pastime for many a suburban youth and bands became an accepted part of 'laddism.'

"With this acceptance of guitars and swagger, Milton Keynes launched two new venues, Bar Central and the Main Arena in Wolverton.

"Cirrus Minor was the first band I ever played in. I joined them without really knowing how to play the drums at all.

"The members all lived on the Lakes Estate in Bletchley and were probably the only musicians in the area.

"My dad took me to buy my first kit from a guy in West Bletchley who had gold discs on his wall. I remember thinking 'One day, I'll have some of those.'

"I think I was 16 when I started playing with Cirrus Minor, although I'm not sure we were even called that back then. We would spend hours listening to The Stone Roses, The Charlatans and sometimes Barrett-era Pink Floyd, while drinking herbal tea and consuming other substances.

"We used to rehearse at the Compass Club underneath Bletchley Leisure Centre, but we never gigged - our singer would

Adam with his Babyshambles bandmates (left and below)

never sing!

"Away from music, I was sliding into a very dark time.

"After failing every qualification at Leon School I managed to get a small bursary to move to Harlow College in Essex.

"That was the start of my music studies and the end of my time in the band. I subsequently moved back to London for a music degree, PGCE and MA.

"In London I continued playing in different bands before landing the drum seat in Babyshambles.

"My world took off overnight and all the hours practising, playing to empty rooms, blagging and struggling paid off.

"At the same time I landed my dream job, my mother passed away from cancer. "It had an immense impact, but I repressed it with the aid of my breakneck new lifestyle.

"I didn't really visit Milton Keynes for a few years - to let me escape the pain.

"But I did visit when we were set to support Oasis at The Bowl. We were outside the gates when our manager called to say Pete was in Paris with Kate Moss and would miss the show. This obviously

"I dedicated the song Bletchley Park to the place on my second album"

pissed the Gallagher's off and we were sent on our way.

"That was the end of our relationship with Oasis. I tried to speak with Noel on other occasions, but we had blown it. Well, Pete had!

"The band continued for a while but after seven years signs of tension were present, and the usual demise came about.

"I'd had a great time but it was over.

"I continued to release solo albums and was able to tackle the painful task of acknowledging my mother's death, and the many other areas of ill-health I had picked up from 'making it.'

"I am still releasing records and touring, but I'm also a psychotherapist specifically with musicians.

"I now come back to my beloved Bletchley regularly and dedicated the song Bletchley Park to the place on my second album.

"I still hold dear memories of growing up in Milton Keynes and the limited yet rich musical heritage it held for me.

"It will always hold a special place in my heart."

Alison Bancroft

"When The Stranglers came on I was at the front. It was so loud and fast.
From that moment I loved the music and sought it out."

When punk broke through the glam rock cracks, it engaged a nation – inspiring some, infuriating others.

Pop music was being turned on its head and being a teenager in the mid '70s was an exciting time. Being a youngster meant freedom of expression, passion, and two-fingered salutes.

But being a teen enjoying new music in a brand new town?

That was really something.

Alison Bancroft was there. She remembered her introduction to this new scene and its sounds.

"I used to listen to punk at my sister's flat, really liked it, and started buying some myself," she said.

"One of the first singles I bought was We Vibrate/Whips and Furs by The Vibrators.

"It was a step on from loud glam rock. It seemed to go that extra bit that I was looking for.

"When I was 15, in May 1977 I went to see The Stranglers at Bletchley Leisure Centre.

"When they came on I was at the front.

"It was so loud and fast and I had never experienced that at a gig before.

From that moment I loved the music and sought it out.

"I suppose it took a bit of time before I very slowly started to change my look, which began with me wearing a safety pin in my T-shirt.

I started bleaching my hair and colouring it, and wore punk clothes I had made myself.

"I used to go the the Sycamore Club in Fenny Stratford. They had an occasional gig and disco and would play any records you brought along.

"I began working a few hours in a shop in Central Milton Keynes, called Criminal Records.

"It had everything you wanted record

Alison Bancroft: Hair and shoulders above the rest

wise, plus fanzines and badges.

"I started going to Newport Pagnell Youth Club. Paul Davies was a fantastic youth worker and would put on gigs.

"The Peartree Youth Centre was great too. Dick Emmings was the youth worker there, and he encouraged us to get out and form bands, and he let us practice.

"He let our band Ethnik Minority play at the youth club and even gained funding from The Police - the band, not the law enforcers!

"The money enabled a lot of bands from the centre to record the album A Warped Sense of Human.

"There was a gig at the Woughton Leisure Centre and most of the bands from the album played the show. It was such a great night.

"I used to work the door at The Craufurd Arms too, so that I could get in free, and we would have our ear to the ground for any house parties that were happening.

"There were always a couple to choose from at the weekend, especially at the YMCA.

"Some nights there you could go from flat to flat and find a different party."

It wasn't only Johnny Rotten and Sid Vicious who made the newspapers at the time either – Alison had a taste of the tabloids when her wedding made the headlines: "I met my mates outside McDonald's, back when there was just the one in Milton Keynes," she recalled.

"Someone mentioned about me getting married the next day and a guy who overheard asked if I minded him coming along and taking some photos.

"When he arrived at Bletchley Register Office he said he was from The Mirror newspaper.

"They printed the photos and the local media picked up the story.

"We spent the next two weeks doing interviews and being photographed.

"The day after the wedding we went on a CND march in London and were photographed heading to that too. It was a bit of fun.

"Eventually, people moved on and things changed. When a few of my friends had kids, they stopped going to gigs.

"I took the stance you should get an excellent babysitter, treat them really well and you could then have your family, but also go out and have fun.

"A lot of friends followed the 'crusty' route and moved into vehicles. For me, it was the end of punk as it had been.

"It had been a really good time.

"It was fun and if I had my time over, I would do it all again."

> **"I used to work the door at The Craufurd Arms so I could get in free"**

Jeff Donert

Jeff was a tireless champion of music in Milton Keynes in the early '80s.
He was no stranger to the stage either, and then tragedy struck.

Jeff Donert was an essential part of the live music scene in the early '80s, promoting shows at venues including Muzak's and the Woughton Centre. He used music to fundraise and fronted his own band, Kingsize Keen & his Rockin' Machine.

"A band that I had named Safety Valve were looking for local gigs in Milton Keynes, at the start of the '80s," remembered bass player Nick Jones.

"I had a tape of us playing some original songs which I took to Jeff's home.

"Jeff was ill that day, and I left the cassette with his partner Pauline.

"I later saw him at the Woughton Centre during a Sunday lunchtime gig and introduced myself.

'Are you the Dire Straits band?' he said.

> **"Only after Jeff's death did I realise he was the bloke who had been waiting for us!"**

"One of my songs may have had a slight Straits approach, although I never really related to the band.

"Anyway, Jeff gave us a support slot at Muzak's, at The New Inn in New Bradwell.

'You're headlining the next time,' he told us. Great!

"We did quite a few gigs after that. Woughton, Muzak's and The Craufurd Arms became regular venues for us.

"Jeff would sit in when he could and when his own band of that time went on to new things, we became his regular backing band.

"Some years before all this, Bedford-based guitarist Dave King and I went to a place called The Cricketers Arms in Southend to audition for work, via the agent Barry Collings.

"Our drummer Maurice Barratt was too ill to make it.

"While we were there, another local drummer Jeff Willett was also auditioning and he played our set with us.

"When we finished a singer from Southend came over raving about us and said he would get us work with him.

"We came home and didn't think too much about it, not having taken in who the bloke was.

"The next week, Dave, Maurice and I were rehearsing at The Bull in Newport Pagnell before I dropped Dave back at Bedford.

"When we arrived, his dad told us that some bloke had come from Southend to see us and waited all night – he had only left just before we got back. We had just missed

each other. Neither party followed up on this and all was forgotten.

"Only after Jeff's death did I realise that he was the bloke who had been waiting for us!

"The whole time we had worked together it never entered our minds, though the clues were all there – Jeff was from Southend, the Barry Collings Agency, the gigs, the music. It had to be him."

Jeff fell ill after a gig supporting Chris Farlowe in Southend.

He had joked with fellow musicians that if he died, the show must go on. Jeff died later that night of a heart attack.

"I understand that Eric Clapton played a benefit show at the pub following Jeff's death," Nick said.

"Everything had come home, it seemed."

George Webley

It's not buildings that are the fabric of a place, it's those who bring their enthusiasm and make a difference - just like Big George.

George was a Londoner, born in Clapham in 1957. His first introduction to the movers and shakers in the music industry came when he was just days old and the crooner Frankie Laine was made his godfather.

But really, the first time that George was touched by the power of a tune was when Donald Swann, the composer and performer famous as one half of Flanders and Swann, played the piano at his school.

Donald's daughter was in George's class and Donald stepped in when the music master passed away suddenly.

"From the first moment he lifted the piano lid, I knew the direction my life was going to take," George later recalled.

When he left school, George took his burgeoning talent on the road with a show band.

Having written to Herbie Flowers for

> **"If passports still stated occupations mine would say 'composer of music with an average duration of 29 seconds'"**

advice, George became firm friends with him and would regularly accompany the acclaimed bassist on stage.

Speaking in 1980 George recalled their first meeting: "About a year ago I was at a loose end. I'd been playing since I was 15 but didn't seem to be getting anywhere.

"I felt really depressed but I wrote to one of my heroes, a great bass player called Herbie Flowers, who had played with Bowie, Essex and is now in a band called Sky.

"He said come around for a chat and a cuppa. My career has exploded since then."

He wasn't lying: In the 12-month period that followed their meeting George worked on more than 60 singles for various groups.

There were sessions with the London Symphony Orchestra too.

Even in those formative years of his career, George was generous to fellow artists, offering his services as a listener and someone who would lend a guiding hand.

"You need someone to talk to in this business and I'm more than willing to help if I can," he offered.

"Many talented musicians play night after night in their bedrooms, but are just too nervous to make that vital step forward. You can help people by making them easy with themselves."

He kept his enthusiasm and his word, and would later help launch Back Beat Records to aid new talent in Milton Keynes.

He threw his time and his money into the label.

This book's author still remembers when George generously offered her the money for a plane fare to Los Angeles to report on a band with local connections who had moved to the sunny side.

"You can give me it back whenever you've got it," he said as if he was offering the loan of a fiver.

By the age of 30 George was working as a musical director, and then took on the role of bandleader for the Sky television show Jameson Tonight.

His many compositions included arranging, producing and recording the music for the smash hit BBC comedy The Office (with Fin Muir taking care of vocal duties on Handbags & Gladrags), Room 101, and the outro music for One Foot in the Grave.

But one composition more than any other will strike a familiar chord with small screen viewers – George penned the theme for the hugely successful panel show Have I Got News for You.

It has been a constant on our television screens since 1990.

"If passports still stated occupations mine would say 'composer of music with an average duration of 29 seconds,'" he said.

He got his first break in broadcasting on Horizon Radio in the new city, and in 1994 George launched on the airwaves of GLR, presenting the Saturday late show.

In 1996 he had a heart attack on air, which took him away from the microphone for a period of recuperation.

But George continued with other musical avenues – together with his two sons he backed Radio 1 DJ Chris Moyles (who had learned the radio ropes in our area) at a number of outside broadcasts over a three year period.

Chris labelled George a genius, which no-one would argue with - least of all the honchos at BBC Three Counties Radio who employed the man with the big mouth (and the far bigger love of music) as a presenter.

His infectious, uncompromising voice would win an army of fans, and see him nominated for one of the industry's most prestigious awards – a Sony. In 2002 he found himself sitting among a shortlist of five that also included Mark Lamarr, Paul Gambaccini, Classic Gold stalwart Mike Sweeney and Radio 3 darling Sean Rafferty: "And me, the first local broadcaster to be nominated in this

George with Pete Winkelman (above) and Robbie Coltrane (left)

category. To me, that's a win, I've won already!" he remarked.

Win it he did, snatching the title of Music Broadcaster from the grasp of those other big players.

Going by their words, the judges must have found the decision an easy one to make: "Big George has an absolutely peerless passion for music of all varieties, and communicates that passion brilliantly.

"He's one of those unique broadcasters who just keep you listening – you can't walk away from the radio when he is talking."

He was funny too. One peer recalled how the Milton Keynes reporter pack would attend cinema press screenings on a weekly basis and George always sat himself at the front of the showing.

Horror writer Shaun Hutson was among the regulars and sat at the rear of the cinema: "George, why do you always sit at the front?" Shaun shouted.

"So I see the film before you," George retorted, quick as a flash.

George wasn't only in demand for his radio work or for his ability at penning a smashing theme tune though.

Whenever a musicologist was required for an explanation or an opinion, Big George was called upon – appearing on shows alongside John Peel and Nicky Campbell, on Kilroy and Esther, and on colourful morning show The Big Breakfast.

Wielding a guitar, dissecting the art

> **"You can't walk away from the radio when he is talking"**

of the Eurovision Song Contest, he won Denise Van Outen and Johnny Vaughan over. That was George - no airs, no graces, just a 'Take me as I am' confidence. And people responded warmly.

When the regional news programme Inside Out debuted on the BBC in 2002 it was George who presented for the eastern region, a role he held for two years.

He was a man who loved and lived for sound, and his family.

His love of music wasn't filed, chiseled or snooty. It was real.

George was just as happy working alongside musical icons like Barry Manilow or Gil Scott-Heron as he was presenting local events – from the half time pitch entertainment for MK Dons to leading the GO! Awards and filling in on bass for cover boys The Peartree Bridge Family, and MK's big and brilliant players The Blues Collective.

He even took to the MK Theatre stage for the Christmas 2005 pantomime Snow White and the Seven Dwarfs, starring alongside Warwick Davis as Stumpy, the tallest dwarf.

Big George passed away from a heart attack on May 7, 2011. He was just 53 years old.

When news of his loss broke on the station he had called home for five years, BBC London, calls and emails came in thick and fast, from all over the country and as far afield as Canada and New York.

In Stony Stratford hundreds of friends

and associates turned out to line the route as his funeral procession passed through the High Street.

The solemn air was punctured by those that had known and loved George blowing on kazoos as he passed. You can imagine the big man breaking into a little smile.

His legacy is still heard through his countless recordings, and his presence is still felt across Milton Keynes - because he was certainly one of the new town's most fervent supporters.

Wherever he went, George inspired, roused and entertained.

The airwaves are most certainly quieter without him, but anyone who met him will tell you that in our memories, George is still as loud as ever.

"I first met 'Big' George at Woughton Campus in 1984.

George approached me and said 'Hello mate, I'm 'Big' George and I want to put a band around you.'

Within a few weeks I was in rehearsal with Steve Kehoe on bass and drummer Shaun Dytham.

George was holding the reins and insisted I write more songs.

He wanted to call the band Graham Saunders and the Contenders - it was something being used a lot in the industry then; Ian Dury and The Blockheads, Elvis Costello and The Attractions, and so on.

Within a few weeks we were playing support to bands that George was in at The Dublin Castle, Dingwalls and The Mean Fiddler, and I thought the Contenders were about to make an impact on the UK scene.

George set up numerous meetings with A&R people and we were rejected time and again. They didn't like the name, so George and I shortened it to The Contenders, but we also wanted to keep my name linked with the band.

That was the first time I was called Graham D - the initial of my middle name, David.

I still use it to this day, although I have added the 'ee' as it was being confused with the hip-hop-rap thing that was beginning to take hold of the music scene.

I soon realised that George had a heart of gold and the patience of a saint.

It didn't take long before I became extremely close with George and his family.

I remember once babysitting for George and Sheila. He was instrumental in opening my ears to the music of all genres, and had left 10 albums for me to listen to while he was gone. One of the albums was by Michael Bolton. His voice was awesome and I recall trying to emulate some of the vocal licks he was using.

> **"I soon realised George had a heart of gold and the patience of a saint"**

It got to track four and my heart skipped a beat.

I looked at the title on the sleeve and it was 'How Am I Supposed To Live Without You.' I couldn't believe what I was listening to - this was my bloody song, or at least my chorus.

How did he get hold of it, why was it on his album and WTF was I going to do?

George asked if I had the original of the song, which of course I had - it was on a C90 tape and had been recorded in my bedroom in 1980.

This was the start of a brief, but bizarre episode in our relationship.

George was working on the Jameson Show on Sky Television and Michael was booked to be on the show in a few weeks time.

He was also booked on Wogan and Des O'Connor.

Once we contacted his label and made our claim to the song he was pulled from all UK appearances.

It was a no-win situation as we couldn't prove anything. All we had was a cassette of a 17-year-old kid sitting in his room singing a song about lost love.

All I ever wanted to be was a songwriter and this would have been an opportunity to fulfill my ambition.

I was never after money, just recognition, of which to this day I have never received.

I toured with George, laughed 'til I cried and got up to all sorts of harmless mischief.

I miss him very much and would've so wanted him to listen to the music I am recording today.

It has him stamped all over it."

Graham Dee

"George's legacy is not the long list of critical achievements but the unseen and unknown influences he had on the city's artistic fraternity.

We worked on many projects together, including our own record company.

For our misfortune we created Back Beat Records – a company we thought would go on to rival the great indie record institutions of Rough Trade and 2 Tone. It never rose to such dizzy heights, but it did provide a chance for us to cut our first EP at Abbey Road studios.

We were quite simply beside ourselves as we drove down the M1 in George's beat up and rusted old 1970s Volvo, listening to a specially prepared Fab Four cassette tape.

As we pulled up outside, an EMI doorman opened George's car door and we both expected him to inform us, 'You can't park that wreck of a car here.'

But instead he politely asked, 'Pink Floyd, Sir?' George, never being slow on the uptake replied, 'Yep mate' and gave him the keys and we both watched the immaculate doorman park George's beleaguered Volvo for us.

Once inside, the cutting of the EP became secondary to our main intention of the day, to find and personally witness The Beatles' legendary studio.

Luckily, we had a sympathetic cutting engineer with keys to the historic room. There was a piano in the corner and George took the opportunity to play a few bars of Let It Be, a song I now find hard to listen to.

As we left Abbey Road, the doorman superbly reversed George's Volvo back out for us. As we drove off we couldn't help but notice Nick Mason's bright red Ferrari parked out on the street and laughed ourselves stupid all the way home.

His finest attribute was whenever he discovered opportunities and made personal strides forward he always left the door open behind him for others to follow."

Lee Scriven

"I grew up in Milton Keynes in the 1980s. There wasn't much to do, so people took it upon themselves to do things, and the result was a thriving music and alternative night scene.

George was a proper muso, someone who'd been paid to be a session player and that really captured the imagination of us aspiring kids. He got involved in the local scene, helping bands and musicians and that's where I first came across him.

I'm grateful to George for encouraging me to have the confidence to dive into the creative world and not be intimidated by the idea of being encountered by 'experts' who'd somehow suss us out.

George was a catalyst, encouraging the careers of a number of folks.

Later, I was able to line him up to do the music on 'Have I Got News For You' and that turned out to be a nice way of repaying his support."

Tim Searle, head of animation, Beano Studios

Owning the airwaves:
George with Trevor Marshall (top)

Freddie Burretti

"He was one of the most talented spirits I had the honour of working with - we changed our world, small as it was, to what we thought it could be."

Freddie Burretti, the man who styled Bowie through much of his Ziggy Stardust period was, for a short time, a Bletchley boy.

Milton Keynes author and film-maker Lee Scriven explored the Burretti/Bowie story with a documentary, and then in 2019 he debuted the musical The Man Who Sewed The World.

"I first heard about Freddie back in the decadent 1980s while I was pretending to be a part time pop star in The Blues Collective," Lee said.

"Hammond Organ player Wixie was, and still is, proper rock 'n' roll both on and off the stage.

"The dressing room was his domain, and Wixie would hold court telling wonderful tales of his and others rock music exploits. His favourite recital was about a boy he knew from Bletchley who sprinkled his stardust on David Bowie and helped him become the famous superstar we all loved and cherished.

"It sounded like a fairytale; a boy from my Bletchley who became Mr Bowie's best mate and co Ziggy Stardust creator. Hence, why the rest of the band and I didn't take too much notice of such a wild claim."

But 25 years on, an acclaimed BBC4 documentary on Ziggy Stardust confirmed Wixie's story.

"My fuse of curiosity had been ignited, and I felt compelled to tell Freddie's story. "It was, and still is, a nigh-on obsession of mine to find out everything I can about this fascinating man.

"I also wanted to use my documentary to build a relationship of trust with Freddie's remaining family and with Mr Bowie and his management. I'm proud that the documentary succeeded in doing that. The critical response to the film did surprise me - it was just made on my overdraft, basically three cameras and 1,006 edits!"

Freddie with one of his closest friends, Daniella Parmar. She inspired the famous Ziggy haircut

With the 'reel' stuff taken care of, Lee turned his attentions to the musical. Burretti - The Man Who Sewed The World enjoyed its stage debut in 2019.

More than 30 actors, dancers and musicians brought their best to the piece, which was directed by Caz Tricks.

Getting involved in Lee's project was a no-brainer for her: "Scribbo creates a collective with a heart and a soul. "Whenever he has one of his 'ideas' I am up for it," she said.

A huge amount of work went into the delivery, and much like the man it was

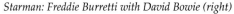
Starman: Freddie Burretti with David Bowie (right)

'Freddie possessed real integrity' - Lee Scriven

written about, it stood out.

And of course it had a soundtrack of Bowie brilliance at its heart.

"I felt a great sense of pride when the musical was finally staged.

It was something I honestly never thought would happen," Lee said. "Obviously, I didn't do it alone, my wife was absolutely pivotal to the completion, and I owe all the people who brought it to life so much."

Freddie's flair was in his amazing eye for fashion. And he loved to boogie!

"He would drive my old man nuts with his dancing," remembers his younger brother Stephen Burrett, "Dad would be trying to watch the TV and all he could hear was Freddie banging around dancing in his bedroom.

"He just loved to dance. At family gatherings, weddings and parties he'd walk in and start dancing straight away, you couldn't stop him. He was in a little world of his own."

David Bowie recalled his style guru fondly: "He was one of the nicest, most talented spirits that I have had the honour of working with," he said, "Freddie and I changed our world, small as it was, to what we thought it could be."

Quite possibly, Freddie wouldn't appreciate the attention that his name continues to attract.

"If I'm really honest, I think he would play it all down," Lee said.

"He might even be embarrassed about the worldwide adulation he constantly receives in the fashion and rock industry.

"He wasn't a man who felt he needed to brag or publicly claim anything, hence why I believe Mr Bowie held him in such high regard.

"He also never cashed in and remained a true friend to Mr Bowie.

"Freddie, above everything else, possessed real integrity. It was a trait Mr Bowie shared and that's something I personally strive for with this project."

The Man Who Sewed The World enjoyed three sold-out performances in Milton Keynes, and yet the show is far from over.

Things are just getting warmed up.

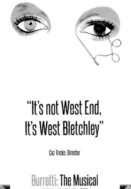

"It's not West End, It's West Bletchley"

Caz Tricks: Director

Burretti: The Musical
MAY 16th 17th 18th May 2019

Mick Abrahams

*"Cameron Crowe worked for Rolling Stone magazine and had covered
Blodwyn Pig… he must have had the track in his vaults!"*

Mick Abrahams could've written a book on the subject of friction between band members. The one time Jethro Tull guitarist, who was briefly replaced by Tony Iommi pre-Black Sabbath, has experienced the chart highs and the musical lows of band life during a varied career that saw him walk away from the scene and his guitar more than once.

But the lure of the strings always called him back.

Mick said: "My first group was The Jesters, which later turned into The Hustlers, then Original Hustlers. There was nothing original about it though - we did Shadows covers and rock 'n' roll!

"The Toggery Five came after, named after a shop called the Toggery that I was led to believe was somewhere in Stockport.

"Nearly all the band came from the Luton and Dunstable area; we all lived in Manchester at the time and made loads of road trips to Germany where we spent some time living.

"Eventually I returned home to

my mum's cooking and got a job as a warehouseman in a cold store - I was starving and broke!

"I kept playing though, and did sessions with people including Neil Christian and Screaming Lord Sutch.

"I got a group together called McGregor's Engine and then joined a unit called the John Evan Band - and that's when everything changed.

"The John Evan Band disappeared into thin air when everyone went back home leaving Ian Anderson, Glenn Cornick and I, so I rang my old mate Clive Bunker and he joined us.

"Following a few gigs under different names we finally settled on Jethro Tull.

"After the massive success that came from the Sunbury Festival, the first Jethro Tull album - This Was - was sitting around the No.3 position in the British charts in 1968, but I had different outlooks and views and the atmosphere between Ian, Glenn, and I was very bad.

"I left the band, gave in a formal notice,

and was rewarded by being sacked!

"I had a rest over Christmas and then formed Blodwyn Pig with Jack Lancaster, Andy Pyle and Ron Berg. We played our first gig at Cooks Ferry in Edmonton, filled the place and went down a storm."

The first Blodwyn Pig album, Ahead Rings Out, was recorded at Morgan Studios in Willesden and went to No.2 in the charts.

"We carried on touring Europe until the next album Getting To This was recorded.

"It reached No.3 and put us on Top Of The Pops with our single Same Old Story - it went in at Number 29 and dropped out the very next week!"

But more changes were ahead for Mick.

"We toured Stateside a second time, but when we returned to the UK I was sacked from my own band. That must be a record!

"Determined to carry on I formed the Mick Abrahams Band, continued touring the UK and Europe and made two albums, but the rot set in again and band squabbles broke out.

"I finally felt I'd had enough, and swapped the guitar for a ladder - working as a window cleaner, then a lifeguard and a car salesman. Jobs that felt normal and ordinary.

"During the late '80s I got a taste for music again and rescued the old guitar from the loft where I had once deposited it in disgust - I had come to terms with the fact that the business was the problem, not me.

"I reformed Blodwyn Pig with various incarnations and then the Mick Abrahams Band, and continued to gig through Europe and the UK.

"I even made several appearances with Jethro Tull and played reunion concerts, just for the fun of it."

But towards the end of 2009 Mick suffered serious health problems: "I had two heart attacks and a stroke. It took a severe toll on my health, my lifestyle and most importantly, my coordination with the guitar."

But his music keeps finding new ears, and a great song written by Mick in 1969 enjoyed a revival in 2000 – when it featured in the box office smash, Almost Famous.

Mick originally penned the track Dear Jill for a Blodwyn Pig album and its resurgence was a pleasant surprise.

Mick said: "I've been assured that it was actually director Cameron Crowe's idea to use the track – he worked for Rolling Stone magazine and had covered Blodwyn Pig in the past, so he must have had the track in his vaults!"

Mick (right) with Jethro Tull's Ian Anderson and Martin Barre

Bernie Marsden

"You think, 'Wouldn't it be great to be in a big band,' and then you end up in one of the biggest bands in the world..."

He is a rock and blues master of the guitar who has travelled the world gracing stages with many a familiar face, but Bernie Marsden has never forgotten his roots. He was raised in Buckingham, and it is still his home today.

As a youngster with a keen interest in music, Bletchley proved to be a beacon for Bernie: "It was a bit of a hub – you would go there to see the bands at Wilton Hall. I never knew where it was really – I just remember getting into a car with somebody and suddenly you were there with lights, and lots of people dancing. I thought 'this is good.'

"I was playing guitar then, but only a bit. Watching a band close up every couple of weeks I'd be thinking, 'I'd like to do this,' and I guess it's one of those things that stays with you subconsciously."

Even without realising it, Bernie was picking up what would become his lifelong trade.

"It was a learning curve, and it was exciting. Then when I played there, I'd think of all the famous people who had played the venue. It gave me a good feeling."

Bletchley Youth Centre had a huge impact on the young Bernie too: "That was the big thing for me, because they put my band on there. They put a festival on in around '69 and I met Elkie Brooks – I ended up playing with her 30 years later.

"Barrie Field, the promoter, put my band Skinny Cat on that day, and I'll always be grateful for things like that.

"We probably played at the Youth Centre every six weeks. I think we used to get five quid or something. It wasn't much, but it was good because you got to open up for these headline bands, and hang out and see how they worked, and I did learn a lot from that. You couldn't have bought that experience."

In Bernie's musically keen mind, the cogs were turning: "I went to work and played for fun in those days, thinking and dreaming that 'maybe one day I could do this for real,' but then pinching myself and

Bernie with Whitesnake 80/81 and (below) with Billy Gibbons from ZZ Top, Brian May and a Skinny Cat advert

saying 'get real!'"

But for Bernie and his tremendous talent at the fret, the future would be a great one.

He went from working with the aforementioned Buckingham-based Skinny Cat as a teenager to playing with UFO in 1972. And from then on, the music just kept happening – including a gig with Cozy Powell's Hammer and work with Babe Ruth, and then in 1977 he became an original member of Paice Ashton Lord.

The career defining moment followed when he formed Whitesnake with David Coverdale.

Bernie worked on the first five studio albums with Whitesnake, and co-wrote some of their biggest hits, including Here I Go Again and Fool For Your Lovin'. Monstrous songs that stand tall today.

Bernie left Whitesnake in 1981 and numerous projects, bands and solo work followed. In 2011 he joined Whitesnake on stage for the first time in three decades much to the delight of fans, and he has since popped up with them at festivals and various other shows.

But Bernie's own career of plenty has seen him stage share with rock 'n' roll luminaries including Robert Plant, Ringo Starr and Paul Weller, and too many others to mention.

His most recent solo opus, 2014's Shine included guest appearances from Whitesnake frontman David Coverdale, and Joe Bonamassa.

With such a rich history of work, it was small surprise when Bernie decided to document it; his self-published biography 'Where's My Guitar? was lauded by fans and has since been snapped up by publisher Harper Collins.

Bernie has lived the dream, and he's not through with it yet.

"I am still living the dream," he says with a laugh.

"I never wanted to be a pop star. I wanted to be a guitar player, and then I became a songwriter. Then you think, 'Wouldn't it be great to be in a big band?' and then you end up in one of the biggest bands in the world.

"You couldn't make that up, could you?"

Mike Stevens

Everyone remembers pop's 'big five,' but Take That's 'sixth member'
was a long-time resident of Milton Keynes.

Mike Stevens lived from a suitcase, travelling extensively with pop phenomenon Take That during the '90s. But at the end of those touring schedules, he would swap the high life for sleepy Newport Pagnell.

Wisbech-born Mike moved to the town in 1985.

"At the time I was working with various function bands and had a job playing at Hammersmith Palais. I was living in Birmingham, so the move was an ideal opportunity to be nearer London - and Newport Pagnell was the only place I could afford to buy a house!"

At the tail end of the '80s, Mike recorded at Linford Manor studio with the dance group L.A Mix who achieved singles chart success.

"That was the first time I had been a writer and producer on a record that went into the Top 40," he recalled.

"It was a very good studio, very old school and really great. A lot of bands really liked going there.

"The Neve desk was one of the biggies."

Saxophonist Mike met up with Fin Muir, a singer who had toured the US with Mötley Crüe and Kiss in rock troupe Waysted. Quickly, 5 Go Jazz was born. "We used to play Dukes Wine Bar and The Point quite regularly. There was a bit of a local following because we were a fun band more than anything.

"We did a combination of things, a lot of Cab Calloway stuff. It was loosely based around jazz, but involved other forms too."

Between London gigs and local sets Mike spent his time working on solo material in his home studio and recorded what evolved into his debut album, Light Up The Night.

The release was eventually picked up by RCA Records.

To support the release, Mike returned to The Point for solo shows, but by this time his work elsewhere was beginning to take off. Then he received a call that would change his career path forever.

"I had been working with David Grant

on a solo album and he knew a session guy who was putting together a band to tour with this pop group, Take That.

"He asked me to get involved and I did. They started to get massive, very quickly."

Before long, Mike found himself taking the reins as musical director for the pop aces.

"It was a bit daunting, a bit unusual, and not what I was used to - the whole screaming girls thing - but you soon get used to it," Mike recalled.

"I was with them pretty much from the start, and by the time of the split in 1996 it was enormous.

"As musical director I had to get the music and everything exactly right, particularly back then - they were very young and inexperienced and didn't know anything.

"They relied on me to make them sound good and make it work. In those days they were very green.

"Gary obviously knew what he was doing though, and even then was writing the songs. I think that was one of the big differences - we were dealing with a band who were very musical because of him.

"But they were young and it was difficult in a lot of other ways, because of what they were going through, and Robbie's problems impacted on everybody."

When the split happened, teenage girls were so traumatised that special helplines were set up to help them cope with the 'loss.'

For Mike, it was a chance to spread his musical wings, and the now London-based ace had no shortage of offers.

"By that time I was starting to work with a lot of other bands,

"It is pretty amazing to sit in a room rehearsing with Paul McCartney"

and it was good to go out and do other things, not be tied down.

"It was tinged with sadness though, because it had been a brilliant time."

Mike kept the musical flame burning - in total three solo albums hit the racks, and when time allowed, he took up position with the reformed 10cc.

But then the call came through for the Take That reunion.

"I got a call from Gary back in 2005 saying they were reforming and doing some arena shows and would I fancy it again.

"I said 'Yeah, absolutely,' not really thinking too much of it, particularly in terms of what it was going to become.

"I remember it was going to be seven arena shows originally, but by the end of it, we had done 30, and then tagged on a couple more at the Milton Keynes Bowl.

A home from home for Stevens: "I loved it, it was my favourite gig of the tour.

"There was something intimate about it and those kind of venues are always the most fun."

Mike's extensive CV includes overseeing the Children in Need concerts and a long relationship working as musical director for Annie Lennox.

He was at the helm for the Queen's Diamond Jubilee concert at Buckingham Palace too.

"I've worked with Paul McCartney and Stevie Wonder...I do feel a little bit of pressure sometimes. It doesn't daunt me in the same way it would have done once upon a time, although it is pretty amazing to sit in a room rehearsing with Paul McCartney!"

Take That

Adam Wakeman

*His dad is prog rock royalty and Adam followed the musical trail - he
is one of Ozzy Osbourne's most trusted musical collaborators.*

As an eight-year-old, Adam Wakeman was already learning classical piano, and by the time he was 17 he had recorded the first of several albums with his father, Rick Wakeman.

They took their creativity on tour together too, playing throughout Europe, America, Russia and Canada.

"I've always loved playing and writing music," Adam said, "I'm not sure what it would be like without having that in my life. Watching my father was a huge part in igniting that passion and the desire to pursue it as a career."

When he was 24-years-old, Wakeman won the Best New Talent Award in American Keyboard magazine which raised his profile further.

He doesn't know whether there is something musical in the genes, but having a musical family "does make it easy if you need to borrow a keyboard or something!"

In great demand for his work as a keyboard player and as a musical director, Adam's talents have been utilised by artists including Robbie Williams, Will Young, Slash, Victoria Beckham and Travis.

For the past 16 years Adam has been ensconced in Ozzy Osbourne's band, and he co-wrote six tracks on Ozzy's platinum-selling 2010 album Scream.

When Black Sabbath hit the road in support of their final album, he took care of keyboard and additional guitar duties and when the rock legends decided to bow out with The End tour, Adam was back in play again.

When time allows, Adam lets his creativity flow as half of the duo Wilson & Wakeman, with songwriter and vocalist Damian Wilson.

They released their debut album Weir Keeper's Tale in 2016, followed in 2018 by The Sun Will Dance In Its Twilight Hour. A session album, Stripped, was released in 2019.

He tours frequently, so Adam is a slave to discipline: "I run most days and try to do more than 100 miles a month," he says, shaming the rest of us, "It keeps me sane and helps me stay a bit healthier on the road.

"I also run my own production library publishing company so that fills up almost every spare minute. We always have several albums in production and music in various TV shows, so there's plenty to fill the time."

With so much time spent hopping from one venue to another, career highlights are almost too many to recall.

Perhaps engaging with 45,000 rabid Ozzy fans in São Paulo? Or headlining the Monsters of Rock Festival with Ozzy and with Sabbath? Or wowing L.A's leading venues The Hollywood Bowl and The Forum?

The list is endless, but two shows stand out in particular: "Live 8 was pretty memorable," Adam recalled, "I had a day off on the Black Sabbath tour and flew from Stockholm to London and then back again so I could play that show. I was so glad I managed to get there.

"But the proudest moment is probably when my three children got on stage with me at The Stables during a concert there and sang backing vocals for me."

For a man often on the road, home needs to be a break from the madness.

That place is a stones throw away from Milton Keynes: "We moved to a village outside Buckingham about 18 years ago and have lived within a few miles of the town ever since. We love it."

In early 2020, Adam oversaw the debut LP release by Jazz Sabbath - 50 years after it should have hit the racks. The band - founded by a certain Milton Keanes - were considered to be at the forefront of the new jazz movement in the late 1960s.

After one listen you'll never think of Black Sabbath in the same way again...

A family affair: Taja, Skyla & Kai Wakeman join Adam (far left) on stage at The Stables

Paul Rivers

"We had to clean 'blood' stains out of the centre before the staff got in the following morning!"

Paul Rivers went from enjoying gigs on one side of the barrier to working shows on the other in 1995. It was the start of a 15-year relationship between Paul and The Pitz venue.

"Once I took over the reins I started to rebuild the name and reputation of the club - by building up a new scene, and searching out great local bands with huge potential to pack out the venue.

"I also wanted to make it a sanctuary for all the music fans and young people of Milton Keynes who didn't quite fit into a very safe, conservative town, and needed somewhere to go where they could belong. Then we slowly began putting on much bigger acts from around the world, as well as the local nights.

"It was always more than just a venue to all the kids that came through in my time. It really was their special place - where they made friends, met partners and played their first gigs.

"Along the way we put on music workshops, released fanzines and five compilation albums, nurtured bands and had a great laugh.

"My time was well spent at the venue and I am proud of what we achieved for the club and for the city.

"I was lucky enough to put on some absolutely fantastic bands - big established touring acts, as well as great local nights. Seeing a local band like Capdown go on to national success was just as important as putting on prog metal legends Mastodon.

"But three shows that stood out for me were The Dandy Warhols, Mark Lanegan Band and Gwar.

"The first time Dandy Warhols played they were buzzing, with songs in the charts and on popular television adverts.

"They brought a powerful projector with them and had no stage lights - they just

> **"It was always more than just a venue to all the kids that came through"**

projected TV static across the stage and the band as they played.

"It was completely mind-blowing for two hours. I was sitting behind the barrier with my jaw on the floor, marvelling at their brilliance!

"Most bands you put on in a club like The Pitz are not necessarily to your personal taste. My job, first and foremost, was to give people what they wanted - a great night and gigging experience.

"But I am a big Mark Lanegan fan from his time in Screaming Trees and for his solo albums. He came with minimal lights, it was really moody, and he has an

Gwar

awesome voice and songs...it was just a fantastic concert.

"I still can't believe I got away with putting GWAR on in an all-ages venue in a family community and leisure centre, but what a spectacle it was!" says Paul, who is still active in the MK scene as co-owner of a band management company, and as an events manager at the Craufurd Arms.

"It was a show full of absolute mayhem and with so much fake blood and monster juices that we had to mop it out the fire doors at the end of the night, and clean 'blood' stains out of the centre before the staff got in the following morning!"

Promoter Paul Rivers

Beanie Bhebhe

"My biggest dreams always included performing on 'Later... with Jools Holland' and headlining Glastonbury. I've managed to do them multiple times."

Around the world, teenagers discover music, decide that a life on the road is for them, pick up a plectrum or a drumstick and dream of being part of the next big thing to wow stadia.

But one Milton Keynes lad combined his talent and passion with a healthy work ethic and turned those dreams into reality.

Beanie Bhebhe first stage stepped at The Pitz as a member of Headfly, who became a decent draw on the Milton Keynes scene for their noisy alt-rock sounds, and he started to hone the skills that would lead him to some of the biggest stages in the world.

At the same time as he was hitting the skins with Headfly he was also feeling the fret as part of six-legged music machine The Ideas. They were finalists in the 2003 Band Blitz competition.

"I learned a lot from the MK scene; I learned about DIY touring, I learned about putting on my own gigs. I learned how to perform well, either using the most basic equipment or by using the clearest sounding PA systems, and I learned about professional recording sessions.

"All of those things were first experienced in Milton Keynes."

And when Beanie wasn't feeding his musical habit on stage, he was a punter supporting his friends in other bands. The scene was vibrant, encouraging and brimming with creativity.

"I remember watching some of the best bands I've ever heard at The Pitz. It really hurt me when some of them stopped performing, for whatever reason.

I just kept thinking 'We have such a uniquely amazing pool of talented people here, so why aren't we trying to show the world?'

"I also got a little complacent, but once I went to Uni in London I realised I needed to try and express what Milton Keynes had taught me, in as many places as possible.

"When I was 19 I met some musicians from Bletchley that ran an indie label called Fortissimo Records.

"Over time, label head and promoter Don McLean became a huge influence and showed me an avant-garde alternative music community around Milton Keynes that I never knew existed. I ended up joining his band Action Beat for an album and a tour, which was an honour. His support of all my leftfield projects since then is something I have always highly regarded, and I will never forget all he has taught me."

Beanie then took on a professional drumming gig which came through a contact of his brother, fellow MK scene dweller, Simba.

He helped hook Beanie up with Australian singer-songwriter Gabriella Cilmi.

In 2008, she had one of the summer smashes with the track Sweet About Me. For a time then, it seemed like radio stations played little else. It was a great gig to bag, and a nice introduction to a fruitful future.

With the spotlight on him, Beanie networked, 'and gained a reputation that meant people were interested in working with me.'

He played bass in Various Cruelties, whose music-making has been described as 'Motown-influenced pop.'

> **"My memories of the scene in Milton Keynes are the ones I truly hold dearest in my heart"**

They bagged a deal with Mercury Records and their debut LP was recorded in LA with producer Tony Hoffer. Beanie took on bass and drumming duties for the release, and made his debut on the BBC's lauded music show, Later... with Jools Holland.

In the same year, he also took the drum stool with London-based drum 'n' bass players Rudimental.

Beanie had been at Uni with Rudimental's Amir and the two had pooled their talents on plenty of sessions together. When Rudimental decided to create a live band, Amir gave Beanie a call. While hoping for success, what followed must have exceeded their own expectations; with Brit Awards, Mobo nominations, multi-platinum album sales and a touring schedule that saw the lad from Milton Keynes hot-footing it around the world bringing their rhythm alive. With Rudimental he toured Stateside and Australia as support to Ed Sheeran.

In late 2016 Rudimental collaborator Anne-Marie snagged Beanie for her band, this time he was able to fret-feel as bass/guitarist. Chart placings and tour dates were fruitful, and then Anne-Marie bagged

Headfly (2003)

her own mega tour with Ed Sheeran in the summer of 2018, which saw MK's fast mover owning stages across the UK, Europe and the USA.

Stadium shows alongside Ed Sheeran became the norm once again.

"My biggest dreams always included things like performing on Later... with Jools Holland, headlining Glastonbury, playing the Coachella Festival in California and playing Wembley.

"Thankfully I've managed to do them all multiple times, which I would never have been able to do without the inspiration I gained from the musicians in Milton Keynes," Beanie says.

"In 2017 I made the front cover of my favourite drum magazine, Rhythm. Mind blown.

"I also felt the same way when Headfly got the front cover of the Citizen's GO! magazine in Milton Keynes.

"Everything I have been able to experience is due to being part of such an incredible place to develop musically and the Milton Keynes scene will never be forgotten. It inspired my intrigue and interest in so many genres of music and I owe everything I ever do in life to MK.

"My memories of the scene there are the ones that I truly hold the dearest in my heart..."

Beanie recording with Headfly at Blinding Studios in Newport Pagnell (top), and with The Ideas (above and left)

Dan Englander

It began with a Prince's Trust start-up loan and now MK's KingUnderground label is conquering decks far and wide.

Since launching back in 2005, independent online record outlet KingUnderground has expanded and is now operational as a record label releasing music from artists all over the world.

"The aim is to release quality underground music on vinyl as well as on digital formats," says man at the helm Dan Englander, who co-founded the business with Peter McCaffrey.

The pair shared a passion for good music, record collecting and hip hop.

Today Dan is the sole owner of KingUnderground.

It still predominantly pushes hip hop, but there's room for some soul and funk too, and more expansion planned.

The growing roster of artists includes players from Norway, Russia and the U.S, and some from Milton Keynes, including Ernest Herb and Simiah.

Simiah's debut release in 2010 was only the second album issued through the label.

One of the most successful label names is one-time Virgin Records signing Lewis Parker, who has produced for the Wu-Tang Clan's Ghostface Killah.

The label is going from strength to strength, and Dan also uses KU as a vehicle for his own music-making, delivering tunes under the name Pings.

Ernest Herb

Tony Platt

"I was given a piece of advice early on that you work with people, not for people."

If you are a rock music fan with a few classic albums in your collection, there's every chance you own something that Tony Platt has had a hand in.

When it comes to music production, the man with more than five decades of work under his belt occupies the top echelon.

A visit to the Radio One studios as a schoolboy, combined with a general love of music helped him into his first positions; working at London-based Trident and Basing Street Studios.

"I knew I wanted to be in a studio playing with tape recorders after that visit to the BBC. I had written dozens of letters to studios asking for a job and got two replies, just before I had given up trying; one was from De Lane Lea and the other from Trident. I went for an interview with both on the same day, got offered both jobs and chose Trident. I then became a 'tea boy.'

Trident and Basing Street were both utilised in numerous recordings, and as an assistant, Tony worked on sessions for The Who, The Stones, Zeppelin and Traffic.

As an engineer, the work kept coming, with luminaries including Free and John Martyn, and the early 1970s saw him mix the album Catch A Fire, and then record and mix the follow-up, Burnin', by an artist who was largely unknown at the time; Bob Marley.

Those releases became Marley's first two gold discs, and took reggae from the sidelines into the spotlight.

It was the beginning of a genre association for Tony that saw him work with artists including Toots and the Maytals and Lorna Bennett. But he

returned to his rock roots and recorded demos for Thin Lizzy and The Stranglers that would prove potent enough to see them both ink record deals.

As producer Mutt Lange's engineer, Tony worked on classics including AC/DC discs Highway to Hell and Back in Black, Foreigner 4 and The Fine Art of Surfacing by The Boomtown Rats.

The '80s saw more hard rock action with bands including Samson (featuring a pre-Maiden Bruce Dickinson), Iron Maiden, Motörhead, Gary Moore, Ronnie James Dio and The Cult.

The studio environment can be a fractious one, with lots of pressures and egos, and the producer can sometimes be the glue holding the process together. Tony makes allowances for artists, but has always tried to avoid confrontation: "I try to spend time with the artist before going into the studio so we can discuss what we are about to do.

"This helps to lay the foundation for what comes next and enables me to get a good idea where the bumps in the road might be," he said.

"Generally I appreciate the pressures the artist will be facing and I am prepared to tolerate quite a bit of bad behaviour from talented artists - less so from less talented ones.

"You manage artists by being considerate and remembering that they are the reason you are there.

"I was given a piece of advice early on that you work with people, not for people."

In more recent times, Tony has worked away from the rock genre for which he is most well-known – driven by a craving to engage with varying styles.

Jazz releases feature heavily, thanks in no small part to a close association with the record label Dune, with albums by Soweto Kinch and Denys Baptiste among the deliveries. He also produced Clare Teal's Don't Talk opus.

"Every session is quite classic in some way or another and it is always tempting to elevate sessions with the benefit of hindsight," Tony admits, "The Bob Marley sessions were a lot of fun and so were the AC/DC ones, but others, like recording John Dankworth in his living room for an album he did with his daughter Jacqui, were special.

"It was one of those times when you have to pinch yourself," he recalled. "Another special session at Basing Street was with Paul Kossoff, John Martyn, Simon Kirke, Rabbit and Tetsu Yamauchi - just a load of musicians who turned up and jammed all night."

Today, Tony's work spans rock to reggae and much in-between, and the man who has travelled the world for sound is quite happy to work from his home close to Milton Keynes when the opportunity presents itself; he has just installed an impressive new mixing room on site.

Tony Platt setting the microphones around Hells Bell with Mike Milsom - the guy that actually made and played the bell - for the recording

The bell foundry was Taylors in Loughborough

The Stables

*The brand new town didn't have a shopping centre, but it would have
a live music venue. John Dankworth and Cleo Laine would see to that.*

"We were living in a very beautiful Georgian house in Aspley Guise when we decided to do the Stables thing," Cleo said, "A lot of people thought we were out of our minds when we told them about it. They would say, 'That's the sort of thing you do when you retire – you can't do that and keep on working.' But we went ahead with it."

The idea behind the venture came to the couple while performing in Cumbria: "A Hungarian gentleman, Miki Sekers, lived there. He was the head of Sekers Silks, a big firm that sold uniform material. He had a very beautiful house and had created a little miniature opera house out of a barn. "We used to work there quite often. We were so enchanted by it and said, 'One day we'll have one of them.'"

Aspley Guise wasn't a suitable spot to set about launching a new venue though – it was too populated.

"We knew darn well that we wouldn't get off the ground without complaints. "Then The Old Vicarage came on the market. As it was a Victorian rectory it was

very dark and gloomy, but the stable was there, so we bought the house," Cleo said.

Hilary Davan Wetton, founder of Milton Keynes City Orchestra said: "There is no doubt that the artistic life of Milton Keynes was changed by John and Cleo's decision to live in the Old Rectory.

"It is also true that the Development Corporation (MKDC) in the early days were quick to grasp how important their presence could be and supported their musical projects. The MKDC made a significant commitment to Wavendon – and later also to the MK City Orchestra – without which the panorama of musical activity that we now take for granted would simply not exist."

Cleo: "We started the music in Milton Keynes, John and I, simply because there wasn't anything here. MKDC realised that and helped us from the beginning.

"They got us a secretary to work in the old Stables, Lavinia Dyer. She knew everybody – aristocrat, peasant and everything inbetween!

"She reminded me of a pantomime

dame – someone who would slap her thighs and say, 'We'll get the job done.'"

Laurie Holloway, whose successful career as a musical director saw him at the helm of Michael Parkinson's chat show, was John and Cleo's pianist at the start of The Stables project.

"When they moved to the Old Rectory it was a very busy time," Laurie said.

"Lots of dinner parties with people of the time, Dudley Moore, John Bird, Eleanor Bron, John Neville, Wendy Toye, Princess Margaret and more.

"I remember the opening of the old Stables. It was all a bit stuck together, but there was an immediate good feel about it thanks to John and Cleo being so involved.

"It wasn't attempted to keep John away from any project that was going on. His stamina and musical genius were awe-inspiring.

"Music was all-pervading at Wavendon. "Every social event was a musical event. "I played piano for so many people at the house. One lovely memory is playing for Cleo's father. He had a good voice and was a bit of a ham.

"Princess Margaret knew the words to most songs. I asked her once how she knew the verses to certain songs and she

> **"I asked Princess Margaret how she knew the verses to certain songs, and she said 'Mr Noël Coward taught me'"**

said, 'Mr Noël Coward taught me.'"

But The Stables project brought many a challenge for its instigators – plenty of them financial.

"John and I had to go to the bank and say we would honour the debts up to a certain amount if it got into trouble, which we did for a very long time," Cleo said.

"Even at the beginning of the new Stables we did that as well. But we never had any regrets. We both really believed in what we were doing."

People thought the couple with the unbridled passion for music were taking things a little too far.

Saxophonist Benny Green recalled the time he saw the venue-to-be: "John guided me across a courtyard, through a door and onto some rough ground on which stood a sort of derelict barn.

"When we got inside John said to me, 'And this is the theatre!' I thought he was off his head!"

But passion would win out against the ridiculous and hard toil would beat those pesky leaks and other ailments by which the venue would be blighted.

"When we first got started we were very hands on – there was nobody else to be," Cleo said.

"There was paint on the carpet for a long time that I spilt and John used to point out to people, 'That's what Cleo did!'"

But many hands made light work, and Wavendon residents helped turn the space once used as a nut and bolt factory with links to Bletchley Park, into a musical hub.

Classical guitarist John Williams, jazz pianist John Ogdon, and Richard Rodney Bennett joined John and Cleo as the first artistic directors of the venue.

The Stables held its first concert on February 6, 1970.

Naturally featuring the sublime talent of the couple with the vision, the Grand Opening Gala also attracted the aforementioned Richard Rodney Bennett, folk artist Julie Felix, jazz singer Marion Montgomery and her husband Laurie Holloway, pianist André Previn and lyricist Richard Stilgoe.

Guitarist John Williams played that

Stables friends: Laurie Holloway (left) and John Williams in 2017

evening too – having spent the day painting the venue ready for curtain up. He performed with evidence of his labouring caught under his fingernails.

"I have heard him play before," John Dankworth is reported to have said, "But never have I heard him play with so much emulsion!"

Almost 50 shows were held in the year that followed. Then, as now, artist pedigree, innovation and diversity ruled.

In 1973 artists including violin virtuoso Stéphane Grappelli, pop star Georgie Fame and the London Chamber Orchestra all graced the stage.

Flick through any number of old brochures and souvenir programmes and the names keep on rolling. In 1980, flautist James Galway, actresses Fenella Fielding and Prunella Scales and trumpeter Humphrey Lyttelton appeared.

Names that were to prove pivotal elsewhere in the new town also played a big part. The Folk at the Stables events were organised by Stony Stratford's music man and honorary Stables trustee Matt

> **"I have heard him play before" said John, "But never have I heard him play with such emulsion!"**

Armour, while Hilary Davan Wetton founded the MKCO.

'The Wavendon AllMusic Plan (or WAP, as it became widely known) has the same goals today as it had when it launched, being 'dedicated to the furtherance of the cause of music of all kinds, and to the breaking down of barriers which hamper its appreciation.'

Vladimir Ashkenazy, Max Bygraves, Dudley Moore, Roy Castle, George Melly, Ronnie Scott, Sheila Hancock, Spike Milligan, Yehudi Menuhin and Joyce Grenfell were among the many varied and illuminating names leaving their mark in the early years.

But The Stables reached further into the community, embracing art in its more literal sense by offering a space to exhibit paintings and prints by artists.

Edna Read was among those showing her creations in 1973 in the exhibition A Different View.

A firm supporter of the venue in its formative years, she recalled accompanying Cleo with both of them on

WEST ELEVATION

103

their hands and knees as they attempted to mop up yet another leak that had sprang at the venue.

Meanwhile, John's sister Avril Dankworth, herself an accomplished pianist, could see potential in the fields that surrounded The Stables.

And those fields were filled with the sound of music when Avril launched her National Children's Music Camps in 1970, known in more recent years as the National Youth Music Camps.

Young people with a thirst for musical knowledge relished the learning events which were healthily infused with adventure and fun.

The summer camps were widely respected and ran on the site for 49 years, but sadly the green area surrounding The Stables was sold for development of housing, and in 2019 the courses were moved to a new venue outside Milton Keynes.

Leading talents who passed through the MK camps as youngsters include Radiohead's Thom Yorke, Sting's guitarist Dominic Miller, songwriter Guy Chambers and screenwriter Tim Firth, the man responsible for the comedy film smash Calendar Girls.

"Imagine coming to the Wavendon Music Camps as a kid and then finding the score to your first TV film was going to be composed by John Dankworth," Tim remembered.

"I was petrified. As a young man I sat and marvelled at the way John was constantly attuned to what everyone around him was offering up, how he heard individual voices and responded, and how he was constantly giving."

In the summer of 1979 work was completed on a £40,000 extension to The Stables theatre.

HRH Princess Margaret, a close friend of the Dankworth family, officially opened the building.

But less than five years later things were nowhere near as jolly; John and Cleo dropped the bombshell that The Stables might close its doors forever because of a financial crisis. Furthermore, they said that if WAP was wound up, they would sell their home and leave the area.

Thankfully, disaster was avoided and the path cleared for the music to continue. But the venue was never going to prop itself up for long. It had withered, was tired and parts were literally rotting.

Plans for a new auditorium were drawn up, signalling a new dawn for the new city's most cherished of entertainment

By Royal Appointment: Princess Margaret at The Stables in 1979

spaces. Raising the substantial funds to make the ambitious project a reality would prove exhaustive.

Dreams became reality thanks to gifts and generosity from The Arts Council of England, from Jim Marshall and from John and Cleo themselves.

Purse strings were tightened and costs reduced in order for work to reach completion.

The new 398-seater Stables opened with a Gala Launch on October 5, 2000. Princess Margaret reprised her earlier role and officially cut the ribbon on a new era.

The Stables would still face financial woes, but each time a black cloud formed, a silver lining would patch the nasty and the venue would continue to shine brightly.

The musical couple juggled hugely successful international careers with the business of The Stables.

Cleo slipped into musicals too - with successful engagements in Showboat, and Colette, which was based on the colourful life of French author Sidonie-Gabrielle Colette.

John wrote Colette for Cleo: "I actually asked Tom Stoppard if he would write

The Stables under construction

105

Stables all-stars: Henry Rollins (above), Amy Winehouse (top) and Craig David

it and he didn't seem in the least bit interested. Then, quite secretly, John wrote the whole thing. I didn't know he was doing it. He just handed it to me and said, 'Here you are.' I couldn't have written it and couldn't think of anyone I thought would do it to my liking.

"I fell in love with him all over again."

In the late noughties, the old bar area at The Stables took on a new lease of life itself. Stage 2 offers artists a smaller space to perform in.

During its 40 year history, many emerging talents and scene stalwarts have bowed to The Stables and its ace acoustics.

The venue has seen everything – from emerging world music artists to seminal bluesmen, comedy A-listers including Russell Brand and Lenny Henry, to jazz royalty like Dave Brubeck.

Some will have been dazzled by the voice of emerging singer Amy Winehouse, or been in the audience the night that Craig David played with the Dankworth Seven.

Seeing the now departed musician John Martyn, who was clearly in ill-health when he took to The Stables stage, and listening to the beauty of the man and his guitar in partnership, was something to savour.

Watching Arthur Lee fronting Love at the venue, cutting into '60s classics like Alone Again Or, and seeing blues legend

The Stables at 40: Dame Cleo and Paul O'Grady

It's a family affair: Sir John and Dame Cleo with children Alec and Jacqui

David Annand's sculpture of Sir John at The Stables entrance

Dr John, Rolling Stone Charlie Watts and Cream aces Jack Bruce and Ginger Baker at work on various occasions are all filed away in the memory box.

The Stables is a special venue that makes special memories and it can stand next to the big boys – it was ranked fourth in the Performing Right Society's Top 100 venues in the country.

On February 6, 2010, exactly 40 years to the day since The Stables first opened its doors for business, a celebratory star-studded gala was planned at the venue, with Cleo and John set to perform alongside artists including Victoria Wood, Timothy West and Prunella Scales, Paul O'Grady, Jennie Linden and Maureen Lipman.

But John had spent the previous few months suffering ill health and wasn't at Cleo's side. Tragically, he passed away at London's King Edward VII hospital, just hours before the curtain rose.

He was 82 years old.

The event, which also featured son Alec and daughter Jacqui, became a tribute to the jazz legend.

A gasp echoed around the auditorium when Cleo made the devastating announcement of his passing.

With great strength and courage, she told the sold-out audience: "I have some sad news for you. John was going to come on and play in his wheelchair for you, but we went to the hospital today and when we got there, John had passed.

"I don't want to bring you down, but I think you should still sit here and celebrate the music.

"We were joined at the hip for a long time and I'll miss him," she added.

"If I had announced it at the beginning of the show it would have put a dampener on the whole night and then it would have been much harder for us to carry on," Cleo told me later.

"Because The Stables was his baby, we couldn't not do it and if that boot had been on the other foot, he would have done the same, I think.

"Music was his life and I always said to people it was music that kept us together. "I would never say to him 'It's me or your music,' because I knew which he would choose!

"Not only did the jazzers admire him, but the classical musicians and the rock

> **"We were joined at the hip for a long time and I'll miss him"**

musicians did too. He gathered all the big styles into his head and his whole physique."

John made headlines in life, but when he passed, column inches saluted him too.

Aside from the British media coverage, John had obituaries in the New York Times, L.A Times, San Francisco Times and in Australia, New Zealand and Hawaii.

"John made his mark and made friends wherever he worked. He took people as he found them, it didn't matter what their background was," Cleo said.

"He always thought that everybody was equal in every way, you see – unless they pointed out that they weren't!"

A memorial service was held at The Stables on March 10, 2010.

Richard Stilgoe presented and guests including Maureen Lipman and Bill Oddie were treated to tributes by Chick Corea and George Shearing.

Today, John still has a wonderful presence at the venue he founded.

In December 2014 a commemorative bronze sculpture of Sir John was unveiled at the venue entrance.

The stunning work was commissioned by the trustees of the Wavendon Allmusic Plan (WAP) and created by renowned Scottish sculptor David Annand.

Dame Cleo was honoured with the Freedom of the Borough of Milton Keynes on March 31, 2011.

Woburn Abbey

"It was last year's 'hippy' invasion all over again. Long-haired girls in sacking and occasional see-through blouses, even longer-haired boys in robes."

Woburn Abbey is an exquisite example of a stately home, revered for its magnificent antiques and art collection and for its colourful past.

Royal visitors to the abbey have included Queen Elizabeth I, King Charles I and Queen Victoria.

The historic pile is officially seated in Bedfordshire, but sits so close to the new city of Milton Keynes that it has an MK postcode.

It is currently home to the 15th Duke of Bedford.

Woburn Abbey might have one foot firmly stuck in the past, but it is a forward-thinking place too.

Nowadays millions of people regularly spend leisure time visiting historical homes, but when the 13th Duke first welcomed visitors through the front door to inspect the grandeur inside in 1955, the concept was a new one.

The paying public was as attractive to the duke, eager to secure essential funding to repair the building and ensure its future, as the building was to visitors who attended en masse to explore the secrets behind the façade.

And after hundreds of years of blue-blooded visitors, the abbey achieved another first when it began welcoming rock and pop royalty to perform there in the 1960s.

Artists including Tina Turner, Dire Straits and Elton John have since delivered memorable moments in the Bedfordshire countryside.

During the August Bank Holiday weekend of 1967, the Festival of the Flower Children presented a sterling line-up

By kind permission of His Grace The Duke of Bedford

A 3-DAY NON-STOP HAPPENING
"FESTIVAL of the FLOWER CHILDREN"

TO BE HELD IN THE BEAUTIFUL GROUNDS OF

WOBURN ABBEY

on Sat., 26th Aug.—Sun., 27th Aug.—Mon., 28th Aug.

with

SMALL FACES, ERIC BURDON, JEFF BECK, BEE GEES, DENNY LAINE, ALAN PRICE SET, MARMALADE

PLUS MANY, MANY OTHER STARS

D.Js. — JEFF DEXTER • MIKE QUINN • TOMMY VANCE

****

Commencing 2.30 p.m., Saturday, 26th August through to 11 p.m., 28th August

DAY TICKETS £1.0.0   WEEK-END TICKETS 30/- *inclusive of*

Camping and caravaning and free access to the beautiful grounds of **WOBURN PARK**

FIREWORK HAPPENING NIGHTLY ! FREE FLOWERS AND SPARKLERS

The beautiful Flower Children in the most beautiful surroundings

Tickets available from: KEITH PROWSE, BETTA BOOKS, TILES, OXFORD STREET
and all IRVINE SELLARS BOUTIQUES

****

Entrance at Ridgmont Gate (di........ ......

By kind permission of
His Grace
The Duke of Bedford.

ALL STAR
"FESTIVAL OF THE
FLOWER CHILDREN"

3-day ticket.

Please retain this
portion for free
access to the lovely
grounds of
WOBURN PARK.

30/-

Nº 05091

By kind permission of His Grace
THE DUKE OF BEDFORD.

All Star Marathon
"FESTIVAL OF THE FLOWER
CHILDREN"

To be held at WOBURN ABBEY on
Saturday, 26th August, Sunday, 27th August,
Monday, 28th August.
Entrance from 12.30 p.m. Saturday onwards.
INCLUSIVE WEEKEND TICKET 30/-
Entrance at Ridgmont Gate
(direct off the M.1).

Free access to Woburn Park; Free camping
and caravaning, firework happening each
night. Free sparklers, flowers.
HUGE PARKING FACILITIES.

A stellar line-up: The show advert and (above) Alan Price and Jeff Beck relax ahead of the show

'By chance the festival was staged during my two-week stay': Ferdinand at Woburn

including the Small Faces, Eric Burdon and Jeff Beck, with Tommy Vance among the DJs attending.

Don Piccard demonstrated the hot air balloon at the event, and the balloon basket was filled with carnations which were distributed to the flower people from the air.

It might have been the Summer of Love, but the bash didn't go down well in the neighbourhood, and the press reports, both national and local were none too favourable about this new type of event:

'Britain's biggest ever 'love-in' is over,' recorded the Beds & Bucks Observer (August 30, 1967).

'With sighs of relief, the natives of Woburn are now able to use the streets of their village for their intended purpose, and not have to do a miniature 'Grand National' over the recumbent forms of flower bedecked 'beautiful children.'

Bus shelters are now almost back to normal, having finished serving their purpose as temporary hostels, and customers at public houses can now walk into bars without being scrutinised by the publican beforehand.'

As the campfires in the woods died down following the three day festival, so too did the ire of residents.

It might have been the summer of love, but the bash didn't go down well with the locals

But those who attended the event said it was less of a 'love-in' and rather a continuous pop concert.

Ferdinand Köther was a young man making his first visit to these shores from Germany at the time: "Just by chance the Festival of the Flower Children was staged during my two-week stay.

"I took a tube train to the end of the line and tried to hitch-hike the rest of the way.

"A bunch of colourfully dressed hippies picked me up at the entry to the motorway, with me proudly wearing my Hendrix-style Salvation Army jacket bought on Portobello Road Market.

'You may leave your things in the car if you want, you can fetch them later,' they said. Ok. So we went from the parking lot to the festival grounds and soon lost sight of each other. Later, I wanted to get my things – the car was gone! 'Shit,' I thought, 'They have stolen all my belongings, except for the few pennies in my pocket.'

"After a while I spotted one of them. 'Oh, hi, there you are, we just had to go and buy some food and drinks. Come along if you wanna get your things now.' "Nothing was stolen - good and honest

The Festival of the Flower Children: Relaxing with the sounds (top, left), and The Move on stage

hippies they were!

"Later that first night The Move started their gig, much cheered for by the crowd. It was dark already, and a generous amount of free sparklers had been given out. "Somebody had the idea to toss a sparkler onto the canvas roof of the stage. Others followed and soon the whole stage was ablaze.

"Hastily, many people tried to save the band's gear. Suddenly a guy appeared in front of me, 'Here, would you please hold this? I'll be back in a minute!' I held a large cymbal in my hand wondering what to do next, when the guy came back carrying some more stuff – and off he went with that cymbal, and more, stolen from Bev Bevan's drum kit during the turmoil.

"Nobody was hurt, somehow the stage was rebuilt and it was a great festival for three days."

In 1968, a little over a year before he would make history with his performance at the legendary Woodstock Festival, the guitar genius of a young Jimi Hendrix headlined the first night of a two-day music parade called The Woburn Music Festival.

It would be his only UK appearance of the year and was another daring move by the duke.

In 1968, the idea of opening up the grounds of a stately home was still a new one, and not without criticism.

On July 6, 14,000 music fans flocked to Woburn to see The Jimi Hendrix Experience. Their long-awaited return to British shores saw them top a bill that also featured Geno Washington, Tyrannosaurus Rex, Family, Little Women and New Formula. Pentangle, Roy Harper, Al Stewart, Alexis Korner and Shirley & Dolly

THE MELODY MAKER IN CONJUNCTION WITH RIK & JOHN GUNNELL PRESENTS THE

WOBURN MUSIC FESTIVAL

BY COURTESY OF HIS GRACE THE DUKE OF BEDFORD

SAT 6th JULY 230-530pm **PENTANGLE**

10s ROY HARPER · AL STEWART
ALEXIS KORNER · SHIRLEY & DOLLY COLLINS

SAT 6th JULY 7-12pm **JIMI HENDRIX EXPERIENCE**
GENO WASHINGTON AND THE RAM JAM BAND

£1 TYRANNOSAURUS REX · THE FAMILY
NEW FORMULA · LITTLE WOMEN

SUN 7th JULY 230-530pm AN AFTERNOON OF **DONOVAN**

12s 6d
SUN 7th JULY 7-11.30pm **FLEETWOOD MAC**
JOHN MAYALL AND THE BLUESBREAKERS

CHAMPION JACK DUPREE · TIM ROSE
15s THE TASTE · DUSTER BENNETT

JULY 6+7

a two-day music festival, but to villagers at Woburn it was last year's "hippy" invasion all over again, declared the local newspaper.

They wrote of 'Long-haired girls in sacking and occasional see-through blouses, even longer-haired boys in robes and fur coats,' passing through the surrounding villages.

'For the people of Woburn the amazing spectacle – and the litter left behind – brought back memories of the "hippy" flower festival.'

Councillor David Woodward, chairman of Woburn Parish Council, viewed the empty bottles, tins and litter in Woburn's streets with disgust.

"The village looks as if it has been bombed," he said.

A ¼ inch reel-to-reel master soundboard tape recording of some of the artists who performed across the two days – including Hendrix and Family - was auctioned through Christies in 2008, selling for almost £50,000.

Hendrix's seven-song set recorded that weekend was released through Dagger Records in 2009.

Neil Diamond twice appeared at Woburn Abbey, in 1977 and 2005.

His Grace the 15th Duke of Bedford can still remember the first visit by the American star.

"My father used to say that it is important for principal to meet principal, so it was important for whoever was in charge at Woburn to meet the artist.

"He would say that if there should be a problem you don't want to be dealing with

Collins had played during the afternoon.

Sunday was devoted to An Afternoon of Donovan, with the evening featuring John Mayall and the Bluesbreakers, Tim Rose and Taste.

Expected headliners Fleetwood Mac never did take the Woburn Stage though - they didn't show up.

Press reports cast the concert as a throwback to the noisy event of 1967, taking a dim view of the show.

'To the organisers and participants it was

Enjoying a gig with a view at Woburn Abbey

Woburn sounds: Russell Watson (top), Dire Straits and Hayley Westenra and Victoria Hart

management, you want to deal directly with the artist."

The 14th Duke and his wife had a four-day wait before Neil Diamond eventually met with them.

But when it came, that meeting was a great success - and trust and confidence on both sides at the meeting led to Neil taking the stage at the abbey without a contract!

"The first time he came here Neil's son Jesse would have been about five years old, and a sand pit was set up for him in front of the house, behind the stage," recalled the duke.

"After the concert I spent the night going around dealing with litter and moving on those people who were trying to camp – we don't have that on site because of the deer in the park.

"I drove up to the front of the house again at something like 5.30am in the morning and there was Neil and my father, feet dangling over the front of the stage.

"They had been sat there talking all night!"

That first performance signalled the start of a friendship between the family and the US superstar that remains strong to this day.

Whenever Neil visits the UK, he stops in on the duke and his family.

"When he comes here he just relaxes," the duke said.

"He wanders around wearing dark glasses and a baseball cap and might go over to the safari park.

"The band always love going around the antiques centre and some of the group do the sculpture gallery.

"It is the same people coming back here now that were with Neil in 1977, it is the familiarity of it all.

"Neil came over for Daddy's funeral too. "We're good friends."

Whenever there have been concerts at the abbey in more recent times the duke has been hands-on, but such involvement means there has been no time to enjoy the spectacle of tens of thousands of fans soaking up the atmosphere of the shows held in his garden.

"You don't actually get to see the show because you are running around dealing with problems the whole time, driving around to see what the traffic is like, checking the litter and all that stuff," he

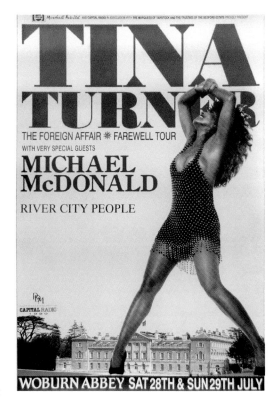

said, "It's work."

And the abbey has to be certain of bringing the right acts to the venue.

"It has got to be the right audience and a safe audience profile.

"Ideally the artists need to be able to do two nights of 40,000 or more to make the set-up costs worthwhile.

"If you go to The Bowl you have the parking and concessions there, whereas it is very different here – it is a greenfield site and costs a lot to set up, so we haven't had any shows for a while but, as and when, we will have them again.

"Because the house is built into a hill we have been lucky - it is a natural amphitheatre. But as we don't do camping, we have to tidy it all up right away and get it ready for the next day.

"I remember when they turned the house lights on after the Tina Turner show and you couldn't see the grass for the litter. "It was just revolting.

"We litter picked all night because the place had to look as good on the second night as it did on the first. It is amazing what people leave behind.

"Barrie Marshall was the promoter then. "He was here for the first night and then

Neil Diamond with His Grace the Duke of Bedford and family (above) and (below right) Jimi Hendrix on the Woburn stage in 1968

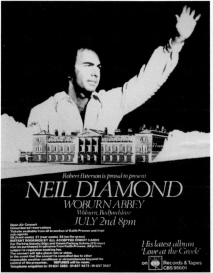

flew to New York because it was the last night of a McCartney tour.

"He flew back in on Sunday night and then he was back here, litter picking.

"It was a hell of an example to set to everyone else.

"Putting the shows on is a different world, and a fun world - you get taken out of what I call 'normal Woburn stuff.'

"Everyone here pulls together for the same cause – from the building department, plumbers and electricians, right through to the parks gang putting up

the fencing to keep the deer out.

"Then you have environmental health and health and safety, and you need to get the licence.

"That's always a tense time. It is mayhem.

"...and you need a pass to get into your own house," he says with a smile.

"You might have tickets for the front door, but you aren't getting past the security unless you have an Access All Areas pass!"

Tina Turner on stage at Woburn Abbey in 1990

The National Bowl

"Our audience were all men with tattoos on their testicles.
They were that tough."

If you walked into the Virgin Megastore, a beast of a music emporium in New York's Times Square a good few years ago, your eyes would have been drawn to an impressive new release display located smack bang in the middle of the entrance.

The album was Road to Revolution: Live at Milton Keynes, by Linkin Park.

The store is now long-gone, but the memory is crystal clear.

Thousands of miles away from Buckinghamshire, Milton Keynes had star billing, and with good reason – during its decades of operation The National Bowl has had more than its fair share of memorable gigs.

In 1971 approval was granted to tip surplus soil from road building during the development of Milton Keynes at the site.

Phil Winsor was an environmental health officer with Milton Keynes Council in 1975, "...and having had an interest in music since my teenage years was in the fortunate position of being in the right place at the right time when MK

Development Corporation sent an architect to California to see the Hollywood Bowl," he recalled.

"His positive approach resulted in the former clay pit being landscaped into a basic grassed amphitheatre that we still have today."

It was perfect for hosting major events and in 1977 the idea of open-air concerts came into play.

But it wasn't bands that offered the first spectacle at the venue – it was a Balloon and Kite Festival on May 26, 1979, though the 'atrocious weather' led to the balloons using an adjacent field, leaving the Bowl free for kite-flying.

A county fair and community technology festival, COMTEK '79, followed before music finally got a footing.

Desmond Dekker played the first date at the venue on September 8, 1979. Other names on the bill included Geno Washington and the Ram Jam Band and Jimmy James and the Vagabonds.

"They played to an audience of about

BANDITS AT 6 O'CLOCK..

Top of the bill — the electric Hi-Tension

There'll be strange flying objects over the Milton Keynes Bowl on Sunday May 27th.

No, invaders but the start of the 1979 Milton Keynes Hot Air Balloon & Kite Festival.

A non-stop action-packed day's fun for all the family. From around 6.00 a.m. (for early risers) right through all the evening.

- Free Admission.
- Free car parking.
- Refreshments available.
- First main event — a mass hot air balloon launch at around 10.30 a.m.
- Appearances by the famous Zanussi Trans-Atlantic Hot Air Balloon and the hot air Airship.
- Main Kite display starts around 3.30 p.m.
- Unusual, large and spectacular kites.
- Dozens of hot air balloons.
- Kite flying displays and balloon launches all through the day.
- It's all happening on Sunday May 27th at the Milton Keynes Bowl (weather permitting of course).

The Milton Keynes Bowl is 2 miles north of Bletchley alongside the A5 near Loughton.

MILTON KEYNES BOWL

A bowl full of fun
Off to a flying start

NEW CITY HEATING

CITY BOWL

EW CITY HEATING

MIRROR, THURSDAY, SEPTEMBER 15, 1983

Jazz and beer festival ends on a sour note

A TOP flight jazz and beer festival was a complete washout at the weekend — thanks to foul weather and the people of Milton Keynes, according to organisers.

DESERTED: Few fans turned up for festival.

Legs & Co...

FINDING THE RIGHT MIX FOR THE BOWL . . .

By JAN HENDERSON

ONE of the highlights of last year in Milton Keynes was the mammoth pop concert at The Bowl, headlined by top rock band The Police.

CROWDS: Flashback to The Police concert.

Rock's all bov

WORK began last week on clearing up the city's Bowl following the Police concert.

Promoters

Members of the team involved in the project celebrate the opening of the site's service building, and drink to the success of the Bowl.

120

Ernie Wise at The Balloon and Kite Festival in 1979, and (left) The Police are announced to play the venue in 1980

5000 which for a large site was sparse, but it was a start," Phil remembered.

Top of the Pops dancing troupe, Legs & Co. were also on hand with some moves. Groups in the running to play in 1980 included Pink Floyd, The Eagles and The Police.

Members of Pink Floyd did visit the venue and were reportedly 'very impressed with what they saw,' but The Police was the only gig that materialised, attracting 30,000 to the town.

Back then the perimeter fence only had a small number of entrances and 30,000 was the maximum capacity permitted.

It was the first big date at the venue, and to this day arguably holds the title of muddiest show too.

Eighteen calls were logged by members of the public complaining about the noise.

Ian Hunter played early in the history of the venue when his own band supported Thin Lizzy in 1981.

He played decked out in top hat and tails, plus his customary dark glasses.

"I remember Phil Lynott offering to babysit our baby son while I played because my wife wanted to watch the gig, and he did, for a few songs anyway. "Also, when I was standing by my car I got mobbed – I was totally shocked as I'm not the 'mobable' type," Ian recalled.

In post-event coverage, the local media said the 12,000 strong audience wasn't enough to make an impact on a venue the size of The Bowl: 'The future of these events must be in doubt unless the promoters can entice more people there for the next one,' they said.

But less than a year later, Queen were holding court.

Promoters banned all bottles and cans of alcohol following an incident in 1980 when one band had been 'canned' so badly they were forced from the stage.

Infrastructure improvements had allowed for 10,000 more ticket sales, but the police weren't worried by an expected 40,000 sell-out show: "Queen are a very popular group and attract middle-of-the-road clientele," they said, confident their team of bobbies "can deal with whatever happens." As it turned out, an audience of

Sting braved a wet and muddy Bowl when The Police played in 1980 (left)

Bowie's Bowl visits (right) saw fans flock to the town

just 23,000 were present.

"It was a very memorable gig," Queen guitarist Brian May said fondly, recalling that show in 1982.

"Outdoors is always a bit unpredictable, because you never know what you are going to get. But for some reason everything conspired to make it a great day – the sound was right on stage and off, and we were just very, very locked in.

"It was broadcast live, recorded and mixed absolutely live, and went out on Tyne Tees Television."

The show would later be released on the CD and DVD, Queen on Fire - Live At The Bowl.

"It is a notable show for things like Staying Power, a song on the Hot Space album. It was a very radical departure, very dry and spacey. People were saying, 'This isn't rock 'n' roll. What are they doing?' But when they heard us do it at Milton Keynes it changed everything. You can hear that."

Still you can't please all the people, and one Milton Keynes resident wrote of their

Queen rock the venue in 1982

annoyance to the Citizen newspaper: 'Does your paper consider £9.30 a reasonable price for tickets for an open air concert that has no proper seats even?'

Genesis played the same year, reuniting with their former lead singer Peter Gabriel for the one-off date and despite more rain and muddy conditions they smashed attendance records. For the first time the venue welcomed 50,000 people through the gates.

In 1983, David Bowie became the first artist to hold court at the venue for three consecutive nights when he brought his Serious Moonlight tour to town.

Police reacted robustly to the biggest shows the new town had ever seen – cancelling rest days and putting 100 officers on duty.

Tickets were sold at £10.30, and there were just 17 arrests over the three days.

Denis O'Regan was Bowie's official photographer and captured some suitably stunning images.

"We were staying in London, so drove up in the bus. I remember the show distinctly because of all the roundabouts in Milton Keynes.

"The police had an outrider at the front and one at the back, and you'd get to the roundabout and the first guy would stop the traffic, the bus would go through and the other outrider would move to the front

and they kept repeating that," Denis remembered.

"It was like royalty – you know the royals are coming when you see the first guy stop. We had exactly the same thing.

"It was a different show – one of the first big ones he did because of the gigantic demand - Wembley Arena was only 10,000 and then he did three in Milton Keynes at 60,000 a night.

"I knew when I took the pictures there that they were going to be quite special for me."

Radio 2 DJ Jo Whiley was in the audience: "It was amazing. I was 18, in the Sixth Form, and I remember Dad taking me and a whole bunch of friends from school.

"Bowie had this massive inflatable globe that went all the way out into the audience.

"It was an incredible introduction to music and probably partly responsible for me doing the job I do at the moment."

But in September the same year, the expected crowds for a jazz and beer festival failed to materialise – organisers blamed foul weather and the people of Milton Keynes for a decidedly sparse turnout, with few fans on site to watch artists including Acker Bilk and Georgie Fame. Ouch.

Millions of people will have their own memories of days spent watching their

Status Quo: 'The last-ever show' in 1984

most favoured at the venue, but The National Bowl conjures up just as many special memories for those who were on the stage looking out.

Status Quo played in 1984 and had the show filmed for release.

After all, the gig – part of their End Of The Road tour – was billed as 'The Farewell Concert.'

It still feels fresh in Francis Rossi's mind: "The amount of things I can remember about that show which you can't print are ridiculous!

"The band were into lots of coke at the time and there was this mirror in the dressing room, which we found out afterwards had a camera behind it. We've never actually located the film since, but various people are in there changing and cleaning their noses, and there are various people's wives checking their underwear and all sorts in front of this mirror...

"Our dressing room was right next to the stage, and Nazareth played. The singer's got that 'Waaaaaaaa!' voice...it was cutting our heads off in the dressing room.

"They were the days when things were much more macho. Our audience were all men with tattoos on their testicles.

"They were that tough!"

All the way from Tennessee, Jason and The Scorchers were among the supporting cast that day and frontman Jason Ringenberg has vivid memories: "When we took the stage, I noticed all of Quo's equipment was covered in plastic and it didn't look like rain!" he says, recalling the weather.

"I soon found out why the plastic was there. We didn't know at the time, but Quo fans had a tradition of completely stoning the openers with the vilest garbage they could sneak in.

"As soon as we started our set, the trash rained down on us like a summer thunderstorm.

Above: Jim Kerr from Simple Minds
Below: Fish from Marillion and Bruce Springsteen

"However, instead of caving in to them and walking off, which is what many acts did in those days, we started yelling at them. Insulting the crowd and egging them on. No pun intended.

"Although the rain of trash never stopped, we did earn their respect and got good press out of it."

Quo's show pulled in 42,000 and it was hot, hot, hot – with more than 300 people overcome by the heat. It was loud too, with villages more than 13 miles to the east of Elfield Park able to hear the band at play.

Michael Jackson famously played the venue in 1988: "That was the big one – tickets sold like hot cakes and the capacity was increased by 5000 to 45,000 – providing the extra tickets were sold to MK residents out of the Civic Office box office facility," remembers Phil Winsor.

Tim Parsons and Maurice Jones were responsible for putting on the original Monsters of Rock Festival at Donington Park. Their company, MCP, also made the most of our venue.

"It was good to go," Tim says, remembering the space.

"You didn't need to create the site, it was already there. It was quite secure and it had really good communications - and it was a lot cheaper than Wembley Stadium, which had a lot to do with it," he admits.

Tim's first big MK show was U2 and the great British weather rained down on the parade – 100 Red Cross staff were kept busy with concert-goers suffering the effects of the cold.

Others who had slipped in the mud bath were sent to hospital with broken bones. There were 500

casualties in all.

"It was going to be an annual event called The Longest Day, but Simple Minds did it the following year and they didn't want to be associated with a U2 lyric, so we couldn't do that.

"Playing there was probably the pinnacle of Simple Minds' career. "Although they had played at Wembley, the two gigs at The Bowl were really, really something and the bills were fantastic.

"I used to really enjoy putting the bills together.

"I remember having Blur, Radiohead and The Cranberries all supporting R.E.M one year, and then getting Radio 1 to broadcast the whole thing and watching how the album sales picked up on the back of it.

"When Radiohead supported R.E.M it started a really great relationship, and they went on to support R.E.M throughout America which was a really big deal."

More infrastructure improvements allowed for a capacity of 65,000 and the gigs kept on coming with many artists choosing to return again and again.

"When we did Bon Jovi with Manic Street Preachers, Billy Idol and Little Angels I thought that was an incredibly strong show," Tim said.

"Manic Street Preachers hated us with a passion because they thought that Bon Jovi was the wrong gig for them. Richey (Edwards, MSP guitarist) and James (Dean Bradfield, MSP guitarist) used to give me a serial panning because we put them on that show.

"But this is the thing – there were 60,000 people out there who thought they were fantastic. The fact that they didn't like the 60,000 people was their problem."

Tim subscribed firmly to the ethos of work hard and play hard.

"You would start on a Monday. You generally used to have the same companies working with you, so it was a great week constructing the stage and putting in the infrastructure, right up to the day before the show when the band would come in and soundcheck.

"Invariably you were working with your mates. One of the great things at showcase events like that was all the managers were there, the record companies were there, all the liggers were there...as long as you are making money, it was a very pleasant way to spend your day!

"It was always a really rewarding

"You tell someone like Axl Rose there is a strict curfew and he will do all he can to break it"

experience putting on the Guns N' Roses and Metallica's of this world, because we had known them for absolutely yonks.

"That didn't mean that we didn't have problems with some of them, but what was nice was that not only were they realising their ambitions, but we were realising our ambitions for ourselves too.

"Guns N' Roses at the National Bowl were less of a problem than they would be at Wembley Stadium, which had a strict curfew of 10.30pm.

"You tell someone like Axl Rose there is a strict curfew and he will do all he can to break it. "Somewhere like MK Bowl had a curfew that wasn't written in stone, so you could do MK with them and actually have a really good time.

"I can't remember the specific show but we were letting off fire extinguishers and making margaritas in baby baths and getting completely trolleyed during the course of the day, swapping clothes with the local policemen and putting in a little bar under the stage for a laugh...it was great fun!"

When they sold MCP, they retained an interest in the venue purchasing 50 per cent of the Bowl with the company that

Michael Jackson on the BAD tour (1988)

UB40 frontman Ali Campbell live on stage at The Bowl (1994)

David Bowie at The National Bowl - Sound and Vision tour (1990)

Erasure played their biggest ever show at The Bowl in 1990

Keith Flint from The Prodigy on stage at The Warrior's Dance Festival in 2010

took over: "So while we weren't promoters we were co-owners of the lease."

In 1999 Metallica brought their Big Day Out to town, but it was one of the special guests on the billing who grabbed the lion's share of the headlines. In the aftermath of the Columbine High School massacre, media outlets suggested the perpetrators had been motivated by the music of Marilyn Manson.

Manson was an easy, unjustified, scapegoat. The panic didn't stay Stateside though and there were calls for him to be banned from appearing at the new town date.

Milton Keynes MP Phyllis Starkey rose to his defence: "The atrocities in the USA were the result of their lax attitude on guns, and anything else is just an excuse," she said.

Sense prevailed, and Manson played the show.

Queens of the Stone Age played that day too. Commercial fame was yet to find them and they were low down the billing on the second stage, which was headlined by Terrorvision.

All did not go swimmingly.

When QOTSA left their belongings in a dressing room over the allotted time, someone from the Terrorvision camp allegedly dumped their gear in the dirt.

"To be honest, although I wasn't there I took the fall for it," former QOTSA bassist Nick Oliveri remembers.

"Our singer Josh got mad and rocked a couple of people. As I'm walking back to the room I saw Josh had bloody knuckles."

Josh relayed the story to his bandmate, but assured him that everything was dealt with.

"I said 'I'm gonna go to the bathroom.'

"But really I sneaked off and went to the room on my own.

"I picked this bag of ice up and threw it at one of the guys Josh had rocked really hard.

"I knew it was him, because his eyes were all puffy. I threw it in his face and said 'Do you need some ice with that?'

"One of the guys jumped on me and I flew on my back with him on top of me.

"The cops came, had me down and put me in jail. I was sitting in a little cell

> **"The cops came, had me down and put me in jail. I was sitting in a little cell in Milton Keynes"**

in Milton Keynes. But I got the suite so it wasn't so bad!

"Then the guy said he wasn't going to press charges so we paid the dude fifty bucks and that was it, done."

Queens of the Stone Age returned to the venue in 2001 for a show that was just as memorable for Nick, but for all the right reasons: "When we played with AC/DC it was a dream come true for me," he said.

"AC/DC was the soundtrack to my childhood - everything I did first; the first time I had sex and the first time I smoked a joint, AC/DC was playing.

So it was a big thing for me. I really love that band and it was a dream to play with them."

In 2003, Eminem enjoyed three nights in the town. It was a huge deal for rap music, and Eminem delivered the goods, although Milton Keynes didn't seem to make its mark on him: "Word up, London!" he said, addressing his audience.

When the Gallagher brothers were still talking they spent a sun-drenched weekend here in 2005. Their appearance came in the same week that the nation was rocked by the 7/7 bombings, and Liam dedicated Live Forever to those who lost their lives. A sobering moment in a pretty perfect rock 'n' roll show.

Pop royalty Take That enjoyed a two night stand back in June 2006.

Nick Oliveri

Bon Jovi first rocked the Bowl in 1989 and made several returns

"We had just come back together and were playing a few arenas then, and it escalated to being stadiums, playing to thousands and thousands of people. It really was amazing," Mark Owen recalled.

"Originally we were going to be doing Wembley Stadium, but they hadn't finished it. The Bowl was such a beautiful venue and lovely the way it spread round in front of you.

"It felt exciting to be playing places like that. I'd spent a lot of years looking at a lot of my favourite acts who had played there like the Foo Fighters and Eminem... and I was at the stage then when I was playing to a couple of hundred people and never thought I'd get to play in front of audiences like that again, so it was incredible to play there."

Green Day, Linkin Park and The Prodigy all played their largest headline shows at the venue, and all followed Queen and Status Quo by releasing their performances to DVD.

The Prodigy's Warrior's Dance Festival was a show that would take not only the band, but the genre, to new heights.

Two stages boasted sets from musicians including Pendulum, Chase & Status, and Gallows throughout the day.

Enter Shikari had already supported Linkin Park at the venue when The Prodigy invited them back for more.

"It's one of the most legendary venues in the country, with countless huge names to have graced the stage. To be put on such an outstanding bill and be playing in the presence of such distinguished musical history was an absolute pleasure and an honour," said drummer Rob Rolfe.

It was another day of magic at the special venue. A fact certainly not lost on those players causing all the commotion.

"It was important to us to bring a proper festival day and night for the people to remember and bring the same intense atmosphere like when we play Brixton Academy.... and it was," remembered Liam Howlett.

"We put a lot of work into the whole way it looked so people really felt like they were stepping into our world, we really like the venue because it is a bowl and different to playing in a flat field.

"We used that to our advantage.

"Standing on that stage was a truly triumphant feeling for us as the whole place kicked off.

"We looked out and saw everybody there for us, we were fuckin' proud."

Bon Jovi hold the record for the most visits to the venue.

They have filled the Bowl on five different occasions; in 1993; 1996; 2001 and 2006. But the first time they rocked up they arrived with a supporting cast of Skid Row, Vixen and Europe on a sun-drenched August day in 1989.

Monsters of Rock: Alice Cooper and Deep Purple played in 2006

Ozzfest 2001: Ozzy Osbourne (above), Zakk Wylde, Black Sabbath's Tony Iommi and Max Cavalera from Soulfly, and (below) Slipknot

Projekt Revolution 2008: Linkin Park's Chester Bennington (top) and Jay-Z on stage

Rolling with it: Liam Gallagher in 2005, and (above) Muse had a production run-through at the venue

"Oh man, the first time we played there was amazing," former Bon Jovi guitarist Richie Sambora said fondly, "That was big, big, big for us back then.

"I really thought I was playing Woodstock - that's the way it looked to me! "I remember there being a bonfire on my side towards the back on the right side of The Bowl and I was very fixated on that. I thought it was cool.

"Steve and Joe from Aerosmith came up and jammed with us too. That was awesome and we became good friends after that.

"Our shows there were very, very memorable gigs – not just for the band, but for the audience."

Foo Fighters made their first UK appearance since their record-setting two-night stand at Wembley Stadium in 2008 with a weekend MK stay in July 2011.

It was special for the whole band, not least guitarist Pat Smear, who got to follow in Queen's footsteps: "It's really exciting to play, because there was the famous Queen concert at the MK Bowl," he said.

"Whenever we play somewhere like that I have the film of Queen playing, which is extra exciting.

"I know the venue so well from the video footage. It feels like 'Wow, really? Us? We're really doing this place?'"

Guitarist Chris Shiflett remembers the weekend fondly too.

"I have very specific memories and I can honestly say that those shows were two of my favourite Foo Fighters shows that we've ever done in the UK," he said.

"When we go on tour now, especially in the summer, we all bring our wives, our kids and our families and for that whole European run we had our families over. "For the Milton Keynes shows I had my mum and stepdad over, who had never been to a big Foo Fighters show.

"We don't do big shows like that in America - it's really in Europe and Australia that we do stadium-sized shows.

"I regretted that I hadn't brought my mum over when we played Wembley so I flew my mum and my stepdad in, and my wife's mum and stepdad came, and it just became this big thing.

"Then a bunch of our close friends came over with their friends and we had the best backstage set up we have ever had.

"Our tour manager Gus put together this incredible thing backstage, mostly for the kids - we had this crazy play area.

"When we were playing I would look

Iggy Pop supported Foo Fighters in 2015, and (below) Pearl Jam headlined in 2014

over and see my whole family - my kids, my wife, my mum, my stepdad and it was amazing. I really like the way that venue is set-up.

"It's really amazing the way that you have that big open space and then it goes up at the back like a big giant amphitheatre."

In February 2012 work began to remove the stage structure at the venue in a move to increase capacity on the site and overcome safety risks associated with the old stage.

The iconic 'house roof' had supported the lighting rigs, sound systems and video walls for world famous artists for two decades, but as productions became ever more spectacular and complex it was no longer sufficient to safely accommodate the necessary weight of equipment.

The first show at the venue following the removal took place the same year with electronic music supergroup Swedish House Mafia in control.

In 2014, Kings of Leon passed through, and Seattle stalwarts Pearl Jam used the venue to wrap up an 11-date European tour.

And dance fans enjoyed another treat with the Electric Daisy Carnival.

A colossal force on the world's dance stage it made its debut on Milton Keynes soil in 2014, the result of a powerful partnership between the Cream and Insomniac brands.

That inaugural visit – with appearances by Avicii and Calvin Harris - saw the world's largest 360 degree digital lighting installation in use, and DJs performing across four stages.

The colossal state-of-the-art production was splattered with theatrical performers and fairground rides and boasted the largest flame units ever used in Europe.

When the curtain fell at the end of a remarkable day, a whopping 440lbs of colourful confetti showered the crowds.

Unsurprisingly, EDC returned in 2015 with the best staging perhaps ever hosted at the venue.

The kineticCATHEDRAL stage towered over proceedings, standing an enormous 90 feet tall and 240 feet wide, with EDCs

"I really thought I was playing Woodstock - that's the way it looked to me!"

symbolic owls watching over the dance disciples.

More than 35,000 revellers checked in for the 11-hour electronic party featuring sets by Tiesto and Hardwell.

But EDC aside, the venue looked like it was going to be a quiet one in 2015.

And then the misfortune of one of rock's finest frontmen turned into the Bowl's good fortune.

When Dave Grohl took a tumble from the stage in Gothenburg on June 12, 'the snap heard around the world' left the Foo Fighters with no choice but to cancel upcoming live dates.

Planned shows at Wembley Stadium and a bill-topping set at Glastonbury were pulled.

Addressing fans, Grohl issued a statement and a promise: "You have always stood by our band, and we will always stand by you.

"Like I say at every show, we wouldn't be here if it weren't for you guys. And I mean that. I thank you from the bottom of my heart.

"And I will do everything I can to come back and give you a night to remember for the rest of your lives as soon as possible."

And true to his word, a little over a month after the fracture the band announced two dates at the National Bowl, for September 5 and 6.

Grohl famously played the shows seated in a custom-built, Game of Thrones-inspired iron throne, adorned with guitar necks and flashing lights.

Designed by Grohl himself, it was ridiculous and wonderful in equal measure.

As for the future?

In late 2019 Milton Keynes Development Partnership and MK Council reached an agreement with MK Dons to allow the football club to develop a new state-of-the-art training facility at the venue.

Twelve football pitches, changing, fitness and medical facilities will all feature in the ambitious plans.

MK Dons chairman Pete Winkelman said: "The Bowl is an iconic venue which has played host to some of the world's biggest and best and we will do all we can to respect and nurture the site."

143

Take That and Robbie Williams (right) both played their own shows at The National Bowl in 2006

Green Day on stage at The National Bowl (2005)

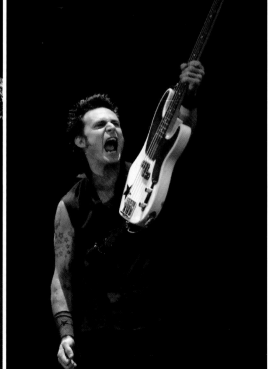

For those about to rock: AC/DC headlined in 2001 (above and below left), with support from Queens of the Stone Age (centre), The Offspring (below right) and Megadeth (bottom)

*Dance delights: Calvin Harris and (below) Steve Aoki
at the Electric Daisy Carnival*

150

151

Bowlography

1979 (Saturday, September 8): **Desmond Dekker & the Aces**, Chairman of the Board, Geno Washington & The Ram Jam Band, Hi-Tension, Jimmy James & the Vagabonds, Legs & Co

1980 (Saturday, July 26): **The Police**, UB40, Squeeze, Skafish, Sector 27, John Peel and Jerry Floyd (compères)

1981 (Saturday, August 8): **Thin Lizzy**, Judie Tzuke, The Ian Hunter Band, Q Tips, Trimmer & Jenkins

1982 (Saturday, June 5): **Queen**, Heart, Teardrop Explodes, Joan Jett & the Blackhearts

1982 (Saturday, October 2): **Genesis**, Talk Talk, The Blues Band, John Martyn

1983 (Friday, July 1, Saturday, July 2 & Sunday, July 3): **David Bowie**, Icehouse, The Beat

1983 (Saturday, September 10): **The British Jazz and Beer Festival, Acker Bilk and his Paramount Band**, Georgie Fame and the Blue Flames, Humphrey Lyttelton, Pete Thomas' Jivin' Jump Band, Bitelli's Onward Jazz, The Temperance Seven, The Georgia Jazzmen

1983 (Sunday, September 11): **The British Jazz and Beer Festival: Georgie Fame and the Blue Flames,** Morrissey Mullen, Gonzalez, Breakfast Band, East Side Torpedoes

1984 (Saturday, July 21): **Status Quo**, Marillion, Nazareth, Jason & The Scorchers, Gary Glitter

1985 (Saturday, June 22): **U2**, R.E.M, The Ramones, Spear Of Destiny, Billy Bragg, Faith Brothers

1986 (Saturday, June 21): **Simple Minds**, The Bangles, The Cult, The Waterboys, In Tua Nua

1986 (Sunday, June 22): **Simple Minds**, Lloyd Cole and the Commotions, Big Audio Dynamite, The Waterboys, Dr and the Medics

1986 (Saturday, June 28): **The Garden Party, Marillion**, Gary Moore, Jethro Tull, Magnum, Mama's Boys

1988 (Saturday, June 18): **Amnesty International Festival of Youth**
All About Eve, Aswad, The Icicle Works, Howard Jones, Runrig, The Rhythm Sisters, So, Martin Stephenson & The Daintees, The Stranglers, Joe Strummer

1988 (Sunday, June 19): **Amnesty International Festival of Youth**
Aswad, Aztec Camera, Big Audio Dynamite, Bhundu Boys, The Damned, The Men They Couldn't Hang, New Model Army, Joe Strummer, World Domination Enterprises

1988 (Saturday, September 10): **Michael Jackson**, Kim Wilde

1989 (Saturday, August 19) **Bon Jovi**, Europe, Vixen, Skid Row (and guests Steven Tyler and Joe Perry from Aerosmith)

1990 (Saturday, August 4 & Sunday, August 5): **David Bowie**, Gene Loves Jezebel, The Men They Couldn't Hang, Two Way Street

1990 (Saturday, September 1): **Erasure**, Was (Not Was), Adamski, Electribe 101

1991 (Saturday, July 6) **ZZ Top**, Bryan Adams, The Law, Thunder, Little Angels

1991 (Saturday, August 24): **Simple Minds**, The Stranglers, O.M.D, An Emotional Fish

1993 (Saturday, May 22): **Bruce Springsteen**

1993 (Saturday, May 29 & Sunday, May 30): **Guns N' Roses**, The Cult, Soul Asylum, Blind Melon

1993 (Saturday, June 5): **Metallica**, Megadeth, The Almighty, Diamond Head

1993 (Saturday, September 18 & Sunday, September 19): **Bon Jovi**, Manic Street Preachers, Billy Idol, Little Angels

1994 (Saturday, August 13): **UB40**, Jamiroquai, Chaka Demus & Pliers

1995 (Saturday, July 29): **R.E.M.**, Blur, Belly, Magnapop

1995 (Sunday, July 30): **R.E.M.**, Radiohead, The Cranberries, Sleeper

1996 (Saturday, July 6): **Bon Jovi**, Joan Osborne, Gun, Seven

1996 (Sunday, July 7): **Bon Jovi**, Joan Osborne, Gun, Vivid

1998 (Saturday, June 20): **OZZFEST**, **Black Sabbath**, Ozzy Osbourne, Foo Fighters, Therapy?, Pantera, Soulfly, Slayer, Fear Factory
Stage 2: Coal Chamber, Life of Agony, Human Waste Project, Entombed, (Hed) p.e, Pitchshifter

1999 (Saturday, July 10): **The Big Day Out, Metallica**, Marilyn Manson, Placebo, Ben Harper & the Innocent Criminals, Ministry, Sepultura, Creed
Kerrang! Stage: Terrorvision, Monster Magnet, Pitchshifter, Symposium, Queens of the Stone Age, Mercyful Fate

2001 (Saturday, May 26): **OZZFEST: Black Sabbath**, Slipknot, Tool, Papa Roach, Soulfly, Disturbed, Mudvayne, Amen, Black Label Society, (Hed) p.e, Union Underground, Apartment 26, Raging Speedhorn

2001 (Friday, June 8): **AC/DC**, The Offspring, Megadeth, Queens of the Stone Age

2001 (Saturday, June 16): **Bon Jovi**, Matchbox 20, Delirious?

2001 (Friday, July 20, Saturday, July 21 & Sunday, July 22): **Robbie Williams**, Toploader, ABC

2002 (Sunday, June 16): **SUMMER XS** Ronan Keating, Blue, Beverley Knight, Mousse T, Jamie Benson, Darius, Rik Waller, The Lighthouse Family, Moony, Alcazar, Zoe Birkett, Ree, Claire Sweeney, Rhianna, David Charvet, Sugababes, Liberty X

2003 (Sunday, June 15): **SUMMER XS** Simply Red, Blue, Busted, Sugababes, Atomic Kitten, Mis-Teeq, Lisa Scott-Lee, Appleton, Big Brovaz, Blazin Squad, Kym Marsh, David Sneddon, DJ Sammy, Daniel Bedingfield, Triple 8, Darius, Abs, Tantalize, Cheeky Girls, Billy Crawford

2003 (Saturday, June 21, Sunday, June 22 & Monday, June 23): **Eminem**, 50 Cent, Cypress Hill, D12, Obie Trice, Xzibit

2004 (Sunday, June 20): **SUMMER XS**, McFly, Natasha Bedingfield, The Calling, Blazin' Squad, Lemar, Matt Goss, Emma Bunton, Bellefire, Beverley Knight, Javine, Mania, Mark Joseph, The 411, Vs

2005 (Saturday, June 18 & Sunday, June 19): **Green Day**, Jimmy Eat World, Taking Back Sunday, Hard-Fi

2005 (Saturday, June 25): **SUMMER XS**, McFly, Texas, Charlotte Church, Daniel Bedingfield, Lucy Silvas, Jem, Rooster, Blazin' Squad, Chesney Hawkes, Tyler James, Ben Adams, The Faders, Rachel Stevens

2005 (Saturday, July 9): **Oasis**, The Zutons, Secret Machines, 22:20s, Redwalls

2005 (Sunday, July 10): **Oasis**, The Coral, 22:20s, Secret Machines, The Soundtrack Of Our Lives

2006 (Saturday, June 3): **MONSTERS OF ROCK, Deep Purple**, Alice Cooper, Journey, Thunder, Queensrÿche, Ted Nugent, Roadstar

2006 (Saturday, June 10 & Sunday, June 11): **Bon Jovi**, Nickelback, Spin

2006 (Saturday, June 24 & Sunday, June 25): **Take That**, Sugababes, Beverley Knight (and guest Lulu)

2006 (Thursday, September 14, Friday, September 15, Saturday, September 16, Monday, September 18 & Tuesday, September 19): **Robbie Williams**, Basement Jaxx, Orson

2008 (Sunday, June 29): **PROJEKT REVOLUTION**, **Linkin Park**, Jay-Z, N*E*R*D, Enter Shikari, The Bravery, Inner Party System, Pendulum

2010 (Saturday, July 24): **WARRIOR'S DANCE FESTIVAL**, **The Prodigy**, Pendulum, Enter Shikari, Chase & Status, Does It Offend You, Yeah?, Zane Lowe
Stage 2: Gallows, Lethal B, David Rodigan, Doorly, Caspa, Hounds

2011 (Saturday, July 2): **Foo Fighters**, Biffy Clyro, Death Cab For Cutie, Tame Impala, DJ Bob Mould (and guests Alice Cooper and Roger Taylor)

2011 (Sunday, July 3): **Foo Fighters**, Biffy Clyro, Jimmy Eat World, The Hot Rats, DJ Bob Mould (and guests John Paul Jones and Seasick Steve)

2012 (Saturday, July 14): **Swedish House Mafia**, Pete Tong, Calvin Harris, Alesso, Madeon, Example, No_ID

2014 (Sunday, June 22): **Kings of Leon**, Haim, Twin Atlantic, The Last Internationale

2014 (Friday, July 11): **Pearl Jam**, Black Rebel Motorcycle Club, Off! (with guests Dhani Harrison and Simon Townshend)

2014 (Saturday, July 12): **Electric Daisy Carnival**, **Avicii**, Calvin Harris, Steve Angello, Steve Aoki, Nicky Romero, Martin Garrix, Showtek, Bassjackers (KineticField)
Marco Carola, Dubfire, Joris Voorn, Hot Since 82, Davide Squillace, Timo Maas, Nick Curly, Miguel Campbell, Route 94, Andrea Oliva, Kerry Chandler (CosmicMeadow)
Paul Van Dyk, Ferry Corsten, Ørjan Nilsen, Simon Patterson, Andy

Moor b2b Lange, Ben Gold, Jordan Suckley b2b Bryan Kearney, Jaytech b2b Ilan Bluestone, Paul Oakenfold, (CircuitGrounds)
Tidy Boys, Bk. Feat Cortina, Andy Whitby, Alex Kidd, Cally Cage & Kim Ayres, Rob Tissera, Maddox & Townsend, Max Mozart & Audox, Trap Two (TidyArena)

2015 (Saturday, July 11): **Electric Daisy Carnival**, **Tiësto**, Dimitri Vegas & Like Mike, Steve Aoki, Carnage, Sick Individuals, Hardwell, Dirty South, Philip George, Kill The Buzz (KineticField)
Art Department, Jamie Jones, Marco Carola, Visionquest, Claude Von Stroke, Route 94, Richy Ahmed, Miguel Campbell, wAFF (NeonGarden)
Paul Van Dyk, Ferry Corsten, John O'Callaghan, Markus Schulz, Cosmic Gate, Simon Patterson, Pure NRG (Live), Jordan Suckley B2B Bryan Kearney, Ilan Bluestone, Will Atkinson (CosmicMeadow)
Pendulum, Subfocus, High Contrast, Mistajam, Friction, Sigma, Shy FX, Matrix & Futurebound, My Nu Leng, Kove (CircuitGrounds)

2015 (Saturday, September 5 & Sunday, September 6): **Foo Fighters**, Iggy Pop, Royal Blood (with guests Roger Taylor and John Paul Jones, Sep 5)

2016 (July 9): **Electric Daisy Carnival**, **Avicii**, Axwell ^ Ingrosso, Martin Garrix, Oliver Heldens, Eric Prydz, Robin Schulz, Martin Solveig (KineticField)
Paul Van Dyk, Ferry Corsten presents Gouryella, Markus Schulz, John O'Callaghan, Andy Moor, Ilan Bluestone, Standerwick, Simon O'Shine, Aly & Fila (CosmicMeadow)
Pendulum, Noisia, Caspa b2b Rusko, Sigma, Roni Size & Krust Presents Full Cycle, Friction, Culture Shock, Goldie MBE, René LaVice (CircuitGrounds)
Duke Dumont (DJ Set), DJ EZ, Galantis, Lost Frequencies, Philip George, 99 Souls, Jauz (NeonGarden)

The Pitz

"The most difficult part was the armed guard sat outside the green room as threats had been made on their lives."

Originally The Bunker was going to be a touring club of sorts, offering local and regional music to venues including the Woughton Centre, the Courtyard in Great Linford, Lovat Hall in Newport Pagnell and Bletchley's Compass Club.

The first meeting was in June 1987 and by September the club, now known as The Pitz, was launched.

"Promotion was carried out across the city, but most of the posters and flyers were torn down by the council, with threats to fine us if we did it again," promoter Chris Kemp said.

"I spent one evening scraping posters off an underpass with the threat of court action hanging over my head."

Wolverton-based band New Mutants headlined the first date.

"In those days Woughton had no curtains, no PA and aside from a few theatre lights it was just a brick box with a wooden floor," Chris recalled.

"We had real tickets, a 24-can rider for the main band, archaic lighting, a 3K rig, no barrier and no security.

"One hundred and eighty people turned up to see support act Claire take the stage."

But turn-outs elsewhere weren't as successful, with less than 50 people supporting shows at the Compass Club.

"After the first two months it was clear that only Woughton was drawing the crowds and the organisation of The Pitz reverted back to me as the Woughton promoter and venue manager.

"Other gigs such as Madcap in Wolverton were putting on more dance and grunge-based artists and packing out, including a show by Black Flag front man Henry Rollins."

Pitz promoter Chris Kemp

and thrash charts.

"From the large amount of money I had made from the series of thrash promotions, I was able to buy Volvina soundproof curtains for the hall. They cost £16,000 in 1988 – a huge outlay.

"I also invested in a rock lighting system and a Zero 88 Demux lighting desk – state of the art."

The Pitz was establishing itself and with Chris typically promoting bands on a 50/50 split, money was coming in nicely. But with major agents starting to put bands through the venue, that fell to an 80/20 split after costs.

"It was almost impossible to make any money unless you charged for all the assets, so we did – costing out the curtains and the lighting in the package."

Crew members were employed not for hard cash, but on the promise of a band t-shirt from the performing artist.

When the venue needed to increase its crew size, auditions were held – and 160 people turned up. Twelve were recruited.

"We had no health and safety training, no breaks, and they might have been working from 8am in the morning until 3am the next."

Security personnel brought their own problems: "After a few abortive attempts at doing our own I paid £4 an hour to a local company to provide security and stewarding.

"I would later regret this, after sacking four companies for taking money and drugs off people and recycling them."

The Pitz catered for the public's appetite – and as musical fashions changed, so too did those on the Pitz stage – from rock to indie and back again, before embracing more thrash metal, grunge and chart-friendly artists.

"When the Pitz started, the main agent was a shady guy from Birmingham who carried wads of cash in his rucksack and pushed the likes of Marshall Law, Wrathchild, The Tattooed Love Boys and other new wave of heavy metal acts."

But Chris started introducing folk and blues at weekends with Roy Harper, The Climax Blues Band and Walter Trout among the names.

"There was also a huge market for old

Then Chris booked his first national band, pseudo-goth rockers Balaam and the Angel: "I learned my first big lesson in the music industry – never book music you like, only music that sells," Chris recalled.

"I hired in lights and a bigger rig as specified by the rider in the contract, and for the first time realised what the overheads for a show would really be.

"Three hundred and fifty people turned up to the gig and it was a fantastic success, but bar takings aside I lost about £400.

"However, that wasn't as bad as the £4,000 I would lose years later on Shakin' Stevens.

"If we were going to be successful I needed to invest in some good gear and learn how to negotiate contracts.

"The gigs were doing fairly well but it seemed impossible to sell-out no matter who I booked.

"Then one of the agents I used introduced me to a phenomenon known as thrash metal.

"The first such band I promoted was called Raven, and it sold out.

"I then began to put thrash on at least twice a week and as the local scene started to blossom we had sell-out gigs continually for three months.

"We were approached by more reputable agents and started to put on major headline acts with singles in the charts or top five albums in the rock, metal

> **"I learned my first big lesson in the music industry - never book music you like, only music that sells"**

rock like Wishbone Ash, Magnum and Hawkwind.

"At the time, I was working with four of the major London agents including John Jackson who looked after Iron Maiden, Nick Peel who looked after Jools Holland, and Rod MacSween who looked after Pearl Jam."

Chris had cultivated a place with a vibe and pull that demanded live music four nights a week.

"It was fun, it was fast and it was furious. The acrid smoke, the stench of beer on the floor and vomit down the curtains was an everyday hazard."

But trouble came knocking when one band took exception to being paid by cheque: "The manager from Gaye Bykers on Acid refused to take our cheque and decided that unless I paid up in cash there would be trouble."

Chris refused, and thought no more about it. Arriving at the venue the next morning he found the cleaner collapsed in the changing rooms.

"The band had allegedly defecated in the showers and used paper towels to push it all over the walls and floors of the cubicles.

"Poor Nancy had been overcome by the smell and fainted.

"Although fun, rock 'n' roll promotion has many hazards, and each gig brings new problems – fighting, over indulgence

in drugs and drink, temperamental artists, lack of the right staff, and tour managers who want the world."

But The Pitz was growing with artists like PJ Harvey, Happy Mondays, Squeeze, The Stranglers, Jools Holland, Sam Brown, Joan Armatrading, Magnum, Terrorvision, Thunder and Romeo's Daughter selling out.

"I started to diversify too, with acts like The Soup Dragons, The Wedding Present, Chumbawamba, The Cardiacs and Thousand Yard Stare all hitting the stage to great acclaim. Belly, The Cranberries and Babes In Toyland followed hard on their heels."

A show by thrash metal titans Exodus sold-out three weeks in advance and on the night of the show the usual audience of 40-somethings was replaced by a wave of 16 to 20-year-olds.

"There were people diving off the stage, off the speakers, surfing onto the audience and going absolutely crazy.

"I lost count of the bleeding noses and crumpled shapes and was fascinated by the sound and the energy."

By now, 'the little club with the big name' was pulling in crowds from across Europe and the UK and the capacity of the venue was increased – from 412 to 500.

The sports hall was utilised for the larger shows, allowing 1000 people to engage with the artists. Being midway between Birmingham and London meant it was perfectly placed to slip in an extra date

Physicist Brian Cox (far right of pic) played The Pitz with rock mob Dare

159

FEBRUARY
27TH 2 DIE 4 8PM
MARCH
5TH CNN 8PM
12TH BLUES & TROUBLE
21ST CHUMBAWUMBA
28TH SHONEN KNIFE
APRIL
4TH MY LITTLE FUNHOUSE
14TH WILDHEARTS 8PM
18TH DREAM THEATER
23RD 1000 YARD STARE
30TH MONSTER MAGNET
MAY
7TH NUCLEAR ASSAULT
14TH POISON IDEA 8PM
21ST MARSHALL LAW
31ST LINDISFARNE
WOUGHTON CENTRE
MILTON KEYNES
(0908) 660392

FEBRUARY
23RD NAPALM DEATH + SCAT OPERA
24TH COLLISTER & GREGSON
27TH STRANGLERS SOLD OUT

MARCH
3RD MAN
9TH HAVANA 3AM
22ND DUMPYS RUSTY NUTS
23RD BLUR + THE BEYOND + SHC

PITZ
AUGUST
3RD MINDFUNK
SEPTEMBER
14TH LIMBOMANIACS
20TH TATTOOED LOVE BOYS
27TH GARY NUMAN
29TH MORDRED
WOUGHTON CENTRE, CHAFFRON WAY, MILTON KEYNES
0908 660393

THE PITZ
JULY 5TH
GILLAN
THE ONLY UK DATE THIS YEAR £8
JULY 24TH
LAWNMOWER DETH
1ST PERFORMANCE OF THE NEW ALBUM
+ MUCKY PUP £6 & £4
TON CENTRE, RAINBOW DRIVE, MILTON KEYNES
(0908) 660392

PITZ PITZ PITZ
NOVEMBER
8TH LAWNMOWER DETH + REANIM
+ H FROM ACID REIGN'S NEW
13TH SAM BROWN
20TH THERAPY + WHIPPING BOYS + IN DUST
25TH THAT PETROL EMOTION + SU
WOUGHTON CENTRE, MILTON KEYNES (09086603

PITZ WOUGHTON CENTRE, MILTON KEY
(0908) 660392

MANOWAR
SATURDAY 5TH FEBRUARY
8PM TICKETS £6 & £5

WOUGHTON CENTRE
MILTON KEYNES
THE PITZ
JULY 2ND
ZIL Z APPA
ET
TURING FZ'S IMMORTAL BAND
JULY 9TH
FREAK OF NATURE
FEATURING MIKE TRAMP
WOUGHTON CENTRE, RAINBOW DRIVE
CHAFFRON WAY, MILTON KEYNES.
(0908)660392

PITZ JUNE
1 Jools Holland £6.50
8 LAWNMOWER DETH £5 £3 £4
9 ECHO & THE BUNNYMEN £6 £5
13 £6 £5
14 RIVEDRIVER £5 £4 £7
23 £7
28 RUBY TURNER £7
Woughton Centre, Rainbow Drive, Milton Keynes 0908 660392

PITZ
MAY
Woughton Centre, Rainbow Drive, Leadenhall, Milton Keynes.
Tel: (0908) 660392

1 curve £4
5 WISHBONE ASH £6
7 KINGS X £7
10 HEADS UP £5
17 Atomseed £5
25 MORDRED £5

PITZ
JUNE
1ST JOOLS HOLLAND
7TH CUD
8TH LAWNMOWER DETH
9TH ECHO AND THE BUNNYMEN
11TH SOHO
13TH MANFRED MANS EARTHBAND
14TH SWERVEDRIVER
28TH RUBY TURNER
WOUGHTON CENTRE,RAINBOW DRIVE 0908660392

PITZ
DECEMBER
£7 & £6
THE SELECTER
£6 & £5.50
BLUES 'N' TROUBLE
NEW BREED 3 £3
£7 & £6
IAN GILLAN
ETS CENTRAL LIBRARY BOX OFFICE BEDFORD
A DISC NORTHAMPTON BOJANGLES DAVENTRY

THE PITZ MAY WOUGHTON CENTRE

4 XENTRIX LAWNMOWER DETH + THE BEYOND £4 MEMB £2·50

20 CELTIC FROST £6

25 DRIVE SHE SAID £5

30 TIGERTAILZ £5 & £4·50

PITZ ONSLAUGHT WOUGHTON CENTRE

THE GREATEST LITTLE CLUB THE PITZ VIP PASS

MUSIC FOR THE PEOPLE THE PITZ MUSIC CLUB

THE PITZ FEBRUARY Woughton Centre Milton Keynes

GANG GRENE CORROSION OF CONFORMITY GUN RUBY TURNER

zubop

Woughton Centre 0908 660392

NAPALM DEATH Saturday 23rd February 1991 Evening 8.00

UNRESERVED £5.00 £4.50 No 0150 Retain This Portion Conditions Overleaf

at the start or end of a tour.

Publications flocked to see what the fuss was about, and Kerrang! magazine placed The Pitz as one of the top five rock clubs in the UK.

"We were riding high and the music was getting faster and faster," Chris remembers.

The highlight of the thrash-era was the arrival of Nuclear Assault."

They had played to 5000 in London and when they walked into The Pitz the lead singer called it a shithole, saying 'we are not playing here.'

"The gig had sold-out in a day and 300 ticketless fans were locked outside the club. After much cajoling, threatening and pleading by the tour manager, they played.

"When the gig started it was packed, and as the night wore on, less and less people seemed to be able to get back in to watch the gig.

"Looking out from the lighting control box, the hall was packed from wall to wall with no space at all."

It transpired that a roofer from Newport Pagnell had led fans over the outer roof, into the courtyard, through the back windows and down the back stairs into the hall.

"Instead of the normal 500 in the hall, we had close to 900," Chris remembers.

Napalm Death left a bad taste with Chris though.

"I was warned but paid no heed...

"It was during the World Cup and we had a portable big screen player from Sony.

"An obscure match was playing and the drummer from the band walked up to the screen, put his fingers down his throat and threw up onto the screen.

"Things went from bad to worse. We had asked the band to talk to the crowd about not diving off the stage, and that the new barrier was for their safety.

"The band came on, and the lead singer shouted, 'Everyone up on stage, there is going to be violence.'

"The crew at the front were assaulted by the crowd and then assailed with kicks and punches from the band behind them. "I spent some time trying to restore order, and finding it too difficult, I withdrew the crew from the pit and a free-for-all took place.

warm up for tour

Concert
video

"If I had tried to stop the show there would have been a riot.

"At a later gig, Death Angel's crew tipped chilli con carne into our new piano and my crew were threatened by the tour manager, so it was getting hairy.

"I had a call the next day from their German tour manager asking if we had found his filofax which contained his life.

"I asked the crew and they said not, but I later saw them making a small fire with what looked like pages from a diary. I turned a blind eye.

"As thrash began its demise, a new iconic sound was beginning – grunge. Foolishly, I'd turned down R.E.M and the Chili Peppers, but we made up for it with a series of brilliant gigs including Mordred, Paw, Gang Green and Poison Idea. After a small romance with rave and a smaller dalliance with pop, probably the biggest club gig to hit Milton Keynes took place.

"John Jackson, who then worked for agents Fair Warning, rang on the off-chance I could put on a gig for The Holy Smokers. They were returning from a Japanese tour having played in stadia. And now they were going to play a gig to 500 at The Pitz.

"The Holy Smokers was the code name for Iron Maiden.

"I wasn't allowed to announce the gig until the day, which I did, at 9am in the morning.

"By 9.30am every ticket had sold out. Three pantechnicons full of gear turned up at the venue, and the full stage and Eddie the mechanical robot mascot were all used.

"A special TV documentary was made and it was the highlight of the history of The Pitz.

"When Blur played to a less than packed house, the guitarist launched his guitar into the crowd and unfortunately hit an unassuming punter, splitting his head open.

"The resulting hospital trip and other pressure on the night prompted me to issue a banning order on the band.

"The next day we featured in every newspaper as the venue that banned Blur.

"To this day it hasn't been forgotten. "Bassist Alex James and frontman Damon Albarn mention the night in their biographies, and when they received their first Brit Award they thanked everyone, but singled me out for my act of supposed unkindliness."

Other memories that stand out?

> **"The Holy Smokers was the code name for Iron Maiden"**

Pitz players: The Zappa brothers, and Babes in Toyland

"PJ Harvey played for just 18 minutes before ending her set sharply.

"I expected a riot but the fans were so blown away by the performance that they left open-mouthed.

"Working with Frank Zappa's sons was surreal as the full Frank Zappa band supported them.

"I spent a few hours talking with them about various gigs and nights and they signed a piece of wood in exchange for my CNN T-shirt.

"The most difficult part was the armed guard with a submachine gun sat outside the green room as death threats had been made on their lives.

"Blaze Bayley, the lead singer with Pitz darlings Wolfsbane was so disgusted with the food we cooked the band that he went on stage with his foot in a chicken carcass in protest, and Ian Gillan from Deep Purple ran onto the stage in his slippers by mistake and beat a hasty retreat to put on his boots before returning!

"I have had dinner with Tom Robinson, Lawnmower Deth and Wolfsbane, and been asked to find interesting people for Belly to talk to.

"I was asked to provide drink, drugs and sex for numerous artists, all of which I refused to do.

"I swam with Babes in Toyland, was accosted by a Page 3 girl, and threatened by Andy Taylor from Duran Duran.

"I was bottled off the stage when announcing that a band had failed to show up, and been held up against the wall by the guitarist with Wishbone Ash.

"I spent virtually no time sleeping, lived on pure adrenaline and turned down a job for Rod MacSween at ITB to be the booking agent for Pearl Jam, Tori Amos and Morphine.

"The low has got to be watching the Tattooed Love Boys with 25 other punters, and the high would be standing at the side of the stage watching 1,000 fans going berserk, thinking 'I did that.'

"Working on the edge was always difficult and making ends meet for the budget even more so. But I wouldn't have exchanged my 10 years as a promoter and venue manager for anything.

"I put on more than 3,000 acts and loved every minute of it."

After leaving The Pitz Chris became a Professor and Pro vice Chancellor at a university and then formed his own consultancy working across the world in music and sporting events.

He also mentors Olympic Coaches in leadership.

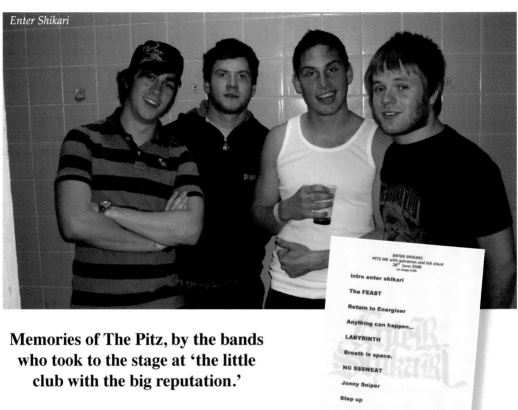

Enter Shikari

ENTER SHIKARI
PITZ MK with galvatron and fell silent
28th June 2008
on stage 9:00

intro enter shikari

The FEAST

Return to Energiser

Anything can happen...

LABYRINTH

Breath in space.

NO SSSWEAT

Jonny Sniper

Step up

Intro - Sorry you're not a winner
....
mothership
Okay time for plan b

Memories of The Pitz, by the bands who took to the stage at 'the little club with the big reputation.'

"I think every memory of playing this venue is a fond one. It's the place we first met the band Fell Silent and from there a relationship blossomed between us into a happy and fruitful one.

We also toured together. It was also the first place I had ever heard the term 'enter shitkari'. I overheard it in a conversation between two punters. I don't think they realised I was standing right behind them - or maybe they did and just didn't care. "Either way I thought it was genius and have been using it ever since.

One of the last times we played there it had been a very successful gig with many attendants going home happy. Or pissed. Or happily pissed.

"We were about to do the same.

"We had been paid, said our goodbyes, loaded the gear and were about to be on our way when it occurred to us that we were a member down, Rou.

It turned out he had gone back inside to look for a garment of some sort, I can't remember what it was but I assume it was his jacket – it would have been pretty silly to forget your trousers in the dressing room.

In doing so he had got himself

locked in the building with the key master safely on his way home.

Took us an hour and a half to locate the key master, bring it back and rescue Rou. And it wasn't the last time it happened."
Rob Rolfe, Enter Shikari

"I remember one time there when we played with Acid Reign and the mobile bar came through, so we took it in turns to lie on the floor underneath it and try to drink beer straight from the pump.

I remember choking and generally getting beer everywhere except in my stomach!

I'm sure we had an indoor footie match with other bands as well. I remember H being quite sporty and competitive. Me? I've always been crap at footie, so sat that one out.

We always went down really well there and loved playing every single time.

The warm-up at The Pitz in 2009 was special to me as it was the first time I

Lawnmower Deth

played with the band since around 1991 and the first gig played as a six-piece. I had a blast.

It set us up perfect for Download really."
Gavin O'Malley, aka Schizo Rotary Sprintmaster, Lawnmower Deth

"I remember having an industrial size tin of baked beans tipped over my head when it was my birthday in about 1992 – the photo was in Kerrang!"
Chris Flint, aka Explodin' Dr Jaggers Flymo, Lawnmower Deth

"It was the one and only venue where some girls got their jugs out and wobbled them around a bit!

One of them had three boobs!"
Stephen Nesfield, aka Concorde Faccripper, Lawnmower Deth

"Milton Keynes was pivotal in the UK thrash scene. I can't think of a tour where we, or any of the bands of our ilk didn't roll through the Pitz.

I remember some classic bills back in the day, Lawnmower Deth, Sabbat and Acid Reign on one, and Lawnmower Deth, Acid Reign and Xentrix on another.

That's why, when we did the Download warm-up show it was great to play the Pitz again and put together a line-up that in some way represented 'how it used to be.'

Adding Virus, H and Metal Messiah to the bill made sense.

That said, the venue did seem to have shrunk!

When you consider that people now talk about the circle pits at Download, I remember where we first saw them – 20 years ago at The Pitz.

That's what I really remember. Serious audience participation and serious dancing.

I don't seem to remember any other venue in the country behaving in quite the same way.

I went down to quite a few gigs there too, just to be in the audience.

I remember seeing Little Angels in there for a warm-up supporting Dread Zeppelin, before their Bowl gig with ZZ Top.

Then, yes, I remember the same things as the rest of the band – beans and bad behaviour…"
Pete Lee, aka Qualcast Mutilator, Lawnmower Deth

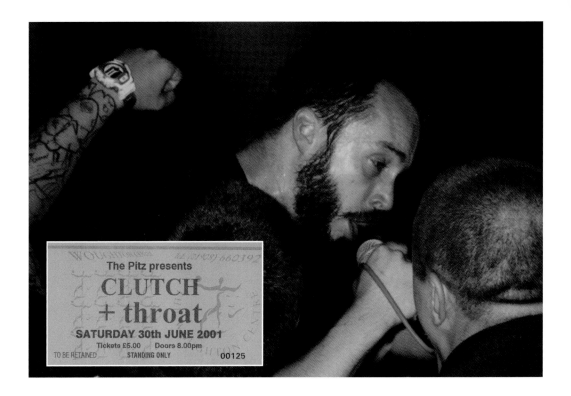

The Pitz presents

CLUTCH
+ throat

SATURDAY 30th JUNE 2001
Tickets £5.00   Doors 8.00pm
TO BE RETAINED   STANDING ONLY   00125

"A scene unfolded after a show at The Pitz. Myself and some of our crew were casually assaulted by a troupe of 12-year-old schoolgirls.

They stole our beer and some cigarettes and enquired how big our willies were.

I've been in some truly unexpected situations, but THAT one scared the shit out of me."
Neil Fallon, Clutch

"The first time we played Milton Keynes was also the first time any of us had been there, so it was all the usual rubbish about concrete cows and an incomprehensible road system.

We didn't see any cows but when we eventually found the Woughton Centre we were surprised to be playing at a sports hall and swimming pool in the middle of a housing estate.

We had only played pubs and sticky floored rock clubs, so a leisure centre was a bit of a change of scenery.

That first time we played to about 40 people but went down brilliantly.

We must have played the Woughton Centre seven or eight times after that and sold it out every time.

One our favourite places to play."
Jase Edwards, Wolfsbane

"When we played at the Pitz in 1990, we had released the album A Bit Of What You Fancy and already had a couple of hit singles so we were really on the crest of a wave.

I was only 21 at the time and being (relatively) local from Bedford it was the nearest thing to a homecoming gig for me.

I remember going out to see my mum with her friends before the show and she was slightly horrified at how 'road worn' I was! I remember that Kerrang! or Metal Hammer magazine was there doing a feature and photoshoot with us and Ozzy Osbourne,who was there with his wife (and our manager) Sharon.

Quite a surreal night.

It's not very often that you see Sharon and Ozzy in a Milton Keynes leisure centre!"
Guy Griffin, The Quireboys (pictured)

THE PITZ

Woughton Centre
0908 660392

THE PITZ
Kings X
DATE 7/5/91
TIME
UNRESERVED
PRICE £ 7.00
No

DATE 18.4.
CONCERT Dream Th...
ACCESS SAMMY JON...

GUEST

WOUGHTON CENTRE
TEL No. 0908 660392
presents
DOGS D'AMOUR
SATURDAY 12th MARCH 1994
Doors open 7:30pm
£ 6.00 £ 5.00   TICKET No. 00499

ACID REIGN
SAT 31ST MAR/90
8.00PM
£5.00/£4.50
Woughton centre,
Chaffron Way,
Leadenhall,
Milton Keynes
TEL:

Woughton
Centre!

WOUGHTON CENTRE
LEADENHALL,MILTON KEYNES MK6 5EJ
TEL No. (0908) 660392
THE PITZ
Presents
N.E.U.K.
on
FRIDAY 1st NOVEMBER 1996
8.00PM
DOOR £3.50 ADV. £2.50   TICKET No. 00004
TO BE RETAINED

SUNDAY LUNCHTIME — THIS SUNDAY
"ITSY BITSY BAND"
SATURDAY, MAY 4, 8pm, £2.50 (£2)
THE GREATEST
SHOW ON LEGS
"Funniest routine I've ever seen on
television" — Clive James
FRIDAY, MAY 10, 8pm. £3 (£2.50)
IVOR CUTLER
One of the most original minds of our
time . . . hilarious" — Time Out
SATURDAY, MAY 18, 8pm. £3.00 Advance
NEW MODEL ARMY

WOUGHTON CENTRE
LEADENHALL, MILTON KEYNES MK6 5EJ
TEL No. 0908 660392
THE PITZ presents
STILTSKIN
+ SUPPORT
SUNDAY 2nd OCTOBER 1994
Doors 8:00pm

MILTON KEYNES
WOUGHTON CENTRE
THE
STRANGLERS
WED 27 FEB

WOUGHTON CENTRE
LEADENHALL, MILTON KEYNES MK6 5E
TEL No. 0908 660392
THE PITZ presents
CANNIBAL
CORPSE
+ SAMAEL & DESULTORY
SATURDAY 10th DECEMBER 1994
Doors 8:00pm
£ 6.50 £ 5.50   TICKET No. 00163
RETAINED

BOX OFFICE (0908)660392
the PITZ Rocks
MILTON KEYNES

Woughton Centre
0908 660392
THE ALMIGHTY
Sunday 23rd June 1991
Evening 7.30
UNRESERVED
£7.00   £6.50
No   0107
Retain This Portion Conditions Overleaf

NEW PITZ ROCK CLUB IN MILTON KEYNES
CATERS FOR ROCK FANS EVERY WEEK WITH
BANDS, A DISCO AND CHEAP BEER.
ARE NO RESTRICTIONS & DRINKS ARE
B PRICES. IF YOU BECOME A MEMBER
U GET DISCOUNTS OFF EVERY GIG.
MEMBERSHIP IS ONLY £3 A YEAR.

FORTHCOMING EVENTS
MARCH
26TH HEADSWIM + REVHEAD   £4 & £3
APRIL
4TH   IGNORANT   £3
10TH NEW ENGLAND   £3
16TH ADRIAN SMITH   £4 & £3
18TH DREAM THEATRE   £6 & £5
25TH ROCK NITE BANDS TBC £3
30TH ROADRUNNER NITE   £3
MAY
...OUR   £6
...NBOW DRIVE MILTON KEYNES

IT'S
THE PITZ!

MUSIC fans might not be expecting too much of a new venue for
Milton Keynes, because it's really
The Pitz.
But organisers behind the new rolling show reckon that the catchy name
won't reflect the standa...
...the shows they a...
Wednesday...

Wednesday, September 2, booking in
at the Woughton Centre for a gig
featuring local favourites The New
Mutants and Claire, plus a special
guest for the inaugural night who has
yet to be announced
Tickets for the opening are available
at the Woughton Centre, and later gigs
will be advertised throughout the ci...
on poster sites.

THE PITZ
WEDNESDAY
8.00PM
£1.50
001721

HILATOR
...1993

KING
PLUS SPECIAL GUESTS
MINDFUN...
NOTTINGHAM ROCK CITY TUE...
CAMBRIDGE CORN EXCHANGE WEDNESDAY 1ST MAY...
£6 Box office tel 0223 357051
MANCHESTER INTERNATIONAL 2 THURSDAY 2ND MAY...
£6 Box office tel 061 273 0834, Piccadilly Box Office tel 061 839 0850
BUCKLEY TIVOLI SATURDAY 4TH MAY...
£6 Box office tel 0224 550742
GLASGOW MAYFAIR SUNDAY 5TH MAY...
£6 from Virgin Records, Union St, Glasgow and usual TOCTA agents
tel 0931 557 6969, credit cards and info same number
NEWCASTLE RIVERSIDE MONDAY 6TH MAY...
£6 Box office tel 091 261 4386
MILTON KEYNES: WOUGHTON CENTRE TUESDAY 7TH MAY...
£7 Box Office tel 0908 660392

TIC
17th January 1991
Doors Open 7.30pm
ED
advance
0248

5/7/92
GILLAN

THE
PITZ
DATE 3-8-91
CONCERT MINDFUNK
ACCESS
GUEST

Biffy Clyro

Mondo Generator's Nick Oliveri

WOUGHTON CENTRE
LEADENHALL, MILTON KEYNES MK6 5EJ
TEL No. (01908) 660392

THE Pitz Presents

PLACEBO

PLUS DEUS

MONDAY 3rd FEBRUARY 1997
8.00pm

£ **7.00**

00387

MONDO GENERATOR

21.08.04
8.00pm
Tickets £8

00118

TO BE GIVEN UP

MARK LANEGAN BAND

21.08.04
8.00pm
Tickets £8

00001

TO BE GIVEN UP

LLERS

NUTE + Linea 77

Metal Night with

MASTODON

Cerberus & Labrat

Deck Cheese Records Showcase with

Not Katies

KRA Y KLA
BB
SPOOKHOU

THREE FILMS BY CAMERON JAMIE
WITH LIVE SOUNDTRACK MUSIC FROM THE MELVINS
UK TOUR NOVEMBER 2003

The Pitz crew

The Wildhearts

169

Band Blitz Competition

An annual staple in Milton Keynes for more than a decade,
The Band Blitz was the only competition worth bothering with.

With the resurgence of big budget musical talent shows in the noughties, a whole host of music competitions started to appear - from the smallest club assembly to national enterprises, all hoping to uncover 'the next big thing.'

But in Milton Keynes, the Band Blitz preceded prime time drear by a few years.

The Blitz was an opportunity for local acts to stand on a stage, perform for their mates and hone their style a little. If they were willing to take it seriously, they could leave with some useful pointers and, if they were good enough, maybe a few prizes too.

The Blitz ran every summer. Five heats, four bands in a heat, and a grand final.

Judges lost track of the evenings spent sweltering in the hosting venue of The Pitz, nursing a lukewarm pint, but it was great fun and really helped to unite a burgeoning scene.

The Blitz was launched as a joint initiative between The Pitz and The Citizen newspaper, and we harnessed some terrific support right from the get-go.

In the early years, winners secured a recording session at Linford Manor studio. It was a fabulous chance to record in a stunning location with expert tuition, following in the footsteps of artists like Jamiroquai and PJ Harvey.

They received more support from Marshall Amplification who provided equipment, and in the pages of The Citizen which backed the bash week on week.

Throw in a cash prize, a headline gig at The Pitz, together with the profile the competition gave rise to, and it was a great chance to make some serious gains. Bosomunkee took the title in 2000, and promptly inked a deal with Precious Cargo records.

75% Lip walked away with the top prize in 2001.

"Growing up, I lived and breathed The Pitz. Teenage girls who listened to

A winning combination: 75% Lip took the Band Blitz title in 2001

punk rock weren't as common as they seem now and it was the only place that had something to do for those not solely interested in boys and make-up," said guitarist Jo Harrison.

"I spent almost every Friday night at The Pitz between the ages of 14 and 16 with my good friend and bandmate Kat.

"We'd make friends with strangers and spend half our time persuading anyone over 18 to get us a drink from the bar.

"It's where we met our drummer, Andrew.

"When sitting on the stairs in the atrium he tripped over my shoelace, falling flat on the floor. He looked up and said 'Alright love, are you looking for a drummer?' How could anyone turn that down?

"After spending years talking and dreaming about making a band, we finally had one and went on to win the Band Blitz.

"My memories from the night of the final are somewhat blurred. Nervousness caught up with me and I downed a bottle of wine before going on stage.

"A couple of years after, I bumped into one of the sound technicians from the night. He reminded me that at one point during the gig, I accidentally kicked my pedal into the crowd.

"He was never sure if it was an

elaborate stage act or whether I was drunk.

"The night of the final might have played out like a well-choreographed movie, but the aftershow was more like a nightmare. Andrew decided to change his name to Drew, a pseudonym he still uses to this day, and our ex-bassist got caught performing a naked striptease in Drew's garage.

"I forgot to tell my mum where I was all night, resulting in a post-victory good old-fashioned family bust-up! Still, it was worth it!" Jo added.

"I remember our heat being very closely fought - Liberty X, True Element, Ego Testical and us," said 75% Lip's Kat Ross.

"The highlight for me was when the crowd got their lighters out for our song No One Cares. In the final, we were up against Fozz, Krain, Minus (I) and Rougus.

"Our performance was a lot stronger than it had been in the heat, and we made an effort to put on a good show.

"We opened with a techno version of one of our songs played on keyboard, which amused half the crowd and confused the rest. When Jo and I began the opening riff to our first 'real' song, we didn't realize Drew was still in the loo.

"He burst onto the stage just in the nick of time to start the drum beat, and this

The PITZ Club in association with M.K CITIZEN and MARSHALL AMPLIFICATION presents...

BATTLE of the BANDS HEAT THREE

FRI 13th AUG
DOORS 7:30p.m
TICKETS £4
BOX OFFICE NUMBER
01908 660392

THE SO CALLED

waffle

AUDIOSIDEPROJECT

THE Dynamics

MARSHALL AMPLIFICATION PRESENTS

BAND BLITZ FINAL

FRIDAY 16th SEPTEMBER/ TICKETS £6
DOORS 7p.m/ BOX OFFICE NUMBER 01908660392

RED CRASH
LIGHTS & SITES

STORM THE GATES

DESPERATE CYCLE

HELLO HALLELUJAH

BiG Fu**iNG SKULL

THE PITZ CLUB IN ASSOCIATION WITH M.K CITIZEN AND MARSHALL AMPLIFICATION...

PRESENTS

THE BATTLE OF THE BANDS
HEAT ONE

KILL DISNEY

ActionBeat

RuN LiKE FuN

ONE LAST CHANCE

PSYCHO UNLE

FRi 30th JULY
TICKETS £4

THE PITZ CLUB IN ASSOCIATION WITH MARSHALL AMPLIFICATION & M.K CITIZEN PRESENTS...

BAND BLITZ 2004 HEAT FOUR

FUDGE

ZiP SHOT

AURORA

SiX POINT FiVE

DOORS 7.30 p.m

FRi 20th AUG

TICKETS £4
BOX OFFICE NUMBER
01908 660392

apparently looked extremely well-timed and planned. It wasn't.

"Not all of the highlights of our performance were accidental - we had some well-choreographed booty-shaking in the breaks of our songs, giving Jo ample opportunity to show off her 'naughty nurse' outfit.

"The smoothest part of our performance by far was the perfectly timed execution of a 'triple Huey', where during a dramatic musical pause, Helen, Jo and I flicked each of our plectrums into the air, caught them and carried on playing.

"This manoeuvre had achieved roughly a five per-cent success rate in rehearsal, but somehow it worked on the night. I like to think it was that more than anything else that won us the judges' approval."

fidjit took the champions title in 2002.

"Up until a few weeks before the Band Blitz, fidjit were playing shows, but didn't have the extra 'bounce' that was connected with our later performances," recalled bassist Steve Scott.

"The motivation that drove us to perform and turn our gigs from a 'band on stage' to a 'show on stage' came from the knowledge we would be playing to packed crowds in front of local and industry judges that we admired.

"Both the heat and the final put us up against bands we respected musically and it was humbling to finish ahead of those talented acts.

"The experience we gained from the recording prize at Linford Manor was invaluable; we expected to be treated like amateurs and were amazed to be given the same recording hours and professional help that major label bands got."

In 2003, a trio called The Ideas came second in the grand final.

Beanie Bhebhe was a part of that six-legged machine, and nowadays earns his money doing things like playing drums for Rudimental, working as guitarist with singer-songwriter Anne-Marie, and delivering his own cool sounds.

The Blitz always had a colourful judging panel, including representatives from the businesses partnering the bash, and over the course of its history more than 200 bands walked onstage under the BB banner.

We had rock bands, indie troupes and occasional pop players, death metal moments, acoustic interludes, men playing in pants and others in gas masks!

Bands and sponsors came and went, but two constants remained at the helm - The Pitz and The Citizen.

In 2008, after 11 years of talent spotting, we brought the curtain down on the area's biggest and best competition.

But the little contest had a great reputation, and its legacy lives on.

"fidjit split up, but the members are still involved in the Milton Keynes music scene," Scotty added.

"This has a massive amount to do with the support we received from the scene and drives us to support others starting out on their musical paths."

Striker

Fenside

Bosomunkee

75% Lip

fidjit at Great Linford Manor with engineer Sam Miller

174

Acacia Close

Aurora's Shadow

Six.Point.Five

Hello Hallelujah

F.I.N.K

THE PITZ CLUB IN ASSOCIATION WITH M.K CITIZEN AND MARSHALL AMPLIFICATION PRESENTS...

TICKETS £4
BOX OFFICE NUMBER
01908
660392

BAND BLITZ
2004
HEAT FIVE
FRI 27th AUG
DOORS 7.30 P.M

BATTERED COD

ALIAS

P.O.t.d.P

the ENIGMA

The Band Blitz judges

176

The Sanctuary

"It was basically an indoor riot of 4,000 people and an event hijacked by some seriously bad boys."

It was a place where dance dreams came true and it was a venue that more than occasionally courted controversy and fought the law.

The Sanctuary was a whacking great warehouse on the outskirts of Bletchley, at Denbigh North.

Dance fans loved the space and the vibe and it soon became a mecca for ravers – where they could mix with thousands of like-minded individuals and have the best time.

The Sanctuary opened its doors at the tail end of 1991, when it played host to the first ever Dreamscape promotion.

At a time when illegal raving was filling tabloid columns, here in Milton Keynes The Sanctuary would let music lovers soak up the sounds with no fear of being moved on or cuffed up.

And it let them party hard for longer - with 10-hour sessions a regular draw for punters from all over the country who

flocked to this 'new warehouse concept.'

Tony Rosenberg came across the place when it was still in its infancy, and within months had persuaded financiers to offer the necessary support to enable him to take over the venue.

He made waves from day one too: One of the first bookings was a date that had to be honoured from the previous management, a World Cup Sound Clash.

Little did they know when they opened the doors for the event that clash would be such an apt word...

"I think that night in February 1994 is still talked about by all the ex-Sanctuary security staff, Thames Valley Police, MK Council EHO, and anyone over 40 into reggae music and living within 100 miles of Milton Keynes," Tony says.

"It was basically an indoor riot of 4,000 people and an event hijacked by some seriously bad boys."

Thames Valley Police rapped his

knuckles and then Tony got back to the job in hand.

His hard work paid off too, with a decade of promotions banked in the memories of the estimated million plus people who Tony believed stepped through the doors.

Dance fans were thrown a feast of favourite names - Gatecrasher, Godskitchen, Slammin' Vinyl, Cream and Fantazia all held nights at the venue.

They were big events too, with a single capacity of 3,000. And when the venue made use of the Rollers facility 6,000 punters could be accommodated.

Throw in a Chill Out marquee, open up the Denbigh leisure site and a whopping capacity of 8,000 was granted.

Tony Rosenberg

Massive stuff.

Although known for its raving exploits, The Sanctuary did deliver bands too.

In its early days Pop Will Eat Itself and The Prodigy were among those gracing the stage.

Modfather Paul Weller played, Cast and Backstreet Boys appeared, and Ocean Colour Scene may or may not have caught the train for their date in 1999.

The funniest not-so-funny bash at the haunt will surprise some though – a night in the company of comedian Bernard Manning...

The Sanctuary wasn't just another venue. It was a hub, a community, and a home for a generation of youths.

It was renowned and respected nationally.

Of course it also encountered its fair share of problems and had to put up with complaints from local residents.

Somehow though, it always seemed to swat away the whingers and the authorities!

It would take something with more force to silence the sounds for good. It was the arrival of top-flight football to Milton Keynes that finally did it.

Wimbledon's re-homing (and subsequent renaming as the MK Dons) needed retail support and the Denbigh site was spied for the operation.

The venue eventually shut up shop on July 10, 2004, and went out on a high with thousands of dance heads soaking up one final new city meeting with Slammin' Vinyl.

Where The Sanctuary once enticed ravers, furniture superstore Ikea now stands, beckoning you inside to purchase a flat-pack for assembly.

But memories of the venue still live on in all those that spent hot, pounding nights there. Four years after it was closed and razed to the ground and the venue was in the headlines again.

In 2008 some of the devoted paid homage with an impressive mini-rave in the Ikea store.

The flashmob blew their whistles and danced their butts off during a five-minute session.

"It was sad to close," said Tony, "But everything moves on and I was beginning to feel the dance scene had shrunk and wouldn't be able to sustain the overheads of the place.

"I am really happy to have been part of such a British youth revolution, and despite not having an emotional attachment to the scene I was far happier walking among 3,000 ravers than I was going for a drink in any Wetherspoons."

Slammin' Vinyl

Slammin' Vinyl is one of the biggest independent dance names in the UK and during a six year period it promoted many tasty events at the venue.

It also ran the last ever Sanctuary event, bringing the curtain down on the venue before the bulldozers moved in. Slammin' Vinyl director Grant Smith remembers the warehouse where dance ruled.

"It was basically a big tin warehouse, rapidly transformed into one of the meccas of rave culture in the early 1990s when this type of music was sweeping through the UK.

"With a versatile 3,000 capacity main room, a second room upstairs with a floor that was always threatening to fall in, and a large outside compound area, what more could you ask for?"

The first generation of rave promoters had regularly used the venue, names like Dreamscape, Helter Skelter and World Dance, so Slammin' Vinyl were following in illustrious footsteps.

It held its first event at The Sanctuary in 1998 with a 6,000 capacity mega-rave, and in the six years that followed it used the place for a variety of shows.

"It wasn't a corporate venue like so many places these days, so you didn't have the litany of rules and regulations that sometimes make current day venues seem quite oppressive.

"Mind you, the security team could be a bit tasty and it was rumoured the head doorman might have been in the French Foreign Legion!

"The music policy across our period was drum 'n' bass, hardcore, old skool (back to the golden days), hard trance and techno.

"We booked virtually everyone who was a name in the rave scene, from Grooverider and Goldie to Slipmatt and beyond. "Most of the guys are still carving out a good living as DJs now."

Its central location and proximity to the M1 gave The Sanctuary a national following, and Grant remembers it as a brilliant place where the brand cut its teeth, before the curtain fell for the final time – and it was Grant who hosted that last event at the venue.

"We made the site as big as possible, using the Sanctuary, Rollers, Fastrack Warehouse and a huge big top outside. "I won't say how many we packed in, but we sold out a month in advance and could probably have sold 25,000 tickets if we'd had the space!" he said.

179

Stadium MK

"I'm thrilled the stadium is putting Milton Keynes on the map for music again nationally."

Building a new football stadium in Bletchley signalled the end of the Sanctuary's reign as one of the leading dance venues in the country.

There was no other choice. To make room for the new stadium, it had to go.

But in 2019, music returned to the area, when the space that is now the MK Dons home turf presented some seriously great shows.

And, while it isn't whistles and dance that are leading the sounds as it was back when the Sanctuary ruled the area, Stadium MK is doing a swell job of focusing music industry eyes on Milton Keynes once more.

MK Dons chairman Pete Winkelman ensured the venue was up to scratch with the best audio equipment around from day one. If you want the best, you go to the best, so he called on long time industry friends Gary Garner and 'Big' Mick

Hughes for advice.

The former is an audio consultant, and 'Big' Mick works as the full-time sound engineer for Metallica.

Pretty soon, Stadium MK boasted the UK's first Meyer Sound self-powered system installed in a stadium.

"Concrete stadiums aren't known for their sound quality, but we've got it sorted there," 'Big' Mick said.

"Pete is on the cutting edge!"

With the National Bowl falling quiet in recent years, the emergence of the stadium as a serious contender for live music couldn't have come at a better time.

And Pete had always envisaged the stadium working that way – even before the turf had been laid.

"Music has always been an intrinsic part of who I am, and, just like football, it brings people together," he said, "MK has long had the infrastructure to cope with top-flight music shows, and I'm thrilled the stadium is putting Milton Keynes on the map for music again nationally."

Take That, Rod Stewart and Rammstein all played the venue in the summer of 2019.

"It was a wonderful way to launch the stadium, with real legends of pop, and one of the most acclaimed rock bands from the past two decades, and that was just the start," he added, "I'm so excited for its future as a top-tier live music venue."

In January 2020 fans snapped up tickets to see reformed New Jersey rockers My Chemical Romance at Stadium MK.

The band were set to play three sold-out shows in June 2020, but at the end of April the dates were postponed until 2021 - a casualty of Covid-19.

A new era at Stadium MK: Take That, live in Milton Keynes on May 23, 2019 and (left) support act Rick Astley

Preparations at Stadium MK ahead of Rammstein's huge show (July 5, 2019)

Sound and vision: Pete Winkelman (centre) with 'Big' Mick and Gary Garner

The King Blues live at MK11

MK11

*"Milton Keynes is at a very significant fork in the road
in terms of its development."*

In the 1970s, much of MK as we now know it was a work in progress. The green and pleasant land was being turned over and building sites crept in.

Milton Keynes Development Corporation were at work in Kiln Farm. The landscape was changing and taking the farmland with it.

How many gig-goers throwing shapes at MK11 realise the bustling venue was born from a number of cowsheds and barns?

Post renovation, the space became known as a sports and social club, with squash courts for employees of MKDC.

As Kiln Farm Social Club, it worked well for some time, but by the mid-noughties, with rising costs and a dwindling turnover, the site was sold off privately.

It passed through a few hands before it was refurbished and re-launched as a bonafide watering hole in 2008.

Brothers Marc and Simon O'Brien came onboard to oversee the bar and kitchen, but it was only ever a side-venture for the then operator, and when he decided to return to

his village pub, the siblings stepped up and made changes.

In December 2012, MK11 Live Music Venue was opened.

They assembled a nucleus of locally-based players – tech-folks and promoters who could enrich the space and help add to the sparse number of venues in the new town.

MK11 has been working well ever since, establishing itself on the gigging circuit, and bringing music makers like Grandmaster Flash, Less Than Jake and Ghostface Killah to town.

A recent expansion means that the sports and restaurant side of the business is better served, and the added space and tidy soundproofing is a treat for music fans. Nice work all round.

"Milton Keynes is at a very significant fork in the road in terms of its development. The town could fast become a carbon copy of the commercial elements of every other city in the UK," Marc said.

"We could be left with all the familiar brands on our high streets and in our

Marc and Simon with US ska punkers Less Than Jake

shopping centres, while we collectively scratch our heads as we try to figure out what our cultural identity is.

"Or we can all fight to make Milton Keynes a hub of independent spirit, with local people making businesses that mean something to them and others, encouraging our young people to stay here and be creative, and contribute to the richer culture of our new city."

Simon added: "The story of Milton Keynes is a very exciting one, which is being written every day.

"We hope to be a part of the story and contribute to a successful and vibrant city for all of us to enjoy together."

Pharoahe Monch on stage at MK11

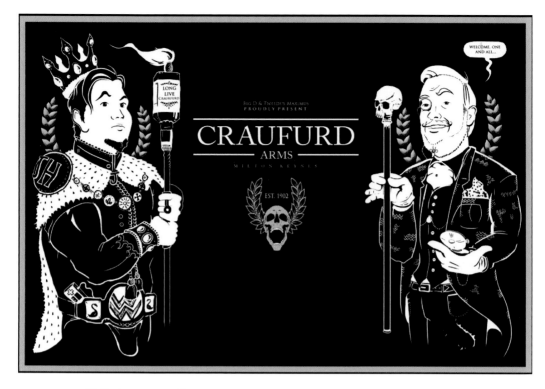

The Craufurd Arms

*"When war came the dances became more frequent - you didn't
sit at home and mope, you got out there and got on with it!"*

Long before plans for the new city had even been thought of, it was the old towns that were the beating heart of local living.
Newport Pagnell, Stony Stratford, Bletchley, New Bradwell and Wolverton are steeped in history and boasted big community spirit.

People worked hard together and enjoyed letting their hair down together too.

Consequently, traditional dances and big band sounds spilled all over in days past.

In Wolverton, venues including The Drill Hall, the Old Technical College, the Old Wolverton Works Canteen and The Craufurd Arms offered live music.

Dennis Lyman was a regular attendee, watching local bands like The Rhythm Aces, who were the premier band on the scene at the time.

"Back then, there was no television and only one radio channel which predominantly offered news and set

shows, and little else, apart from cinema," he said.

"We went for something to do, for exercise, and to meet people.

"The bands always played tunes that you could sing to as well as dance to.

"Because of the lack of anything else to do, you created something else of your own and everyone seemed to enjoy themselves...you would still get the occasional drunks in, but shall we say they were forcefully ushered out.

"The area was full of musicians then, because everyone played in local troupes, like the Bradwell Silver Band.

"That's how many people learned to play, and they would then play the dances in the evenings.

"When war came, if anything, the dances became more frequent - you didn't sit at home and mope, you got out there and got on with it!"

Dennis also recalled harmony singing duo Les Inch and Ben Burbidge being a popular attraction in the local clubs.

The dances remained a force to be reckoned with through to the early '60s when the world was exposed to the new phenomenon of rock 'n' roll.

Wolverton adapted and gradually dances were replaced by the new style.

The Craufurd Arms had opened its doors for the first time in 1907 and frequently hosted live entertainment.

It was built by the People's Refreshment House Association (PRHA), founded in 1896 by the Bishop of Chester. Lieutenant Colonel Craufurd was the PRHA chairman.

Today a pint goes hand in hand with a gig at the venue, but the intention of the men who built the place was to encourage its patrons to become teetotal.

Temperance was to be applauded.

Imagine what they would make of today's well-stocked bars!

In the '60s local bands including The Fenders stepped onto the stage, with the live music a popular draw in both the rear room and the front bar, just as it is today.

In the '70s, music was still strong at the haunt, and artists doing the rounds nationally came through - AC/DC support band Blazer Blazer played the Hammersmith Apollo with the Australian aces before showing up to rouse Wolverton a couple of days later.

But by this point it wasn't only music that was attracting audiences. Comedy names were bringing funnies to the fore

as well - acts like Mike Reid, and Roger De Courcey with Nookie Bear!

Shane Quentin, now a long-standing DJ on CRMK remembers snapping up an original hand-stamped paper sleeve copy of Gangsters, the debut single from The Specials, when they played the venue in April 1979.

On June 11, 1979 another unassuming band of youngsters made it to the stage.

Relatively unknown at the time, with only a couple of singles tucked under their belts, West Sussex players The Cure would go on to shift more than 27 million albums.

The same year, ex-Thin Lizzy guitarist Eric Bell, The Undertones, and Freddie Fingers Lee all touched down in Wolverton to deliver the goods at the Craufurd.

Freddie, who had been heavily influenced by Jerry Lee Lewis, also played with Screaming Lord Sutch and Ian Hunter.

The Craufurd advert referred to the 'One-eyed king of the boogie-woogie piano and a great rock 'n' roll act,' and that was certainly so - Freddie would regularly remove his glass eye and pop it in a pint of beer during performances!

As the decades continued so did the music. Local acts had a platform with everyone from Safety Valve and Foreign Legion to Rat Salad found lugging their gear in and out of the venue.

But in 2009, the Craufurd was taken over by new custodians who have turned the pub into a pulsating beast of live music, and it

The Craufurd Arms team

came at a time when the new city was in desperate need of venues.

Underpass Promotions team Jason Hall and Jenny Fuszard turned the volume up and attracted the punters inside.

Jason takes up the story: "We took over the Craufurd Arms as promoter on May 10, 2009, after two years promoting at Zaks at the Queen Victoria in Wolverton.

"Zaks no longer wanted to offer live music following a change of owners, which meant a change of direction for the venue."

The Craufurd Arms was viewed as a blank canvas where Underpass Promotions could blossom.

After a couple of months, the lease for the venue became available and Jason took over the whole building - two bars, the venue and the hotel.

"We had our sights set on building a music hub for MK to embrace as its own.

"Quickly building a recording studio and rehearsal facility on the site meant that it was available for bands and performers to practice, record, perform and drink in.

It was the perfect place.

"One of my favourite early bookings was Jeffree Star," Jason remembers.

"With his cult Myspace following, it was

our first sold-out capacity show at the Craufurd and we felt like we had progressed to the next level.

"Hosting a Capdown homecoming after their revival was cool too.

"They are one of the biggest exports to come out of Milton Keynes and seeing a capacity crowd screaming every word back at the band from the top of their lungs was quite something.

"In 2011 we had the honour of being shortlisted as one of the top small venues in the country by NME and won the Publican's Best Music Bar in the East of England."

In 2013, Jenny left her position and Max Harvey stepped up to run the venue in partnership with Jason. Things are flourishing.

Big bands gracing the small stage have included Skindred, Soulfly, Living Colour, Slaves, Gaz Coombes, Therapy? and Wolf Alice - the tip of a wonderfully varied list of noise-bringers who have delivered some truly memorable nights.

"We will continue to build on the foundations we have set and firmly establish Milton Keynes on the map for music," Jason promises.

Max added: "The local music scene is a community with all walks of life and we want to be the catalyst that helps it grow into something beautiful."

Live and loud at The Craufurd Arms:
Life of Agony (2019), Therapy? (middle, 2018) and Skindred (2014)

Bletchley Youth Centre

*"When Black Sabbath played it was unbelievable. It sold out,
and I think we got them for £15."*

Black Sabbath, Genesis and Status Quo; all acts who have commanded some major audiences in their time. But if you were hanging at the hip and trendy Esmeralda's in Bletchley during the late 1960s and '70s you could have seen them in the distinctly more intimate venue.

The club, based out of Bletchley Youth Centre, also hosted one of Rick Wakeman's first gigs with The Strawbs, and when Kevin Ayers played he was accompanied by a young Mike Oldfield on bass, before Tubular Bells took him to dizzy heights.

Those who were there, take us back to the dawn of an exciting new era.

These days Phil Banfield is credited with being the man 'who taught Virgin how to sell records!'

That's quite a statement, but one that comes from Richard Branson himself.

During a lengthy career, Phil spent 17 years working as Sting's agent, continues to represent guitar legend Jeff Beck, and manages Ian Gillan.

He also set up the hugely successful booking agency Coda, which merged into US-based Paradigm Talent Agency in 2019.

It currently counts Ellie Goulding, Rag'n' Bone Man and Lewis Capaldi among its monstrous line-up of talents.

But the man who has travelled the world representing the cream of the industry got his first foot in the musical door at Bletchley Youth Centre.

"I used to hang out there and youth leader Barrie Field encouraged me to get involved and help out," he recalled.

"I was about 15 years old. We booked the bands, or suggested the bands to be booked.

"We were very lucky, we had one of the very first shows with Black Sabbath when their debut album came out.

"We also had Wishbone Ash, Genesis, Status Quo...

"I organised a free open air show in the field behind the Youth Club and Marshall Amplification let us have the equipment for it.

"Then I began promoting shows at the Old Rugby Ground at Manor Fields too, and I remember booking Man.

"They were one of those bands that didn't have a certain length of set - they used to smoke a lot of drugs on stage and stopped playing when the drugs ran out, so depending on what they had, it could be a one-hour set or a three-hour one!

"On this particular night it was a three-hour set and we had the management on our backs about closing down the venue because we had gone over the curfew!"

Phil spent a while promoting locally, and was able to build up business agent contacts inside London's exciting music fraternity.

He managed a couple of local bands too – namely Hot Cottage and Milton - and when one of those aforementioned contacts began hunting a new booker, Phil went for it.

"I was 16-and-a-half years old then," he remembers, "Everyone says 'How did you get into it?' and I tell them; 'I lied - I bullshitted!'

"I said I knew what to do, but I didn't, because back then no-one did."

The music industry was changing, and Phil was young enough and open enough to (rock and) roll with its evolution.

He said: "When I booked bands in the early days, you didn't have riders, nothing in the dressing room, you didn't have catering - you just turned up with your equipment.

"Half the time musicians would set up their own PA and lights. Then roadies came, then someone said 'Shall we get some beer in the dressing room? Let's make a rider,' and then it became a two page rider...now it's a frigging book!"

Phil can recall seeing the new city of Milton Keynes springing up around him.

"I remember the days of sitting on Bletchley's Lakes Estate waiting for people to move in so I could run up and try to get them to take Taylors Milk - that was how I had to subsidise working in the music business," says the man who has one of the strongest management-artist partnerships in the industry: His working relationship with Ian Gillan is nearly four decades long. And counting.

"People went to London's Marquee because they trusted it and that was how you discovered new bands.

"Hopefully that's how it was at Bletchley Youth Centre too - we got good

acts. Sometimes we were lucky.

"When Black Sabbath went into the album charts and played it was unbelievable.

"It sold out, and I think we got the band for £15, which was OK - we used to have a budget between £10 and £30.

"It was stunning to have them there.

"There was a buzz about them, and shows hadn't really moved into the Hammersmith Odeon and similar venues then, so clubs at that time were very, very important."

Sunday evening sessions at the venue became known as Esmeralda's.

"Esmeralda's became known on the circuit and the agents would ring us.

"One of those was a guy called Bob Fisher and we built up a relationship with him.

"He would say 'Take a tip, check this band out.' One of them was Man, and another was Black Widow - we promoted them and got very strange phone calls from witches all over the country!

"We didn't always get it right, but nine times out of 10 we did, and that's why people came to the centre - they became fans of the place just as much as who you put on.

"We did have one act turn up, see the size of the stage, then turn around

> "I said I knew what to do, but I didn't, because back then no-one did!"

and leave again - it was Brian Davison, drummer with The Nice and his new act.

"Status Quo were known as a pop band when they came.

"They'd had hit singles, but were moving into rock and wanted to go out and play the clubs.

"We got them and everyone said 'What a

Skull presents at ESMERALDA'S

GENESIS
plus
Capability Brown
Solar Prism Lights

Skull presents at ESMERALDA'S
STATUS QUO
plus
Snake Eye
Solar Prism Lights - Unicorn Sounds
SUNDAY, 23rd APRIL, 7.30 till Late
BLETCHLEY YOUTH CENTRE

NUMBER ___ 63 ___ Members 40p Guests 50p

coup,' but what they didn't know was they were going to see a brand new band of sorts, playing heavy rock, not the hits!

"These days I've gone into semi-retirement and my hobby is breeding and owning racehorses, and it has all come about through going up to Bletchley Youth Centre and getting involved with some rock 'n' roll bands.

"It has been a brilliant, brilliant life."

Barrie remembers

Barrie Field worked as a scientific officer at Cranfield College of Aeronautics before taking a position teaching at Bletchley's Denbigh School.

And on a Friday night, he used to run a youth club. His reason for doing it?

"I considered the youngsters deserved more," he says on reflection.

"The mix of local teenagers - careful, considerate, humorous, steady and tactful, and the new 'imports' from London - flash, quick, fashion conscious, music-loving and friendly was exciting and unique."

After a couple of years, Barrie was offered the post of full-time leader at the Derwent Drive Youth Centre, which had yet to open.

Lord Campbell officially launched the centre in April 1968.

"We stressed it would be a 16+ club, and that we would direct it along the twin aspects of sport and music, and away we went for 12 years of top flight music and entertainment," Barrie said.

"What made the club so successful was the building itself. Potential members and I were involved in its design, and we had a wonderfully aware and well trained set of assistant leaders, up to the minute chart bands, and superb disco and film nights."

Attendances averaged more than 300 people, seven nights a week. The record number was 630, in an era before fire

"He informed me that dancing was illegal on Sundays"

limits were imposed.

"Parents loved what we were doing, and the youngsters were great ambassadors, so there was never much in the way of opposition."

Some memories stand-out more than others though - like the time a dozen American 'draft dodgers' camped in the adjacent sports field.

"They had arrived from Canada having refused to fight in the Vietnam War," Barrie said.

Stackridge played that night, together with French four-piece band Arge.

"They were the first band we had with a laser light, and danced wearing black leotards with skeletons painted on them in ultra blue sensitive paint.

"When an ultra blue lamp shone on them in the dark, all you could see were skeletons moving about...

"That was the evening the police arrived to close us down. The chief had difficulty with me because I had suggested to the 'long-haired weirdos' who were always being stopped and searched that they carried aspirin with them; results from the lab were always predictable!

"He informed me that dancing was illegal on Sundays, as it was then.

"I invited him in and said we ran concert sessions where the youngsters sat and listened to bands, but didn't dance.

"You will appreciate his total disbelief when he was met by some 400 seated members watching skeletons dancing, a laser spot picking him up...and the sounds of some of the strangest music. "The inspector and his men beat a hasty retreat!

"Five minutes later Stackridge went on stage and the dancers took over.

"If the inspectors had seen that, we would have been closed down.

"The highlights were continuous and considerable."

Barrie can remember names including Mike Oldfield, Lol Coxhill and Rick Wakeman among the numbers of unknowns and newbie talents who passed through the doors. For a time the club continued with a vibrant following, an engaging list of artists playing on its stage and a staff as passionate as its patrons.

Rodney Corner - who would later serve as coroner in the area - was chairman of the management team!

But all good things come to an end, and for Esmeralda's the deathknell came in 1980.

"Sunday concerts became legal, universities started booking top flight bands who then charged considerable sums, and the whole economic structure of the country changed.

"Noises were also made about remov-ing one of the full-time leaders. I made it clear I couldn't carry the burden alone and would be forced to move on."

Barrie did move on, for a while working at a youth club at Leon School in Bletchley, but the sweetness of Esmeralda's was over.

"Having left in 1980, Esmeralda's came to an end and the demise of the youth centre began, due to insufficient support," he says.

"The most interesting legacy is that the vast majority of members still live and work locally.

"Meeting with many of them, I am told the effect the centre and its activities had on their personal development and how that helped them raise their families and construct their careers.

"Some legacy, that!"

Barrie Field

Mick Burns was one of the familiar faces at the youth club, soaking up the sounds and the engaging environs.

He time travels back to April 23, 1972.

"I'm walking up Derwent Drive, off Whaddon Way in West Bletchley, on a sunny Sunday afternoon.

"It looks warmer than it actually is, which justifies the full-length army coat I am wearing, along with the skintight loon pants and tasselled moccasin boots.

"I am doing my 16-year old best to look cool.

"My destination, Bletchley Youth Centre, appears at the end of the road where the modern housing estate ends and the fields begin."

Mick's arrival takes a familiar turn and he switches on the jukebox, before heading downstairs into the back room where the Unicorn Sounds equipment is kept.

"Every Friday night while the main hall is packed with the suited and booted dancing to the soul and reggae disco, we - the hairier, scruffier ones, are grooving to loud rock music.

"Unicorn Sounds is Chris, Paul and me. We have pooled our resources and come up with twin decks, a 100 watt valve amplifier, two 4x12 speaker cabinets, a microphone and a pretty awesome collection of LPs.

"In this back room, variously known as The Lab or The Cage, every Friday we play the latest in progressive rock at ear damage volume while some dance wildly and others just watch and nod their heads.

"We also provide the recorded music while the bands set up and change over in the main hall on Sundays when the place is transformed into Esmeralda's.

"Chris and I carry the equipment to the main hall and start setting up.

"As we are plugging in, Dave Hone arrives.

"Dave is your archetypal hippie, tall, thin, dark straight hair, centre-parted falling near to his waist, small dark round glasses and his chick, petite and shy.

"Together, they are Solar Prism Lights, and responsible for changing this rather drab sports hall into the psychedelic vision that is Esmeralda's.

"They do it with a collection of slide projectors, on which are mounted various rotating oil and water filters, creating an ever changing multi-coloured, bubbling vista onto the walls and ceiling of the blacked out hall.

"It's 7.30pm, and Babs and Barrie are on the door selling tickets - 40p for members, 50p for guests.

"A queue of jeans and Afghan coat-wearing beautiful people are paying and the hall begins to fill.

"Around 8pm support act Snake Eye come on. A straight ahead rock guitar band, there is lots of indulgent lead breaks and they are entirely forgettable.

"The audience in the main have sat down on the floor or headed upstairs to the coffee bar.

"I play more rock tunes - some Zeppelin, Neil Young, and a request for some Genesis.

"The hall fills up in anticipation of the headline band.

"Status Quo come on to muted applause, say a quick 'Hello, Esmeralda's' and launch into their three chord head-down boogie with two guitar parts.

"The audience, having been numbed by Snake Eye and then chilled by the intermission music are slow to respond.

"Most are standing now though, falling into compulsive head-nodding.

"After the second number Francis Rossi bellows into the microphone 'C'mon you lazy buggers, get up and dance!'

"They launch into the next thumping tune to which the audience immediately respond.

"For the next hour the room bounces, until the end of the second encore when the overhead lighting is switched on, giving the signal to leave.

"Lots of very sweaty, smiling faces head home with ears that will probably still be ringing the next morning.

"Within 10 minutes the Unicorn Sounds equipment is stashed away in The lab, ready for next Friday.

"I head off down Derwent Drive, stepping out with a purposeful stride to march the six miles home to Wavendon. It's nearly midnight and I have to be up for work at 6.30am. But am I worried? Not a bit."

And looking back?

"I think 'Did I realise how special it was and how lucky we were?'" Mick says with hindsight.

"If you look at the list of acts who played Sunday nights at the youth centre, it is almost a who's who of happening and up-and-coming bands of the time.

"It's quite remarkable, but what I remember most from those few short years of my youth were the great friends I made and the wonderful times we had."

Peartree Centre

"The Police had such a good gig they wanted to give something back to Milton Keynes..."

When Dylan Jeavons' dad took a new job in Milton Keynes, he relocated the whole family to the blossoming area. It was 1978, and Dylan was about to be exposed to riches from an exciting music scene of which he would become an integral part.

He said: "It was known as the city of mud, as only a few estates were up and running.

"We moved into Waterside, Peartree Bridge, which was next door to two very important places: Inter-Action at the Old Rectory, an incredibly arty and productive place populated by hippies and creative types; and the real focus of my attention, the youth club next door, the Peartree Centre.

"Peartree Centre was a formidable place to a 12-year-old, and it took me months to pluck up the courage to enter. You would see groups of scary-looking lads outside the entrance, smoking fags and looking intimidating.

"When I finally went in, I was hounded by one of these older lads, threatening to take me outside and give me a beating.

"Once he found out who my brothers were he didn't just leave me alone, he apologised!

"Not that my brothers were all that, they were just part of the in-crowd, I suppose."

One person who made Dylan welcome was the guy running the centre, Dick Emmings. He was 'a very cool, chilled out, charismatic man,' who turned it from youth club to arts centre.

It became the hub for live music in the town. Bands rehearsed there in the week and played at the weekends.

"On week nights, sat in the bar area playing Space Invaders, I would be surrounded by local musicians grabbing a fag break," said Dylan, "It became my home-from-home.

"The vibrant music scene was intoxicating. I could wander around the rehearsal rooms watching bands hone their sets and was totally impressed by how different one band was from another.

"Pub rock, punk, pop, disco...all kinds rehearsed there.

"It wasn't just bands though, there were dance and theatre groups as well as other characters that could make things happen. You want a promo video for that song you've just recorded? No problem, ask Dusty. You need someone to look through that contract? Ask Steve.

"Anything seemed possible and money was never mentioned; 'You scratch my back and I'll scratch yours' was the policy.

"This period, 1979-80, was still riding the wave of punk music and there was a genuine feeling that anyone could start or be in a band, so many did.

"I had grown up in a musical family where a guitar was always within reach, so I could always knock out a tune.

"It wasn't long before one of those fag-smoking musos joined me at the Space Invaders table and asked, 'Do you know anyone that plays bass guitar?'

"That was it. At the age of 13 I was in my first band The Young Parisians."

The band were considered to be players of post-punk new wave by those on the scene. But Dylan was happy just to be playing in a band.

"The singer Caz Tricks was a girl from school and we became lifelong friends.

"This is how it worked at the centre: I joined the band on the Monday, we rehearsed just about every night of that week and played our first gig at the centre on the Friday night supporting one of the other 'resident' bands.

"The place was usually packed for a gig so to me it was like being on Top Of The Pops!"

Dylan added: "Inevitably The Young Parisians didn't last but we became something better: N.A. Pop 2000. It was 1980 and we were now New Romantics!

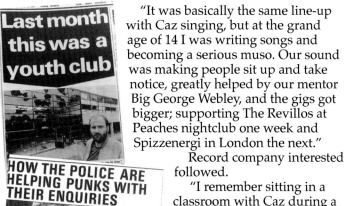

Last month this was a youth club

HOW THE POLICE ARE HELPING PUNKS WITH THEIR ENQUIRIES

The centre that is keeping kids off the streets

"It was basically the same line-up with Caz singing, but at the grand age of 14 I was writing songs and becoming a serious muso. Our sound was making people sit up and take notice, greatly helped by our mentor Big George Webley, and the gigs got bigger; supporting The Revillos at Peaches nightclub one week and Spizzenergi in London the next."

Record company interested followed.

"I remember sitting in a classroom with Caz during a lunch break reading through the record contract we had been offered. It looked like this was it.

"At the time The Police were playing at The Bowl and there was a real buzz around the city.

"They had such a good gig here they wanted to give something back to Milton Keynes. Their manager, Miles Copeland made some enquiries and decided to give the Peartree Centre money towards PA equipment, lighting and recording facilities, but most importantly it would finance the production of an MK compilation album featuring bands that rehearsed at the centre.

"Dick couldn't believe his luck and nor could we!

"The album would be called A Warped Sense of Human featuring ourselves, Fictitious, The Dancing Counterparts, Ethnik Minority and the Ticketz amongst others.

"It all happened incredibly quickly, the album was released in no time at all and Dick brought it to the attention of John Peel, who played quite a few tracks, including N.A. Pop 2000, which really made us feel we had hit the big time."

Dylan became friends with Lee Scriven, who was the drummer in punk band Ficticious at the time. When N.A. Pop 2000 fell apart, Lee asked Dylan to join his new band, HA! They still followed the punk style - and they had two drummers.

They were a hit locally, and by the mid 1980s the two pals were hooked on The Blues Brothers film, so they decided to put a party band together based on The Blues Brothers with a collective of musicians joining forces.

A WARPED SENSE OF HUMAN

WOUGHTON CENTRE

For YOUR leisure and entertainment
Tomorrow (Saturday), 15th August
from 8 pm
A WARPED SENSE OF HUMAN
Live music event promoted by Peartree Records
Tickets £2.00 on the door
Sunday, 16th August from 12 noon
in the Foyer. Hole in the Head Gang

PEARTREE RECORDS PRESENT
TO PROMOTE THE RELEASE OF THE ALBUM.
A WARPED SENSE OF HUMAN
THOSE APPEARING ON THE ALBUM AND ON THE NIGHT :-
OFFBEAT - FICTITIOUS - TICKETZ
ETHNIC MINORITY - N.A.POP 2000
DANCING COUNTERPARTS - KINGSIZE KEEN
& HIS ROCKIN'
MACHINE
AT WOUGHTON CAMPUS
SATURDAY AUGUST 15TH 8·00 pm.
TICKETS AT THE DOOR £2.00 (INCLUDES A 50p VOUCHER TO USE WHEN PURCHASING THE ALBUM)

The Blues Collective was born.

Dylan said: "We packed out venues from the word go. The band eclipsed HA! who fell by the wayside, but all the members were now in The Blues Collective anyway. For years we travelled up and down the country playing massive venues to sell-out audiences. The Edinburgh Fringe became an annual event with a week-long residency. We appeared on Scottish TV and performed to more than 80,000 people at an open-air festival.

"The Blues Collective ultimately became a victim of its own success, with some members more focused on money rather than just having the crack. The band slowly lost its passion, hanging up their black ties and pork pie hats.

"Without doubt, The Blues Collective were the most successful band I have ever been in and provided some of the highlights of my life."

The Peartree Centre had continued to be a great friend to the music scene in the early '80s, but things were changing with high energy dance music and nightclubs being favoured over live music.

The centre became known for The Joint club nights.

"Dick had now moved on and with that the place seemed to lose its soul. It deteriorated physically and culturally over the next few years and by the mid '80s the centre was sadly boarded up."

When news reached Dylan that the old place was to be bulldozed he broke into the building for one last nose around.

There really wasn't much in the way of souvenirs, or so it seemed; just bits of broken furniture, shelving and cupboards.

But buried in the bottom of a cupboard in the space that used to be Dick's office were two boxes containing Warped Sense of Human albums!

Around 100 albums had lain there undiscovered for years. Dylan liberated the albums and gave them away, not knowing that years later they would fetch around £200 on Ebay!

Dick Emmings passed away a few years ago, but his legacy continues.

Dylan says: "If it wasn't for him welcoming me into the club I might never have met the lifelong friends I have and might never have become a musician.

"I continue to play in bands, often with the same musicians I played with at the Peartree Centre at the age of 13.

"I put on the odd gig here and there and when I'm trying to organise these things, I ask myself, 'How would Dick have done this?'

"It has been incredibly frustrating as a dad watching my own musical children grow up, not having a facility like Peartree Centre, nor a mentor like Dick.

"I was extremely lucky to have been around then."

The Point

Teenagers would roll into bed at some ridiculous hour and still make it into school for sixth form classes on the Friday morning!

When it opened its doors The Point was the perfect beacon for the new city of Milton Keynes - big, bold, and futuristic, its red neon lighting could be seen all over the city and for miles around.

For a while it was the hub of entertainment, housing the UK's first multiplex cinema, and Europe's first fully-integrated entertainment venue.

In today's all consuming society, it seems alien to think of a time when you couldn't enjoy multiple entertainment opportunities under the one roof, but it was The Point that demonstrated it first.

No-one had seen a 10-screen cinema complex on this side of the Atlantic before, and the seven-and-a-half million pound structure was a huge deal when it opened its doors in 1985.

"The attendance goal was for 760,000 admissions in the first year. AMC The Point did 1,050,000 admissions in the first year; more than any cinema in the UK for the past 15 years, including Leicester Square,"

said Charles J. Wesoky who oversaw the venture.

"The name is not accidental," said Peter Sherlock, during the launch. He was managing director of Bass Leisure, who funded the project with AMC Entertainment.

"We see this very much as a meeting point where people - families - can come, meet up and then make up their minds what they are going to do."

You could choose from Italian, French or English cuisine at The Brasserie, search for a full-house in the bingo area, be entertained at The Club or sit back with a plentiful supply of popcorn and nachos to engage in the latest blockbusters.

Film premieres brought celebrities to town and the venue went from strength to strength. When The Point hosted a premiere for Rocky IV in 1986, Survivor (whose track Eye Of The Tiger was the theme song to Rocky III) joined pop stars Paul Young and Hazel O'Connor, television favourites Ronnie Barker, Sally James and

The Club at THE POINT

TONIGHT £3
Radio 1's 'Janice Long' spins the alternative sounds (Guest DJ).

TUES 19TH — 'Live Jump and Jive' Soul all the way with **Camdens Eddie Richards & T.B.A.** (Soul Guest D.J.)

WEDS — **Party night at The Club.** Bring your party or just yourself to dance the night away to the sounds of the past.

* * * SOUL NITE II Sun 24th featuring Phil Fearon & Galaxy & Others

Top rock bands at premiere

Charity Premiere of Rocky IV at The Point a week today to help raise money for Oliver Wells Special School in Milton Keynes.

They will join a galaxy of pop stars, showbiz celebrities, actors and actresses for the gala premiere hosted by Film presenter, Barry Norman.

be present, organisers are hoping that his mountainous theme boxing opponent Dolph Lungen will be there.

An auction of tickets for...

Survivor play the main theme from the movie Burning Heart, and have also written tracks for a new Rocky IV LP on CBS featuring various artists including Go...

West ... for the Mirror

MILTON KEYNES *Premier* **ROCK NIGHT!!** ☠
THE **Xposure** ROCK CLUB

EVERY THURSDAY NIGHT
9.00 p.m. - 2.00 a.m.

at

at

402 Midsummer Boulevard, Central Milton Keynes

Now with NO dress restrictions *plus* Reduced drinks prices!!!!

Special Introductory Offer to First Time Visitors
ONLY £2.00 admission between 9 and 10 p.m. any Thursday in August with this flyer

OUR PRICE MUSIC - No 1 for Rock records in Milton Keynes

All set for some heavy weather

THERE are big stars and big stars, and they don't come much bigger than the Weather Girls.

The mighty duo, who have voices to match their fuller figures, racked up a smash hit with It's Raining Men not so long ago.

And now Martha Wash and Izora Armstead (pictured left) are back with their second album, Big Girls Don't Cry, and looking forward to a date at The Point next Thursday.

Favourites

Milton Keynes is just one stop on a globe-trotting schedule for the Weather Girls, who are — to coin a rock phrase — very big in Japan as well as favourites on the European circuit.

Their new city date, at The Club, costs £4.50 on the door and the fun goes on from 9 pm until 2 am.

Getting to The Point: The Weather Girls (above) and Survivor (far left) were among visitors

Christopher Biggins, and film buff Barry Norman to soak up the action on the big screen.

Georgie Fame, Captain Sensible and Marie Wilson lent their talents to the centre in the early days.

In 1991, the venue staged a Summer Festival and while The Brasserie lured in locals with delights including a bucking bronco rodeo, a wind surfing simulator and professional arm wrestling, the kids had Keith Chegwin to entertain them.

At The Club at The Point, Monday was Freestyle with DJ Bob Sennington and Wednesday's Midweek Affair asked that you dress to impress before strutting your stuff to the best of the sounds from the '50s, '60s and '70s.

Friday night was Ladies Night and Boogie Down promised revellers 'the ultimate party night' every Saturday.

Thursday nights belonged to the Xposure Rock Club week on week during the early '90s, thanks to a bunch of impassioned Brummie rock fans who upped their gear and drove down to

Milton Keynes to spill the latest noisy anthems at The Club. Dave Juste and Steve Webb spun the tunes for three years.

Xposure's days here corresponded with Metallica's Black album and the grunge explosion and came at a time when hair metal still had enough glitter to shine.

You could shake your mop to Enter Sandman, get sozzled for less with bargain booze offers and socialize with like-minded rockers through to the early hours.

Teenagers would drink too much, roll into bed at some ridiculous hour and still make it in to school for sixth form classes on a Friday morning!

Today The Point is set to be relegated to memory, with plans to demolish the legendary illuminated pyramid in favour of a new leisure and retail development.

With consumers changing the way they shop, you have to wonder if these facilities are essential.

Milton Keynes is a new town that needs to create its own history.

Demolishing such an iconic part of its fabric isn't the way to do it.

Unit Nine

"We wanted to support the local scene but also bring back established names to put Milton Keynes on the map."

A small warehouse on the outskirts of Milton Keynes mightn't automatically scream 'live music venue' but that's exactly what has become of Wolverton's Unit Nine. Originally, those at the helm utilised the space for a recording studio, and for children's parties.

It's a long way from the ace artist list including Zed Bias and Ian Van Dahl, who have since turned the volume up.

"Our initial idea was to bring more live music to Milton Keynes, of any form," said Jamie Stimpson, who co-founded Unit Nine with business partner Dom Rampello.

"We wanted to support the local scene, but also help bring back established names to help put MK on the map."

Running a venue on an industrial estate can be tricky too, but when the music-loving fraternity arrive to party, there aren't many neighbours to complain about

"Milton Keynes is a tough nut to crack when it comes to nightlife"

the noise here.

"People sometimes get confused as to the nature of what Unit Nine is. As a live music venue, it means we aren't open religiously, only when we have an event on, and we focus on quality over quantity.

"Milton Keynes is a tough nut to crack when it comes to nightlife," Jamie says.

"With no real hub of passing trade, it has been vitally important to find promoters that can attract numbers to make the events pay and keep music live. We also have a great customer base, which has helped massively in the development of the venue."

It turns out that things are developing nicely too: "We have been fortunate and had some huge names play at Unit Nine - one of the biggest nights we had was with the Garage Nation brand, and the H.A.S (Hardcore Appreciation Society).

"Those events have been really eye

Above: Raising hands and raising the roof at Unit Nine

opening. People travel for them not just from across the UK, but from Europe too.

"Without doubt they've been the most consistent in filling the venue and providing an atmosphere like no other," said Dom.

"Then we've had names like Nicky Blackmarket, Ratpack, Ian Van Dahl and Darren Styles...the list goes on and on."

Things are going from strength to strength, and Unit Nine has welcomed a capacity increase, but things are set to get bigger still.

"We've just installed a brand new state of the art lighting system which has gone down an absolute storm, and there is much more to look forward to.

"We have some exciting plans to expand the venue, and are constantly re-investing," Jamie added.

Selfie-belief: Founders Jamie (left) and Dom

Wilton Hall

*Wilton Hall went from a facility for wartime staff at Bletchley Park to
a rock 'n' roll haven with visits by The Stones and Pink Floyd.*

During its colourful history Wilton Hall has hosted more than its fair share of household names. But there have been battles too, between visiting youths and residents and even between dance genres.

The venue was built shortly after the outbreak of the Second World War when the large Foreign Office department arrived at Bletchley Park.

Back then staff were entertained by dances, shows and operas.

Olivia Newton-John's father Brin worked at Bletchley Park and while off-duty would show his vocal flair as a tenor, giving performances with the Operatic Society.

Wartime visits came from notable artists including soprano Dame Maggie Teyte and pianist Dame Myra Hess.

When the war ended, the venue known as The Assembly Hall was gradually let to the public and music continued as a regular fixture. Tommy Claridge and Doug Dytham and his Rhythm Aces were familiar names at the venue during the mid-1940s.

In 1952, Bletchley was visited by the Duke of Edinburgh, and Harold Macmillan, a Prime Minister to be.

The following year another politician on the ascent, Labour's James Callaghan came to town and, along with the rest of the country, Bletchley was gripped by coronation fever.

Before 1953 ended, the Bletchley Gazette ran with the headline 'Council to buy Assembly Hall for £13,500,' but although the council took over the running of the hall the headline was premature and a sale wasn't completed.

Dance band sounds continued with no threat of upset. But change was coming - jiving became a teenage phenomenon and residents close to the hall did not take kindly to the new craze.

Jive lessons were being given by Ron Stanley at Wilton Hall but a headline from November 1955 must have upset local youths: 'Doctors instead of dancers

WILL FIGHT TO HAVE WILTON HALL REMOVED

"Jiving" to be banned?

THERE was plenty of plain speaking at last Friday's conference of Bletchley Councillors, Wilton Hall-area residents, Police officers and Ministry of Works officials called because of disturbances at, and following, recent Saturday night dances at Wilton Hall.

As a result, the Council may soon be deciding on the following suggestions:—

(1) A ban on "jiving"—it takes up room and leads to arguments;
(2) Proper and "stronger" stewarding;
(3) Better lighting outside the hall;
(4) A "vetting" of all organisations running dances;
(5) A proper "soft drinks" and tea bar in addition to the other bar.

But while these measures may be taken to run dances Wilton-avenue residents declare they will fight "tooth and nail" for the removal of the hall as a dance hall, and will not agree to removal of the restrictive covenants on the hall which Bletchley Council say must go before they will take over from the Ministry of Works.

ALL QUIET

Saturday's dance at Wilton Hall passed off without trouble of any kind.

It was organised by Fenny and Bletchley Bowls Club and 300 young dancers were pre-

Mr. M Nicol, of the Lodge, next door to the hall, told the meeting that residents had each received a letter from the Ministry. He believed this was right in saying that resident owners could, by convenient spacing, reduce the number of dances permitted. "If the Ministry did not curb attendances ..."

Council to buy Assembly Hall for £13,500

AND RUN DANCES TO MEET COST

BLETCHLEY COUNCIL on Tuesday decided to buy the Assembly Hall, Wilton-avenue, for £13,500 and to run Saturday night dances there to help to pay for it, members of the public relations and entertainments committee having offered to supervise them for the first six months.

The hall now belongs to the Ministry of Works, and the ... the District Valuer's valuation.

Doctors instead of dancers at Wilton Hall?

"CONVERT IT TO HEALTH CENTRE" — SUGGESTION

IS Wilton Hall suitable for conversion into the diagnostic and treatment clinic which the Regional Hospital Board has included in its future planning programme?

Cllr. C. Head, Bletchley's representative on the Aylesbury Hospital Group Management Committee, put the novel and somewhat startling idea to colleagues at Tuesday's Council meeting, suggesting that if the hall could be used, the hopes of improved "hospital" facilities for Bletchley would be brought near realisation.

The chairman of the public relations committee, Cllr. E. R. Staniford, in reply to Cllr. E. Fuller, had just announced that the negotiations for the purchase of the hall by the Council had got to the stage of asking counsel's opinion on a draft settlement between the solicitors for the Treasury and ...

A "CUT" FOR THE JOINTS

Practically the whole of North Bucks and part of south-west Northants were affected by an electricity breakdown ...

FORECOURT TRADING

The practice of "forecourt trading" is not growing among Bletchley traders, and no undue exception could be taken of what trading there is at the present time.

That is Bletchley Chamber of Trade's opinion as expressed to Bletchley Council following the two bodies on the matter.

The Chamber adds that when the kerb in Bletchley-road is placed nearer the shop fronts traders would co-operate by withdrawing notices of displays which might obstruct the flow of pedestrian traffic.

[Forecourt footnote : the forecourt in front of the Northampton Building Society is to be taken over by the Council. The executors of the ...

---

at Wilton Hall?,' reported the Gazette, suggesting that the hall be converted into a health centre.

That never happened, but Wilton Hall soon had another fight on its hands with trouble and disturbances irking residents.

A meeting was called, and the Gazette reported the affair in June 1956: 'WILL FIGHT TO HAVE WILTON HALL REMOVED

"Jiving" to be banned?" asked the headline.

A conference of Bletchley Councillors, Wilton Hall area residents, police officers and Ministry Of Works officials was called following bother at the Saturday night dances.

Ideas put forward to hopefully bring an end to the troubles included a ban on jiving because it 'takes up room and leads to arguments.'

Other ideas included 'proper and stronger stewarding' and 'a vetting of all organisations running dances' but it wasn't enough for the residents, who declared they would fight tooth and nail for the removal of the hall as a dance venue.

Soon after, a council meeting agreed to employ a uniformed doorman and six stewards. A quote for turnstiles was made. And it was decided that jiving would be banned after all!

In 1958 and '59, weekly dances were still going strong with artists like Ron Horrell and his Band and The Don Pearce Orchestra entertaining the music-hungry.

The change from foxtrot to rock 'n' roll was a slow one that began with the arrival of The Top Pops Club, which opened in September 1959. The Tuesday night session ran for 18 months.

Bletchley businessman Mr P B Harrington was forced to call time on his events due to dwindling attendances and the Gazette reported his regret at the failure: "I am a very disappointed man. "I have done everything I can to help the teenagers. If they have wanted big bands, I have tried to get them. Even so it has run at a loss.

"Now the teenagers have nothing solely for themselves. So many times we hear the scream, as was the case when I came here, that there is nothing to do. When this sort of thing happens, one understands why not."

The venue wasn't about to quieten any though.

London-based promoter Ron King quickly stepped in to fill the gap. Bletchley's youngsters were about to get a crash course in rock 'n' roll from some of the most controversial artists of the day.

Screaming Lord Sutch certainly put tongues to wagging when he livened up a night in the town.

What did the audience think when Sutch showed up on stage dressed in animal skin and sporting a huge pair of buffalo horns on his head?

Wilton Hall, Bletchle[y]

THURSDAY N[...]

7.30 - 10.30 p.m. : Adm[...]

ROCKING

STANLEY [...]

THE H.M.V. [...]

JOHNN[Y]

[...] THE PIRATES

Wilton Hall, Bletchley

THURSDAY, 21st APRIL

7.30 to 10.30 p.m. : Admission 3/- : 7.30 to 10.30 p.m.

ROCKING : STANLEY DALE presents : ROLLING

Return by popular demand

TERRY ANTON

And His RHYTHM ROCKERS

Tonight: JOHNNY KIDD

WILTON HALL

Bletchley

[...]DAY, 22nd JULY

[J]OE BROWN

[and] THE JOLLIES

[...] p.m.   Admission 5/-

[...]4th JULY

[...]R WEATHER BROWN

[a]nd HIS ALL STARS

[...] p.m.   Members 3/6, Guests 4/6

MONDAY, 31st JULY

MICK MULLIGAN

8 - 11 p.m.   Members 3/6, Guests 4/6

SATURDAY, 29th JULY

BILLY FURY and THE BLUE FLAMES

[8] - 11.45 p.m.   Admission 6/6

[...] AUGUST

[...]KIDD and THE PIRATES

R.K. Enterprises (London) Ltd.
Ron King presents at the

WILTON HALL, Bletchley

THIS SATURDAY, 4th NOVEMBER
CLOSED

MONDAY, 6th NOVEMBER

ALEX WELSH

8 - 11 p.m.   Admission 3/6 and 4/6

SATURDAY, 11th NOVEMBER
REOPENING with

BERT WEEDON

8 - 11.45 p.m.   Admission 5/6

SATURDAY, 18th NOVEMBER — CLOSED

Ron King apologises that Gene Vincent will not
as advertised. In his place on SATURDAY [...]
NOVEMBER, a personal appearance o[f]
JESS CONRAD and VERA DA[...]
who will judge a
GRAND JIVING CONTEST
£10 to the winning couple plus a film and scr[...]

As from this date we are open every Sa[t...]

TUESDAY, 28th NOVEMBER
GRAND REOPENING NIGHT

NEIL CHRISTIAN and the Cru[...]
Plus the TOP POPS. 8-11 p.m. Admissi[...]

The dates we are closed are bookings take[n...]
Council before we commenced our series [...]

Ron King presents at the

WILTON HALL, BLETCHLEY

THIS SATURDAY, 7th SEPTEMBER

GERRY and
THE PACEMAKERS
Plus THE CLEARWAYS
Admission 10/-

SATURDAY, 14th SEPTEMBER

JOHNNY KIDD and THE PIRATES

SATURDAY, 21st SEPTEMBER

Screaming LORD SUTCH & The Savages

All Rights of Admission Reserved

WILTON HALL, BLETCHLEY
GRAND OPENING PARTY NIGHT

NEXT WEDNESDAY, 11th SEPT.
8 - 11 p.m.   Admission 2/6

TOP TWENTY DISC CLUB

PRIZES TO BE WON
Record Players, Transistor Radios, Hair Dryers,
Electric Shavers, Mains Radios, Television [...]
NUMEROUS OTHER PRIZES
To be won on "TAKE YOUR PICK"—first time
ever to be seen in England
On production of this cut-out you will be admitted
FREE OF CHARGE ON OUR OPENING NIGHT

[Ron] King presents at the

[...]N HALL, Bletchley

[...]URDAY, SEPTEMBER 1st

[VI]CKY VALANCE

Plus

[...]ranks & The Avalons

[...].30 p.m.   Admission 6/6

[...]ER 8th

[...]BROWN and The Brothers

[...]ER 15th

VINCE [EAGER]

Ron King presents at the

WILTON HALL, Bletchley

SEPTEMBER 15th

VINCE EAGER & The Cruisers
Plus

Rod Price & The College Men
Admission 6/6.   8 - 11.30 p.m.

SEPTEMBER 22nd

Owing to unforeseen circumstances, COLIN HICKS
will not be able to appear. In place of him we have

THE DAVE CLARK FIVE

SEPTEMBER 29th

Helen Shapiro's cousin

SUSAN SINGE[R]

OCTOBER 6th

CLOSED FOR ONE NIGH[T]

All rights of admission r[...]

SATURDA[Y...]
"Come Outside"

MIKE SARNE

Plus

Vern Rogers & the [...]
8 - 11.30 p.m.   Admissi[on...]

SATURDAY, 11th AUGUST

TOMMY [...]

SATURDAY, 18th AUGUST

DOUG SH[...]

SATURDAY, 25th AUGUST

NERO and THE [...]

[Ron King] presents at the

WILTON HALL, Bletchley

THIS SATURDAY, JUNE 13th

THE PARAMOUNTS
Plus JEANIE & THE DIAMONDS
8 - 11.30 p.m.   Admission 6/6

JUNE 20th

VERN ROGERS & The Orbits

JUNE 27th

THE TRENDS

JULY 4th

THE ANIMALS

All Rights of Admission Reserved

TOP TWENTY CLUB
EVERY WEDNESDAY
8 - 11 p.m.   Admission 2/6

Ron King presents at the

WILTON HALL, BLETCHLEY

JANUARY 12th

Emile Ford's ex-backing group, The

ORIGINAL CHECKMATES
Plus CHRIS FARLOW and

"THE THUNDERBIRDS"
8 - 11.30 p.m.   Admission 6/6

JANUARY 19th

"Sun Arise"—ROLF HARRIS

JANUARY 26th—CLOSED FOR ONE NIGHT ONLY

FEBRUARY 2nd

MARTY WILDE
and "THE WILD CATS"

All rights of admission reserved

[...]HALL, Bletchley

[f]or one week only

LORD SUTCH
[and] THE SAVAGES
Admission 6/6

CHRISTMAS EVE
[Ret]urn of the fabulous
[...] INCORPORATED

[...]ENTON and THE FENTONS

DECEMBER 31st — New Year's Eve
WE ARE NOT OPEN

Ron King presents at the

WILTON HALL, Bletchley

THIS SATURDAY, NOVEMBER 21st

CLIFF BENNETT
& The Rebel Rousers
Plus NICKY and THE PAGENS
8 - 11.30 p.m.   Admission 7/6

NOVEMBER 28th

THE BIRDS is coming

DECEMBER 5th

THE WAYFARERS

All Rights of Admission Reserved

TOP TWENTY DISC NIGHT
EVERY WEDNESDAY

[...]EMBER
—One night only

[...]EMBER

[...]SEY SOUNDS

[...]dmission reserved

[...]ED ON WEDNESDAY

[...]nesday, 27th Novem-
[...]pening we are giving
[...]ts for the Christmas
[...]es Show.

Ron King presents at the

WILTON HALL, BLETCHLEY

THIS SATURDAY, AUGUST 8th

TOMMY QUICKLY
and THE REMO 4
Plus THE GANGBUSTERS
8 - 11.30 p.m.   Admission 7/6

AUGUST 15th

THE PRETTY THINGS

AUGUST 22nd

LULU and THE LUVVERS

All Rights of Admission Reserved

Ron King presents at the

WILTON HALL, BLETCHLEY

THIS SATURDAY, 30 NOVEMBER

JULIE GRANT
Plus THE MUSTANGS
8 - 11.30 p.m.   Admission 6/6

SATURDAY, 7th DECEMBER

THE BARRON KNIGHTS

SATURDAY, 14th DECEMBER

THE FOURMOST

SATURDAY, 21st DECEMBER

THE SEARCHERS

Screaming Lord Sutch meets his admirers in Bletchley (1963)

It was a long way from the foxtrot for sure as was reflected in the views of the ticket-holders.

"If anyone else did that he would be locked up. I feel sorry for the bloke," said one, while another was quoted saying: "He couldn't sing to save his life. He frightens the girls and sets the boys laughing their heads off."

But there was positivity too: "He was smashing," said one girl who saw him at work on the stage.

Ron King was an ace at promoting, adding Wilton Hall to a further 17 locations he worked at both in and out of London.

He also had 250 bands on his books. Not bad for a 27-year-old.

Ron had no qualms about taking over the nights where The Top Pops Club had failed.

"I thought I could run them better and had 450 people here on the first night," he said at the time.

"People say rock 'n' roll is dead, but it is taking more money now than it has ever done."

Wilton Hall wasn't just serving the needs of young music fans. It also provided a necessary platform for local amateur dramatic groups and hosted talks (everyone from celebrity gardener Percy Thrower to politician Enoch Powell) too, but Tuesday and Saturday nights belonged to Ron King and the place was positively humming, attracting the stars of the era.

"He frightens the girls and sets the boys laughing their heads off"

A Monday evening jazz club launched in July 1961, bringing artists like Bruce Turner and Mick Mulligan through the doors but 'lack of support' meant time was called on the 'trad nights' before the year was out.

Still, the popular music events lived up to the hype with artists including Neil Christian & the Crusaders, Joe Brown, Billy Fury and Ricky Valence among the attractions of 1961.

The new year brought with it plenty more reasons for Bletchley's youth to cheer. Shane Fenton and the Fentones kicked off 1962 before Shane had a name change to Alvin Stardust. A week later the club charged its highest admission fee to date for heart-throb Adam Faith, a wallet-busting 8s 6d!

"The Roulettes backed him that night and Wilton Avenue was totally overrun with people, plenty of them were girls! You just couldn't move!" one fan recalled.

As 1962 continued, it brought return appearances by Joe Brown, Ricky Valence, Shane Fenton and Screaming Lord Sutch. B. Bumble and the Stingers and the Dave Clark Five were among the newbies popping in and sounding out.

The success continued to build in 1963. Marty Wilde & The Wild Cats, The Barron Knights, The Searchers and The Hollies (frontman Allan Clarke's shoes ended up in the audience when they performed) appearing on a cluttered listing. And, years before his fall from grace, Rolf Harris played too.

The Rolling Stones in Bletchley, 1964

And, following two cancellations, on June 29 it was third time lucky for fans of Gene Vincent when he finally made it to the stage with a young Chas Hodges (later of Chas & Dave fame) in the band.

In March 1964, Wilton Hall put on the show that is still being talked about more than five decades later – The Rolling Stones.

They played before an avid, over-subscribed audience on March 28.

Rather like The Beatles' appearances at the teeny Cavern Club, more people claim to have seen the band at play in the intimate confines than could have possibly fit through the doors.

Mind you, the Gazette's 'Teenage Topics' column reported that not all those who attended were thrilled by the show.

"Pay ten bob to see this lot. Cor, I wouldn't walk to the end of this street," said one who did.

The Gazette spoke to the Stones backstage before they took to the stage for two half hour sets.

Bill Wyman admitted that when he had visited Bletchley Road cafe Mokaris earlier in the day no-one had recognised him.

The band were pretty slow to locate Bletchley themselves: "We couldn't find it on the map for about 10 minutes!" he said.

There was plenty of excited swooning that night and some girls were hurt in the ensuing crush as fans 'squashed themselves into the hall until it fairly creaked,' said a newspaper report.

After the first set by the Stones, girls dashed to the cloakrooms to clean up their mascara streaked faces and re-emerged

Girls dashed to the cloakrooms to clean up their mascara streaked faces

looking fresh and fabulous again a short time later!

Before the year end The Animals, Lulu & The Luvvers, The Hollies, The Troggs, and The Birds (with Ronnie Wood) had all passed through the doors and onto the small stage, to the delight of the teenage fraternity.

In 1965, Manfred Mann and The Who helped to hold attentions before the venue closed its doors in the summer for a seven-week spell of extension and redecoration work.

It reopened on September 11 with The Druids doing the honours, but the bigger date on the musical calendar would have been the arrival on Christmas Eve of The Small Faces.

Admission would have set you back 8/6'.

A new year didn't bring prosperity for Wilton Hall, and although the music continued the venue wasn't attracting the same calibre of artists that visitors had grown accustomed to.

Ironically in April, the town received its most famous visitors and the streets were filled with crowds excited for the arrival of HM the Queen and the Duke of Edinburgh.

But at Wilton Hall the slump continued and Johnny Kidd and the Pirates played their last appearance at the venue on April 16.

Six months later, Johnny would be gone - tragically killed in a road accident.

He was just 30 years old.

Times were changing. By July, it was game over for promoter Ron King, and the plug was pulled on the Saturday dances at Wilton Hall.

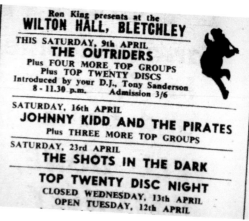

"I think the kids are fed up with what they are getting," Ron told the Bletchley Gazette.

"They hear an artist on record, then when he appears 'live' they are disappointed because he sounds entirely different."

Teenage girls did still have an occasional heartthrob pass their way though; Like when new record shop Disci opened its doors and invited Walker Brothers singer/drummer Gary Walker to do the honours and declare the Queensway store open.

Meantime Wilton Hall received a lifeline when Race Enterprises opened in September.

But the success was short-lived, and save for a November 5 appearance by The Pink Freud (you'll know them as Pink Floyd) the venue never quite regained its earlier boom.

Today's club culture offers plenty of cheap deals to get punters through the doors, but competition was fierce back then too, and The Palace Ballroom in Wolverton (originally opened as a cinema house in 1911) was hot on Wilton Hall's tail.

"All the prettiest girls in Bletchley go to the Palace, and to prove it, admission before 9.30pm for pretty girls is 3/6'," promised the advert.

Zoot Money (with The Police's Andy Summers in the ranks), The Beat Merchants, The Walker Brothers, The Small Faces and The Undertakers all played at The Palace. So did Ian Hunter. Known for Mott the Hoople and The Rant Band, back then he was appearing as Hurricane Henry with the Shriekers.

"The prettiest girls in Bletchley go to the palace...to prove it, admission for pretty girls is 3/6"

Many of the bands would deliver early sets at the Palace before getting back in the van and driving to the California Ballroom in Dunstable to play their second set of the night – it helped that both venues were under the ownership of Edwin Green.

They even had dinnertime dances.

Wilton Hall had once been majestic for music fans, but by the end of 1966 its major rock 'n' pop days were almost done with.

Speaking in late 2018, Ron King, then aged 84, recalled the challenge of taking on the Bletchley venue almost six decades previously: "When I found Wilton Hall everyone I knew said I would do no good there, as others had tried. That was the challenge I needed to make a go of it. I still love a challenge and I am still in the club and bar business to this day."

Ron might have been surrounded by stars but he wasn't impressed by the glamour, or the rock 'n' roll - money was his motivation.

Ron King (2019)

He admitted: "At that stage I wasn't interested in any band or group, only the money I could make because I came from a very poor family and had to battle my way through..."

After Ron ceased promoting at Wilton Hall, the venue continued to operate for community use for years before the building started to deteriorate.

Milton Keynes Council were now overseeing the property, and they were keen to sell.

Step forward Tony Manni who bought the space on June 8, 2000, and turned the venue and its fortunes around.

He upgraded the space to a high specification and Wilton Hall became a go-to for fans of tribute nights.

"A friend told me about the place and when I saw it I knew exactly what I could do with it," Tony said.

"The attraction? It has got character. It has a real warmth, and as soon as I stepped into the place I could imagine the people from the Second World War era dancing there. You can feel it.

"It has a nice aura and a sense of history about it.

"I didn't even look at the plans for the place," he recalled, "As soon as I walked in I decided to buy it. I wanted to make it into a place where you can wine, dine and dance the night away.

"People have always enjoyed doing that, it's nothing new - that is something that the pharaohs were enjoying back in the day."

For 18 years under Tony's guise Wilton Hall continued to flourish.

But in 2018 a planning application was lodged with MK Council to demolish the building and build six detached houses on the site.

"It will be sad, but everything must change," owner Tony told the Citizen newspaper.

In April 2019 Tony passed away.

Local councillors and residents are against the demolition, arguing that the hall is a valuable community facility that is remembered nostalgically by thousands, and that is certainly true.

The planning application states the hall is not a listed building and is of 'limited visual and historic value.'

It also said that there 'are plenty of other community halls and facilities available in the area.'

There may be other facilities locally, but none have the history notched up by Wilton Hall. Its loss will be a blow for those keen to ensure that Milton Keynes keeps another piece of history intact.

Screaming Lord Sutch on stage at Wilton Hall, 1961

Good vibrations at Wilton Hall

Nick Jones was a teenager who had just started playing the bass guitar when Wilton Hall opened its doors to rock 'n' roll, and the lure of the sounds meant he quickly became a frequent visitor.
It was a family affair; Nick's sister Pauline would often attend the concerts and mum Marge ran the bustling cloakroom.

"I saw Neil Christian and the Crusaders support the big names who played at Wilton Hall many times. The band had a very young Jimmy page on guitar, who usually wore a powder blue suit and played an orange Gretsch guitar.
They played rock covers in the main, with Christian prowling around the stage and climbing over the in-house piano during the solos.
At the close of their set Page would play the National Anthem.
American band B. Bumble and the Stingers played in 1962, the same year they went to Number One in the singles chart. As I drove into Wilton Avenue for the gig, a very rotund man stood on the corner in a pair of bright pink tights! That was my first introduction to B. Bumble.

It was a good 15 years or so before anyone heard the word punk, and it made for quite a sight!
Screaming Lord Sutch and the Savages were always a great attraction and had plenty of wild stage antics.
Sutch would sometimes dress as Jack the Ripper before 'disembowelling' pianist Freddie Fingers Lee. He would start a fire onstage, reveal his long hair from under his hat and shake it over the flames while singing Great Balls of Fire.
Nero and the Gladiators were a great instrumental band who dressed in Roman gear and did rock adaptations of classical themes like In the Hall of the Mountain King. Nero was a pianist.
Even today, you don't see many bands dressed in togas and tunics, do you?
I also remember a blues night with bands like Chicken Shack playing - a certain Christine Perfect featured on piano. She later joined Fleetwood Mac and became Christine McVie.
The Jeff Beck Group played in 1968 with Ronnie Wood on bass and Rod Stewart on vocals. I've heard Rod say he never went on stage in jeans, but he did at Wilton Hall, with a big safety pin holding them together!"

Gone but not forgotten

A nostalgic look back at a few of the much missed venues and promotions that served Milton Keynes so well.

Muzak's

A new club launched in the Northern edge of the city in September 1980, it brought an ambitious feel to the still blossoming Milton Keynes.

Muzak's was a fortnightly club located upstairs in New Bradwell pub, The New Inn.

It wanted to shake free of genre constraints and offer folk, blues, jazz, rock, new wave and country & western under the same roof – and on the same night!

The idea – from the brilliantly creative Bill Billings (the late artist responsible for some of MK's most recognisable sculptures and plenty more besides) and OU energy researcher Alan Horton worked well.

The club firmly established itself with musicians and punters, and was taken over by singer and entrepreneur Jeff Donert a year later. For a couple of years it was a staple for live sounds, before that all-too familiar 'audience apathy' failed the

venture. But even when people thought they'd heard the last of the blending brand it returned. In June 1984 it was revived for a special one-off event; The Muzak's Special was the climax of the Great Linford Festival, held in the grounds of the Manor.

The Fox & Hounds

This tidy little watering hole in the heart of Stony Stratford dates back to 1742.

The name above the door in those days was The Hare & Hound, although locals used to call it something else: "Legend has it that it started as a low-grade inn nicknamed The Rag & Louse. It used to be a real dive of a lodging house," said Ken Daniels who took the reins of the venue in late 1993, following a career working for the Foreign Office.

His arrival was the start of a tenancy that would last for nigh on a decade.

"I moved here with the job and the pub became my local. Then it came up for sale and I thought 'I could do that!'" he added.

During his time at the helm Ken booked more than 400 bands, and Robin Chandler & The Howling Tomcats took the stage more than 100 times!

Paul Jones, Tony McPhee and Mick Abrahams all played the haunt under Ken's ownership.

There have been occasional ghost stories too: "Some people said a young victorian woman used to cross between the cellar room and the rear building," Ken said.

"It does, of course, have the 'ghosts' of some world class musicians in its fabric!"

The pub still serves up a good pint, but music is less of a fixture now.

The Joint

Heralded as an Aladdin's Cave of modern music and trends, The Joint operated out of the Peartree Centre, opening in late 1983.

Every Friday a small team could be found turning the centre into a venue, with an inspired use of props including dummies and netting.

It was all the vision of Netherfield man Mark Mason.

Eddie Richards was the club DJ: "We are a musical alternative. Unlike other clubs like Austens, you can wear what you want – anything goes," he was quoted as saying at the time.

"We've got such a good name on the London scene that groups contact us wanting to play here. Groups just can't believe a club like ours exists outside London."

But by June 1984, The Joint – together with dozens of other clubs and organisations that used the space – had been kicked out by The Bucks Association of Youth Clubs. Massive repairs were needed and the association didn't have the necessary funds.

Less than a month after closure The Peartree Centre had been torn apart by vandals.

Ken Daniels, former owner of The Fox & Hounds (above)

Remembering Muzaks and The Joint (right)

The Starting Gate

Based near Secklow Gate in the heart of Milton Keynes, The Starting Gate looked like a motorcycle enthusiast's paradise during the early '80s, with bikes parked up en masse outside and their owners keeping the wet stuff flowing inside.

Marillion were regulars on the stage.

"I remember playing there wearing Britannia make-up, with the Union Jack painted on my face," recalls former frontman Fish.

"Probably the most powerful memory, apart from playing the Genesis song I Know What I Like (In Your Wardrobe) there, which is on a bootleg somewhere, is that it was the only place we did a gig with Marillion as a four-piece.

"It would be around March '82, and Diz Minnitt was our bass player. The rest of the band had turned around and identified Diz as being the weakest link.

In all honesty, I knew that he was, but at the same time, he was my best friend and I was trying to deflect the inevitable.

"Before the Milton Keynes gig, the temperature and the pressure was so much that I ended up having to tell Diz that he was basically being fired.

"He was horrifically upset and I remember being out in the car park with Diz and he said he couldn't do the gig, and that was that.

"We went on stage as a four-piece, and that was just before Aylesbury boy Pete Trewavas, joined."

He added: "We had the van back then, and when we toured we would reach out to places 40 to 60 miles around Aylesbury. We would keep going round and round in that circle and footprint, and the fans would follow us - they would go from Dunstable to Milton Keynes to Berkhamstead.

"I can't remember what we got paid at The Starting Gate, probably £60 or £75 a gig, something like that.

"Remember, this was pre tom-tom days and I used to really fucking hate driving through Milton Keynes - bloody roundabouts!

"The number of times we got lost trying to find the gig.

"It was always a nightmare."

The Countapoint

The Countapoint had that punky DIY ethic perfected.

The wall of apathy that surrounded many a live show was yet to spread to the Bletchley Leisure Centre spot, which sucked up the noisy sounds.

The Countapoint, known in earlier times as The Compass Club, enjoyed its fair share of charged nights. In the late '80s and early '90s Culture Shock, born from punk aces Subhumans, were regulars.

They recorded live shows there, name-checked The Countapoint on their releases, and their gigs were immense, sweat-soaked successes. Culture Shock's music mattered too; they documented their rage at the government, championed animal rights and mourned the loss of a society where people cared.

Not simply social commentators, plenty would say they also had an astute understanding of the path that lay ahead.

The first band I saw at the venue was anarcho-punk mob Conflict. That evening my musical horizon was substantially expanded and things would never be quite the same again.

Bands too numerous to mention blew minds inside that most innocuous of venues.

Chumbawamba were another staple, and used to unite their crowd in motion as they jostled for space on a stage not really made for so many.

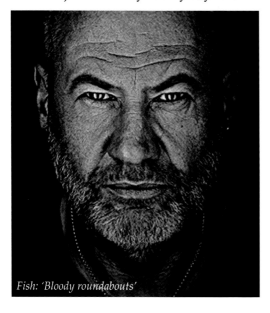

Fish: 'Bloody roundabouts'

Blythe Power, Sofahead, Bolt Thrower, RDF and Snuff. There were so many bands, so many memories.

The Countapoint was a place where friends were made and where interests were piqued.

You could learn a lot too: We've still got a copy of a Squatters Handbook knocking around somewhere, purchased from one of the stalls that would crop up seeking support for causes - support anti-vivisection, ban the bomb, fight the poll tax...

The Countapoint also did a fine line in fine grub to soak up the liquid refreshment that always went down the hatch rather easily.

And when it wanted to come back up?

There were often a few over-indulgers slumped outside looking up at the stars, or face down over the water-edge wishing they'd not gotten quite so friendly with the Pernod.

Janine Haynes was one frequenter.

"With a hunger for punk and with my alternatively dressed friends in tow it was the only place worth going to.

"A small, dark venue with an alternative atmosphere and the type of skinhead or mohawk or dreadlocked, pierced clientele that most parents would worry about their children associating with.

"I never met a kinder bunch of friends than at this venue," Janine said.

"I moshed, sweated, snogged the occasional boy, bought CDs, listened to local and touring bands, learned a little about politics from the lyrics of those punk bands and got into literature after

countapoint. bletchley sat.18thma

speaking to some band members who were very well read. Now, the ghost of The Countapoint brings about delicious memories of Citizen Fish and countless other punk bands that made the difficult task of growing up all the more bearable."

The Skoolhouse

The old adage 'you don't know what you've got until it's gone' is true of The Skoolhouse, a large pub leased as a music venue in 1993.

Tucked out of the way in Fullers Slade, it offered live music five nights a week. Blues, rock, metal and cover bands were the staple.

But that ambitious five night stand had been cut to just three nights by the following January.

Business wasn't so good after all.

Local bands and those working the national pub/club circuit were the lifeblood of the haunt, and they all received a decidedly dark welcome from the venue, whose interior was painted black from head to toe.

The two-tier approach meant you could rock your socks off on the dance floor, or lean over the proceedings with a little more decorum, from the balcony.

During its brief lifetime the venue – later re-christened The Bunker and then The Cavendish Club - welcomed artists like Reef and Skunk Anansie to the stage, but the promises of grandeur never reached fruition and towards the end of its lifespan, the venue had become entangled in club culture too.

Fire eventually engulfed the venue and snuffed out any hopes of a second coming. Had it not been razed to the ground, The Skoolhouse could have made for a fabulous antidote to the current culture of chain names and bland clubs that occupy every street in every town.

Bar Central

Originally opened as Muswell's Cafe Bar, the first floor snug in CMK was sold in 1996 and underwent a total transformation. London-based businessman and nightclub owner Howard Spooner decided the new name would be Bar Central.

"Every Friday and Saturday I'm going to have a nightclub evening called MK1 and I'll be trying to recreate a bit of my London club in Milton Keynes," said Howard, who ran Embargo nightclub on The Kings Road.

"There's competition from Chicago and Flamingos and I think the Oasis Bar in The Point is pretty popular as well," he told the press.

In London, Spooner's star soared and his clubbing credentials were a hit with A-listers and young Royals.

But by 1997 MK was already a distant memory for him – by April that year Bar Central had new owners.

Waterfall Holdings moved in bringing their own DJs.

In 1998, Project B pulled in The Freestylers.

As the new millennium approached, the venue was doing swift business with external promoters taking regular stints at the venue.

Friday night hit Revolver had launched in the autumn of 1997 and was a hit from the off.

It attracted the indie and alternative brigade en masse, with the promise of 'The best in big beat, glam Madchester and indie,' spilling from the decks and filling the dance floor.

And what Revolver did for indie, Sensoria did for dance and trance fans, when it based itself at BC from late in 1999, following the closure of Carriages in Wolverton.

Things ticked along nicely for a few years, but in 2004 the end was nigh, and some of the best-known promos were shown the door – Sensoria, Ignition and Steppers all shipped out: "People demand drum 'n' bass and they demand trance, but then you don't get the attendances," said club manager Neil Gurner.

Lee Smith was resident DJ at the aforementioned Revolver night. Every week the venue would be bursting with punters eager to devour tunes and connect with their mates.

It was the bustling centre of indie-life in the town.

"Trish was a pivotal part in the start of the club. She saw that attendances at the Happy Wednesday's promotion over at The Winter Gardens were starting to

Bar Central promotions were plentiful

dwindle," Lee said.

"As a promoter, she took the initiative and used the smaller venue to create a much greater atmosphere.

"Trish spent a lot of time on promotion and making props and backdrops for the club. I was involved in painting some large colourful backdrops.

"I started on the decks after Lee Scriven let me loose on the Monday night sessions - his love for The Who is something we both shared and built a friendship over.

"Flo Jo and Scissors and Witters were resident DJs along with me. We worked under the names of DJ Resurrection, Smiffy, Beatmaster General and General Lee.

"After learning my trade I made a mixtape and applied to work at Revolver on a Friday night.

"I was 18-years-old and it paid the princely sum of £50 an hour.

"I thought I had died and gone to heaven - I got to spin the best tracks, fill the dance floor and got that haul.

"Back in the 90s that was good pickings...still is, in my eyes.

"The beer was cheap, the attitude was non-existent; wear what you want, be who you want to be.

"Some of us wanted to be other people, and I had Ian Brown's swagger down to a fine art, even making my own famous money t-shirt before they hit the market.

"Bands were a highlight at the venue, including visitors Winnebago Deal and Rachel Stamp, and Cliff Rescue and the Helicopters and Fur Circus locally. I played bass with the latter for a while.

"Resident sound man Nigel was always a good crack and worked well with the bands, and behind the bar Helen could whip you up a plate of chips for a quid."

Lee added: "Every Christmas a number of bands would have the opportunity to play three cover songs and I remember all the bands trying to out do each other with the wackiest covers.

"Remember, this was pre-Live Lounge. "I think my cover of Billie Jean was a good one, but also remember The Final Countdown going down well."

Oceana

The 2,200-capacity nightclub Oceana opened its doors in 2002 in Xscape.

Luminar Leisure invested £5m into the complex which boasted two nightclubs – the Icehouse and the Discotheque room. Different themed bars, including the Aspen Ski Lodge and Parisienne Boudoir, also catered for punters.

In 2008 the venue was given a £2.5m facelift, and though Oceana MK was the first, the brand proved popular enough to be rolled out at venues around the country.

The club eventually called last orders in 2012. With Oceana gone, Xscape welcomed in Wonderworld, who promised 'a new era of nightlife' in the town, but after four-and-a-half years, it too called time.

Keen clubbers have had to shift focus to find alternative weekend entertainment, with the space previously occupied by the young and feisty, now being utilised by a trampolining centre.

Talk about the ups and downs of clubbing life!

Madcap Theatre

Many of the events that took place at Wolverton's Madcap happened under the Green Events banner. Activist Ged Kelly set up the initiative and at first it was used to swell the coffers for the Green Party, Greenpeace and Friends of the earth.

The first Green Gig was actually held at the OU in 1989 with support from the New Mutants and Helicopter and featured five local bands.

Ged then joined the board of Madcap and began a series of monthly gigs, featuring local and regional bands, that continued for many years.

"Nearly all the bands/artists from the area had played the Creed Street haunt, which drew together a dedicated and diverse community of volunteers too numerous to mention," Ged recalled.

Ged was joined in the core group by Paul Capel, Gordon Glass, Philippa Tipper, Guy Jones, Gwilym Gibbons, Tom Kelly, Caz Tricks, Wally (on lighting), Paul Gatiss, Steve Owen, Blain Dawson, Alex Limburg Bond, Rick Hutton and many others truly worthy of a mention.

This creative group evolved to develop a broader range of gigs and other performing arts events, under various banners, to cater for the growing sub-culture in Milton Keynes.

Examples included BIG GIGs, APHELION, the CLUB IT series, the Dub U Like mega series and its successor Tribal Vibrations that continued with psychedelic dub and multicultural sounds through to

the last gig in 2001.

"Over 12 years this ever changing collective promoted more than 250 gigs at Madcap featuring approximately 600 bands, built a professional recording studio in the basement and offered music industry related courses for musicians," Ged said, "Many of those involved with the gigs over the years went on to develop significant careers in the music and cultural industries."

A small sample of artists gracing the Madcap stage included Chumbawumba, Henry Rollins, The Rhythmites, Transglobal Underground, Loop Guru, MR C, Eddy Richards, Asian Dub Foundation, RDF and Dreadzone.

Peaches Discotheque

Located in Bletchley's Brunel Centre, Peaches opened for business in 1978 when it was acquired by the Rank Leisure Group – previously it ran as Tramps.

It was lively and fun, and its two bars and restaurant saw folks flock to the hub.

It liked the odd slogan as well - cheeky little lines like: 'If you don't take her, someone else will.'

Later, Peaches became Martines and then Rayzels.

Directors Wine Bar

Tucked into the opening of Station Square in CMK, Directors offered more than a glass of pinot grigio - you could get an earful of sounds too, everyone from Jonathan E to Safety Valve aired their creativity.

How The Blues Collective's many members managed to fit on its stage, remains one of MKs biggest mysteries.

Dukes Wine Bar

A Winter Gardens staple with a cozy atmosphere that hosted a train of Milton Keynes talents, and artists from out of town; Sex Pistol Glenn Matlock stepped up one night.

"During the 1990s, The Winter Gardens complex housed the great little club, Dukes," remembers Stray's Del Bromham.

"For a time, it was managed by fellow musician, Fin Muir.

"Fin was the singer with rock band Waysted, and to say he liked a drink would be an understatement. The walls of the club were lined with empty bottles of a particular Scottish wine called Buckfast. I have no doubt whatsoever that Fin had consumed the contents of all of them..."

The Empire

It opened in April 1998, taking over the space formerly operating as Golden Flamingos following a £2m refurbishment. The doors were locked in 2002, but in 2003 it reopened for business – this time steered by Sanctuary bosses Fiona and Tony Rosenberg.

Who remembers spending evening's drinking and dancing in the main space and the Spice Room before it closed for good in 2005?

The Winter Gardens

A space famous for its Ultra Vegas spectacles, and its indie success - the mid-week Happy Wednesday's alt-disco celebrated its second birthday in 1997.

Ultra Vegas enjoyed highs in 1999 with Boy George among the music bringers, but dance dreams turned into nightmares soon after, when in the November of the same year, The Winter Gardens announced it would be shutting up shop.

Its closure impacted on many independent promotions. Bad times.

The Main Arena

Known as The Palace in the '60s, The Wannadies were among the artists to perform at Wolverton's Main Arena in 1997, when the haunt staked its claim as a venue once again, and it did ok for a short while, too.

Towards the end of the '90s, the venue was under new management who spruced things up with a new sound and lights system. And they re-christened the place; it would now be known as Carriages.

But in early 1999 the plug was pulled on the venture.

UltraVegas

The 1990s signalled a new beginning for dance aficionados in MK. Instead of chasing styles elsewhere, clubbers had the perfect haven on their doorstep.

Having spent years soaking up weekend dance sessions in warehouses, derelict buildings and fields, Marc Carter decided to turn from reveller to promoter.

In 1990 he created the IQ brand which whetted appetites, and made a certain splash with revellers at Riviera Lights in Bedford: "The venue grew in stature and audiences came from all around to dance until 6am and swim in the pool that was in the club. A swimming pool!

"It went well, but all roads were leading to Milton Keynes being the home of IQ," Marc said.

A year later, it was being hosted at Bletchley mecca The Sanctuary, with Jon DaSilva, Carl Cox, John Digweed, and LTJ Bukem among those delivering at the quality house night.

Massive birthday events were supported by Boy George and Allister Whitehead, with the brilliant resident DJs Johnny G, Jay Marshall, Bruce B, Paul McGilway and the hugely popular 'MK superstar DJ' Nick Norman creating the vibe for which IQ was known.

Eventually, IQ was replaced by ClubTV @ The Sanctuary, the brainwave of Antony Delahaye and Marc.

With the use of ISDN link-ups, world-renowned DJs from all over the globe could play alongside DJs in the club in a

modern Top of the Pops TV studio type environment.

Huge screens and dance podiums and platforms covered the space, and amazing visuals added to the atmosphere at this new visionary form.

Names including Sasha and Judge Jules helped the 'up-for-it' clubbers dance 'til dawn.

"In late 1995 a meeting with local promoters resulted in a co-promoted New Year's Eve party and the decision was made to take things to the next level," said Marc.

"Sitting at a dining table with Richard Long and Gary Smart we decided to join forces; UltraVegas (UV) was born."

The first event was held at The Winter Gardens in February 1996. It was a smash hit, and punters began flocking to the sounds - easy to see why when deck deliverers included Paul Oakenfold, Pete Tong, Paul Van Dyk, Seb Fontaine, Tall Paul, the late, great Tony De Vit, Jon Pleased Wimmin and Boy George.

A-list brands including Gatecrasher and Miss Moneypenny's showed out too.

"The weekly Saturday nights continued and crowds got bigger, sexier and more adventurous.

> **"The word was that UltraVegas was the only night to fill the gap between London and Birmingham"**

"The word on the street was that UltraVegas was the only night to fill the gap between London and Birmingham," Marc said, "The squeaky clean young crowd that had first appeared had grown in confidence, gained knowledge of the scene and were expressing themselves in amazing outfits and makeup – and that was just the boys!

"Women wore just enough to stop them getting arrested and UltraVegas had become one of the main contributors to kickstart another generation of clubbers."

The success could be measured by the volume of numbers who attended, and where they came from – dance disciples headed to Milton Keynes from France, Germany, Holland and Italy to enjoy the sounds.

With the trio leading the brand (Richard later became a resident DJ), Vegas was the place that had it all. But after five years of sensational house events on local soil and elsewhere in the UK, UV ran out of venues in its hometown.

The Winter Gardens changed hands and while Friday nights at The Empire were special, Marc didn't consider it the right fit for the brand.

Spreading the word: Flyers and adverts for the UltraVegas sessions

"The Sanctuary was used once - to promote the fifth birthday celebration. "Every DJ you could imagine played, and were accompanied by Chicane, who were Number 1 in the UK Top 40 that weekend, headlining to nearly 5,000 clubbers.

"What a way to say goodbye to something that nobody wanted to see die."

And then Vegas was gone.

But the dance-heads who soaked up the sounds, plumped up for the parties and enjoyed the outrageous antics refused to let it go quietly.

Nigh on seven years after it stopped, MKs super club returned for occasional reunions; there were eight parties throughout 2009 and 2010, this time with

Marc overseeing everything.

"All those who attended the parties were hell-bent on blowing the cobwebs away, and funky techy house and original '90s house music was smashed out of massive sound systems.

"Original crowds and the new breed of clubbers were on the heaving dance floors - what a feeling," Marc said.

He added: "I did think the UltraVegas puzzle was complete with the final resting place in the green fields of MK, but with the huge resurgence of nostalgia in the club scene over the last few years, I look forward to celebrating its 25th anniversary in 2021 in its home of Milton Keynes with a bang."

223

Sensoria

"We made our dream a reality and provided Milton Keynes with years of clubbing heaven."

❞ We spent a lot of time clubbing in the early '90s, but towards the end of the decade the bigger clubs were taking off and a lot of the atmosphere was disappearing," recalls Trish Munro (inset), founder of one of the most successful dance brands to set up shop in the new city.

"We began staging house parties for ourselves and friends and got so proficient that we decided to turn professional and set up our own night, with the aim of providing an aural and visual experience for all clubbers in a safe, friendly environment where people could relax and have a good time.

"We created our very own Egyptian temple with lots of beautifully painted UV backdrops and over the years we added lots of Egyptian artefacts to the set.

"The first-ever Sensoria was held in the Cellar Bar of the Kilrush, now the infamous Pink Punters (were we responsible for setting that seed in motion?) on New Year's Eve, 1997.

"We then moved to The Main Arena in Wolverton for a couple of years, finally taking up permanent residence at Bar Central in 1999.

"Together with our resident DJs Pete Brown, Keith Hurley, AKA and Andy Bagguley, and our resident percussionist The Techno Pharaoh, we worked together to create our own unique sound and billed it as 'A journey through house and trance.'

"We were always loyal to our local boys and gave many an aspiring DJ a chance to play on the decks.

"We had lots of memorable nights playing host to top DJs, but Sensoria followers were very loyal and it was always our regulars who drew the biggest crowds and kept the dance floor full to the last tune.

"At Sensoria, putting on a good night was more important to us than making a fast buck and our ethos wasn't lost on our clubbers who came early, stayed late and loved every minute of it.

Keith Hurley

"Our chill-out room was always full of happy, chatty clubbers, and many special friendships and relationships began there.

"We had regular dancers and jugglers to spice up the evening's entertainment, and attracted a lot of single females - they said how safe and hassle-free they felt at our club.

"Sensoria was the winner of MKs Best Dance Promotion for three years in a row.

"Our annual summer clubbing cruise down the Thames was always a sell-out and a much anticipated treat.

"When Bar Central decided to shut their doors forever, we made the decision to go too.

"Our last night was held in September 2004 and we went out in a blaze of glory with full capacity and many tears at the end of the night.

"When all is said and done, we were a small club with a big heart and put our clubbers first before making money.

"We made our dream a reality and provided Milton Keynes with years of clubbing heaven."

Beatcheck

*Fed up with a drought of live dance music deliciousness, two MK fellas
decided to bring the noise themselves and Beatcheck was born.*

Beatcheck was the baby of Jason Charles and Dan Selinger, the new-city raised chaps who originally started promoting in Brighton.
"I was a student and Jason was being a hobo," recalled Dan.

"Beatcheck started because we were fed up with having no decent live dance music nights, despite the fact that there were loads of incredible acts doing the rounds at the time.

"We wanted to create a night dedicated to live dance music.

"Bands have soundchecks, dance music bands have 'beat' checks, and so the name was born.

"We put on all kinds of acts, but live drum 'n' bass and hip-hop mainly.

"Highlights were Lo Fidelity Allstars and Carnival Collective, a 25-piece samba outfit that put on a breakbeat set for us.

"It was insane and the punters in Brighton loved it in a big way."

Jason moved back to Milton Keynes to replicate the success: "We saw that people weren't promoting well in MK - they weren't postering, flyering or using online forums, nothing like that.

"We decided to bring some of that promoting know-how home and it worked a treat."

Beatcheck debuted in the town in 2006, at the Old Rodeo Bar. Air Records' Ali B was the main attraction, but the new brand soon moved to Revolution Vodka Bar.

"Some people doubted whether it would work or not, but it did - and better than we had hoped.

"The punters went wild, soaking up a real London and Brighton clubbing environment on their doorstep.

"By attracting some of the people who like decent music to come out into the town for the first time, and mixing them with some of the more open-minded townies, we created an amazing atmosphere.

"Over the next couple of years we managed to pull in some of the biggest names in underground dance music, and at our peak we were getting more than 1,000 people through the doors each night.

"We showed through Beatcheck that you can put on a music-focused night with groups to create one big underground love-in, in the concrete city," Dan said.

"We were the first underground night to bring huge names in dance to MK on a weekly basis, and inspired a handful of other promoters to pick up their game, get flyering and think about the music."

Beatcheck nested at Revolution for three years, before the brand picked up its record bags and beats and moved the short distance to Opus.

"We were the first promoters to put an underground dance music night on in a venue in the Theatre District which was a real coup."

It continued with regular crowds for a while before hanging up its promoting boots, delivering a capacity show with Beardyman.

But the itch needed scratching and Beatcheck resurfaced.

Thankfully, the beats still get checked around town every once in a while.

> **"At our peak we were getting more than 1,000 people through the doors each night"**

Wolverton Town Band

The early years

Long before there was Milton Keynes, there was a flourishing musical scene in the towns and villages all around.

Stony Stratford Town Band formed in the 1860s and was a prominent feature at town functions before the First World War.

But with significant losses during the fighting, by 1919 the music-makers were struggling.

Mr Wilmin was the band leader and every week, on practice night at The Crown in Stony Stratford, he would ensure members paid one shilling subscription.

Times were tough and it wasn't the best way to drive up the numbers!

The band played regular Sunday night open air concerts in the Market Square from late spring until early autumn, but they were only allowed to begin after 7pm following evensong at the church.

With efforts to rekindle interest in the band failing, it played for the last time in 1929.

The introduction of the 'wireless' radio and syncopated music served to spread modern dance rhythms far and wide in the early 1920s.

In the area we now call Milton Keynes many bands formed to play to ballroom dances - some diversified, fusing modern and old-time sounds, and earned the nickname of 50-50.

Joe Lovesy's Orchestra, and the **Bright Knights** concentrated on old-time, while the likes of **The Rhythm Aces** and **The Ambassadors** kept things modern.

Venues were plentiful too - in Wolverton couples could go 'in motion' at the Science & Art Institute, Drill Hall and The Works Canteen, which were all big enough to accommodate more than 200 dancing couples.

Smaller venues offering a service included The Craufurd Arms and the Victoria Hotel.

From the late 1920s through to the early '30s, patrons of The County Arms Hotel in New Bradwell were treated to the unique sounds and talents of **The Blue Bird Mouth Organ Band**, who played every Saturday.

It might have been grand if you

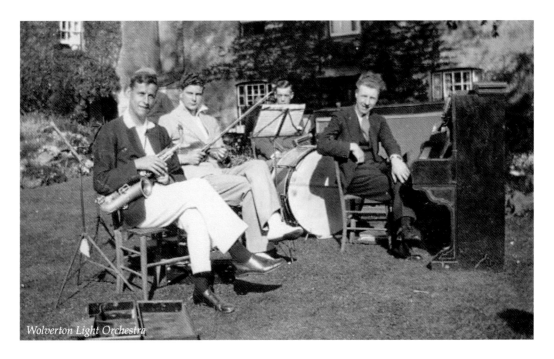

Wolverton Light Orchestra

were upstairs listening to the music, but downstairs in the bar, those quaffing knew only a din, thanks to some decidedly old and creaky flooring: "It sounded like a herd of cattle moving around," one patron recalled.

In 1938, the hotel was completely altered and a new dance floor put in - The Blue Bird Band would return too, re-emerging as an accordion band.

Wolverton Town Band's origins can be traced back to the 1st Buckinghamshire Volunteer Rifles; a breakaway group formed by three rifle members, Mr Fred Grace, Mr Jack Bates and Mr Carvell would eventually become known as the Wolverton Town Band.

In 1920 they entered the National Brass Festival in London, competing in the 4th Section with Verdi's Il trovatore, which saw them take a very respectable third place at Crystal Palace.

When they repeated the success two years later, the proud people of Wolverton rewarded their own, issuing each member of the band with a medal.

With the onset of the Second World War the band stood down, and members became part of the Local Defence Volunteer Band.

In 1940 the **Wolverton Home Guard Military Band** was formed, with Doug Dytham in the role of bandmaster - in a coup for the area they were the only Home Guard band in the country.

An old ambulance room in the railway works served as its HQ, and Doug's brother Syd was the band sergeant.

Bandsmen from Wolverton, Bradwell, and Stony Stratford were involved, together with one or two from the Newport Pagnell band - at full strength there were 40 players.

They led the stand-down parade in Wolverton at the head of the battalion at the end of 1944, before being relegated to history.

When the war ended, normal service was resumed with Wolverton Town Band.

"When I joined it was called Wolverton Town and BR Band, a title adopted in order to obtain the use of the British Rail works canteen and a tiny cupboard 'under the stairs' where all the equipment was kept," remembered Bob Mills.

In 2014 Jane Lloyd became the first woman to take up the post of musical director with the group.

Wolverton Town Band remains musically active in the area, and the mixed ability group of players is always looking to expand its number, if you are up to the challenge.

The Wolverton Light Orchestra was founded in 1927 as the Frank Brooks Orchestra.

Post-war it reformed as the Wolverton Orchestral Society, and then in 1977 it settled as the Wolverton Light Orchestra.

In the early 1930s the band's regular concert spaces included the New Empire Cinema in Wolverton and the Electra in Newport Pagnell.

Wartime depleted band numbers, though a few concerts were still performed annually.

Ill health forced the resignation of founder Frank Brooks in late 1945, and the mantle passed to Harold Nutt, music master at Wolverton Grammar School. Success continued for a time, but by the mid-1950s interest was waning and the orchestra downed its instruments for six years or so, before new enthusiasm revived it in 1961.

The WLO still performs today. Mike Crofts is the musical director - a role he has held for the past 25 years.

Bradwell man **Tommy Claridge** was a musical virtuoso who was able to play several instruments.

His first band **The Amazons** were formed in 1934, but when war broke out Tommy joined the Royal Engineers - taking his accordion with him.

In France, he was among the last to be evacuated from St Nazaire in June 1940. Tommy had been aboard the ill-fated liner, Lancastria. The ship was bombed and sunk with the loss of thousands of lives.

Tommy Claridge's was spared that day - but his accordion was lost, and now rests somewhere on the seabed.

Post-war, he formed a new trio before the band was reformed as **The Tommy Claridge Orchestra**.

When they later split, Tommy joined Doug Dytham's **Rhythm Aces**.

Newport Pagnell-born **Tommy Papworth** served with the railway Royal Engineers during World War One and while carrying out his military duties succumbed to shell shock.

He later set up shop as a fruiterer in Bletchley, but his music-making was renowned in the area.

In the 1920s he started the sextet **Apollo String Orchestra**, which accompanied silent films at the cinema.

In the late 1930s **The Papworth Trio** was formed.

Pianist Tommy, drummer Joe Underwood, and violinist Cliff French quickly became a big draw.

During World War Two any means to maintain public morale was important and dances proved extremely popular, with the trio among the best regarded – and they entertained by playing everything from the Lancers to the hokey cokey.

The band continued until 1956, when Tommy passed away.

In the 1940s dance bands entered the fray, and helped boost the mood. Among the frontrunners, you would have found **Vera Stapleton and her Rhythmic Band**, the aforementioned **Tommy Claridge and his New Lyric Dance Band** and **Joe Lovesey and his Orchestra**.

In 1947, **Bletchley Town Band** played their way through six streets, hoping to collect 210 clothing coupons for their trouble.

Bad weather curtailed their efforts but the vouchers rolled in, enabling some of the adult personnel to be decked out in new clobber. It was necessary too; having been kept in storage during the war, the uniforms had been ravaged by moths!

Later the same year, Bletchley magistrates granted a music licence to Norman Green, for Greenway's Cafe, who wanted a small orchestra to play for customers.

Light music would be played on Sundays: 'Not jazz or anything of that nature, but a better type of music,' was the assurance.

Bradwell Silver Band

Children aren't supposed to open their Christmas presents until they've heard the BSB at play; a tradition dating back to 1902!

Milton Keynes might be only half a century into its own history, but the village of New Bradwell – which now occupies the northern edge of the new city – boasts a team of music-makers who have been delivering nice noises for much longer.

The village was founded primarily to house workers from the London & North Western Railway company, which had its workshops in nearby Wolverton.

On January 15, 1901 a meeting at the girls' school discussed the formation of a brass band.

A week later, and following various suggestions (Bradwell Excelsior, Stantonbury St James, Bradwell Town and Bradwell Recreation Brass Band), a name was settled on: the Bradwell United Brass Band.

The name was used through to 1955.

An early purchase was a trombone, which cost the quite considerable sum of seven pounds and 10 shillings. It was engraved for an additional two pounds and 10 shillings.

The trombone survives today, although it has since been retired from musical duty!

Bradwell Silver Band (BSB) has an unbroken service record, surviving through World War I, and World War II. When the village was targeted during the blitz and suffered fatalities, the band continued.

In 1958 the band played on the pitch at Luton Town Football Club, fundraising in the wake of the tragic Munich air disaster (which took the lives of 23 people, including eight Manchester United players), and in 1990 they performed at The Point multiplex in the company of Sarah, Duchess of York, at the Royal premiere of the Harrison Ford film Presumed Innocent.

There have been numerous other live engagements, community events and charity shows, a trio of CD releases and successful appearances at the British Brass Band Championships.

Many players who learned their craft with the Bradwell Silver Band have taken their talent forward, including Ben Godfrey who started playing cornet with them when he was 10 years old.

He later studied at the Royal Academy of Music and, post-graduation, freelanced with many of the UK's leading symphony

Bradwell Silver Band's first bandmaster, Gilbert Locke in 1901 (above left), and in 1954 with then president Dr Margery Fildes (above). Below, the band in 2017. BSB circa 1930 (facing page)

orchestras and in West End shows.

It is Ben's playing that is heard daily on the theme tune for Channel 4 news.

Bradwell Silver Band doesn't just play for today though – it nurtures the talent of tomorrow through its development band, teaching the next generation of players who will keep the brass band alive. BSB provides free tutoring and loan of instruments.

Every Christmas morning since 1902 the band has played carols around the streets of New Bradwell and Bradville, from 6am.

Traditionally beginning with the shattering strains of Byrom's Christians, Awake! Salute The Happy Morn, the music always arrives with plenty of impact, as one resident recalled: "The time-honoured custom began with the first blow at the corner of Bridge Street and Church Street... the first time I heard it, I nearly shot out of bed wondering what the hell had happened. But the tradition is loved by all Bradwellians, young and old."

Residents keep the players toasty during the cold winter morning by providing hot drinks and snacks.

The music goes on come rain, shine or snow, and according to tradition, children aren't supposed to unwrap their presents from Santa until they have heard the band at play!

The Rhythm Aces

After decades spent blowing their trumpets (and trombone and post horn),
Syd and Doug Dytham had their musical achievements recognised in 1973.

The siblings, bandsmen with Wolverton Town and BR Silver Band, were awarded silverware and a radio for their half century of music making on the North Bucks music scene.

The duo both had specific solo pieces that proved popular at shows; Syd's was the traditional Post Horn Gallop while Doug would deliver rasping trombone piece The Joywheel.

Although not on board from day one, Doug was also at the helm of The Rhythm Aces, a leading local dance band who formed in 1934.

At the time, quartets in the district were a familiar sight and sound, and would come together for Sunday morning jazz sessions in The Craufurd Arms in Wolverton.

During one such meeting, it was decided to form a band from the most eminent players among them, explaining the 'aces' in the name. Doug - who also played the violin alongside the trombone - took over as leader one year after their inception. At the time he had his own band too – as did the nine other original members.

They would continue to perform with their own groups but would get together for special concerts.

The Rhythm Aces were called upon to entertain many a distinguished audience, and would perform annually at Cosgrove Hall, for Mrs Winterbottom's renowned Christmas Eve house party, and her Boxing Day Ball in Stony Stratford's Regent Hall.

The Rhythm Aces were still going strong with three gigs a week nearly half a century later.

Doug said that he had never needed to advertise the services of his band – his diary was full with engagements until The Rhythm Aces retired in 1984.

Doug worked as a chief foreman at Wolverton Works (which made railway wagons and repaired coaches) so wasn't called up for service. It meant that in between the 'day job' and helping out the police force, he was able to maintain his music-making throughout the war.

Things weren't nearly as conservative as you might have imagined during those early days either – the aces operated from behind some pretty saucy silhouetted music stands!

MUSIC by FRANK SPENCE

RODEXICON CRICKET CLUB (W. O. Peake Ltd.)

GRAND DANCE

ASSEMBLY HALL, WILTON AVE
(By kind permission of Col. Platt, O.B.E.)

SATURDAY, FEBRUARY 1st

8 to 11.45 p.m.

BLETCHLEY

GRAND DANCE

ASSEMBLY HALL, WILTON AVE
(By kind permission of Col. Platt, O.B.E.)

WEDNESDAY, FEBRUARY 12

From 8 p.m.

Douglas Dytham and his Rhythm Aces

ADMISSION 2/6   H.M. FORCES 2/-

REFRESHMENTS   Committee reserve the right of admission

A HAPPY NEW YEAR

Terry Carroll and his Rockets

Ballroom dancing was the call in Wolverton in the mid-1950s - until the Rockets brought skiffle and rock 'n' roll to town.

Terry grew up in Wolverton, and was always drawn to sound: "I could get a tune out of tin whistles, mouth organs and the like," he remembered.

He took violin lessons from his uncle Doug Dytham, leader of The Rhythm Aces dance band, and when his parents became tenants of The Coffee Pot Inn in Yardley Gobion, piano lessons were granted.

"The Coffee Pot was a familiar hang out for the local youth and when I acquired a PYE record maker, they were already there and waiting to have a go.

"They wanted to sing songs in the hit parade; Tommy Steele's Singing The Blues and Bill Haley's Rock Around The Clock, but some ballads were also included.

"Arthur Jacquest had returned from

> **"Organisers had used soap flakes instead of talcum powder on the floor"**

national service where he had acquired a guitar and he and I provided the backing.

"We performed our increasing repertoire to Coffee Pot customers to some acclaim and ventured out to play for the real public in the village hall for the youth club.

"We needed a name and The Rockets seemed to us to be a natural progression from Bill Haley's Comets.

"I don't think the dance bands of the day had amplification.

"We were ahead of the game and the PYE record maker was a versatile beast.

"By fitting a different stylus it could play ordinary records and act as an amplifier.

"The speaker was in the detachable lid, which was hung from the curtain rail of the stage.

"The microphone was a little spherical

crystal affair which didn't look good.

"But when it was housed in our microphone stand consisting of a length of curtain rail screwed to a hub cap with a Sun-Pat peanut tin on the top and all painted silver, it was cool!

"Apart from my brother Rod on drums, the only other instruments were things you could shake or rattle.

"I don't know how we made ourselves heard but the young audience loved it.

"Not content with shaking and rattling, Rod bought an alto saxophone and Michael Ford bought a clarinet and later a tenor sax.

"Both took lessons and became quite proficient," Terry said.

"David Williams took over on drums, lead singer Roy Church got a guitar and we were on our way.

"We played most of the village halls and venues including The Craufurd Arms and Victoria Hotel in Wolverton and the mecca of the district; Wolverton Railway Works Mess Room."

In those days, it wasn't simply a case of the band piling into a van and heading to shows, though, and things could prove difficult.

"Transport in the early days was a problem," Terry admitted.

"An early trip to a do at Hanslope Park saw my brother with most of the instruments in an open-topped, two-seater, Austin Seven Special, followed by me with the bass drum in my motorbike and side car, with Michael bringing up the rear on a moped where the foot cymbal was strapped across the carrier!

"When we were playing at Yardley Gobion and my cousin Nicky Dytham could join us, he would arrive on a United Counties double-decker bus with his double bass."

It was worth the dodgy journeys though – the band were pulling large crowds wherever they went.

"Things got better when Rod traded the Special for a Humber estate car which we could all get in.

"On at least one occasion there were 12 people and the double bass inside.

"Not surprisingly, the steering finally failed and we ended up in someone's front garden.

"The steering finally failed and we ended up in someone's front garden"

"One evening we were in full swing when we became conscious that Roy's voice was beginning to falter and members of the audience were beginning to cough.

"It turned out that the organisers had used soap flakes instead of talcum powder on the floor.

"The hall was evacuated and swept through before we continued.

"On another occasion we played at Yardley Hastings on a freezing cold evening.

Their pipes had frozen and burst.

The stage was running in water and there was no heating."

But a chill of a different kind was in the air before too long.

The band had started being noticed for the undesirable youth element that seemed to follow them around; the type who preferred to show off their ability with their fists rather than any kind of fancy footwork.

It meant that Terry and the Rockets came to the attention of the boys in blue.

"I have very little memory of any troubles apart from the very occasional scuffle, when we would refuse to carry on playing until it subsided," Terry said.

"My cousin always told the tale of a huge mêlée in the yard outside the County Arms: As we came out of the hall with our instruments someone shouted 'It's the band.'

"The crowd parted like the red sea for Moses, let us through, and then resumed fighting.

"It's a good story, but I don't remember it happening!"

Promoters became loathe to book The Rockets, and the damage had been done. But the music didn't stop altogether.

Terry added: "We made our final appearance as The Rockets at the second charity concert at the Mess Room, gave up rock 'n' roll and went on to play traditional jazz throughout the trad boom years, finally becoming the very respectable Blue Streak Combo."

Terry sadly passed away in early 2015.

The Danesborough Chorus

This vocal ensemble have been bringing tuneful sounds to the stage for more than four decades, and boast a long 'Dankworth connection.'

Choral society The Danesborough Chorus formed in 1975, and still give three concerts every year.

Since its inception hundreds of voices have aired as part of the collective, which performs in and around Milton Keynes, traditionally utilising the assets of Woburn Parish Church and Milton Keynes Theatre.

Ian Smith celebrated four decades as musical director with the Danesborough Chorus on July 1, 2017.

One of the leading conductors in the area, he also worked as director of music, as head of expressive arts and as an assistant headteacher at Wootton Upper School, as a trustee of The Wavendon Allmusic Plan, and a member of The Stables Theatre Board.

His 40th anniversary with the chorus was marked with a performance of Mendelssohn's choral drama Elijah.

Sir John Dankworth was the choir's only president from its inception until he passed away in 2010.

He was a passionate supporter too – and composed two works for the choir to perform; Thy Kingdom Gone and All The World's A Stage.

"We gave All The World's A Stage its world premiere in Woburn Parish Church on June 25, 1988," Ian recalled.

"Sir John believed in blurring the boundaries between different musical genres, and this work is a perfect example of jazz, folk and classical fusion!"

The libretto is the well-known description of the seven ages of human life from Shakespeare's As You Like It.

Sir John employed his characteristically ravishing choral vocabulary to produce a piece of work that was both witty and moving.

Following his death, the choir once again performed the work in tribute to him.

The Dankworth union continues to this day though; Sir John's daughter Jacqui took over as president in 2012.

MK City Orchestra

For more than four decades MK City Orchestra provided the finer soundtrack to the new city. But in 2019 the baton was put down for the last time.

Hilary Davan Wetton was instrumental in putting classical music on the map in Milton Keynes.

He first came to the town in 1974 as head of the Music Centre at Stantonbury, and the campus director of music.

"I was inspired to do so by Geoff Cooksey, whose vision of the arts in education and the community was compelling, and by Cindy Hargate, the Development Corporation's art manager, who believed that anything was possible in Milton Keynes.

"My first year was extraordinarily exciting. We set up the Music Centre; initially with nine students, but with more than 200 by the year's end."

He also founded a choir, the Milton Keynes Chorale: "It grew from 30 to 70 members in its first year," he said.

"Finally, in February 1975 the Milton Keynes City Orchestra gave its first concert – which could easily have been its last – in the Stantonbury Theatre.

"We had a full audience, and a group of enthusiasts quickly allowed themselves to be cajoled into forming a committee to promote its concerts.

"The orchestra was the first wholly professional group to be centred in Milton Keynes, and speedily established an annual series of concerts in the theatre.

"In the late 1980s the Development Corporation and its successors sponsored a series of recordings, mainly of little-known British 19th-century symphonies, which received both national and international acclaim."

In June 2015, the orchestra celebrated its 40 year anniversary, and the champagne kept on coming – a month later MKCO presented Much Ado about MK, a concert to mark a milestone birthday for Hilary, and he conducted his concert of music.

"When the orchestra played its first concert, failure was not an option, but in retrospect it is little short of a miracle

Hilary with MKCO members, and (facing page) Damian Iorio in control

that the orchestra is still going strong," Hilary said at the time.

"There have been golden periods; our series of recordings of rare English symphonies, our tour of the eastern USA, the opening season in the theatre where our audience averaged 90 per cent and collaborations with major international artists whose enthusiasm for the quality of the orchestra was always a delight – and a reassurance.

Leaders: Hilary Davan Wetton (above) and Damian Iorio

"The survival of the orchestra is due to three main factors. Firstly the quality of the players, secondly the support of the orchestra's voluntary board and finally the loyalty of the patron and the MK audience, who have kept the aspirations of the orchestra and its conductors alive with warmth and encouragement."

But sadly, the orchestra was unable to manoeuvre through a changing landscape and the company performed its last

concert on June 23, 2019 at MK Theatre. In a statement, the orchestra said: 'It is with deep regret that the Board of MKCO has made a fully considered decision for the orchestra to close at the end of the 2018-2019 season. Over the last six years there has been a proactive fundraising and creative re-organisation to bring greater quality to performance and education work. However, audiences haven't grown significantly, the company is not resilient and there isn't sustainable financial or resource support for professional classical music performance in MK.

It is devasting to close a cultural organisation with a 44-year history, but amongst the terrific highs and memorable classical concerts there have been financial and resource concerns over many years. This is a difficult decision and it is truly heartbreaking for those involved who have given so much.'

Musical director Damian Iorio was at the helm for the very last concert, a rousing performance of Totally Tchaikovsky.

The Fenders

The Fenders entertained film fans at the Granada cinema in Rugby, but one member would eventually occupy the big screen himself.

The Fenders started out as a Wolverton Youth Club group, based around guitarist Nick Malone in the early 1960s.

After various line-up changes, things settled down with Martin Hyde on rhythm guitar, drummer Maurice Barratt, bassist Nick Jones, and singers Dave Lee and Mick Riley.

Nick Malone was still at the helm.

Gigs were constant at the many local clubs and pubs, and the band were steered by manager Laddie Bunker.

They didn't only service the local area though – Rugby Granada cinema was a regular haunt and The Fenders would play the interval spot between films.

They played the famous 2i's coffee bar in Soho too, where Cliff Richard and The Shadows, and other pop stars were discovered. In 1963 Nick Malone bowed out and went to London to find work. He later got creative with Billy J. Kramer, and one-eyed boogie boy Freddie Fingers Lee, making two albums with him.

Nick appeared in the film Blue Suede Shoes, about a rock 'n' roll weekend at a holiday camp.

The rest of The Fenders went their separate ways working with many other musicians over the years.

Nick Jones found most of his musical work in and around Bedford, working with prominent players there for more than 40 years.

Everyone presumed he was a Bedfordian – thanks in no small part to his long musical union with guitarist Dave King. But he's one of ours.

Unit Six

The foundations of Unit Six were laid down in 1959, and six decades later the band is still going strong.

The roots of one of Milton Keynes' longest-running bands stretches all the way back to the late 1950s, when it was originally called The Nomads.

Drummer Nigel Deacon came up with the name.

"As a teenager growing up listening to all the pop bands on the radio, I just wanted to be a part of it.

"I loved the music and looked around to see if I could find other people who shared my interest to join me," Nigel said.

Guitarist Jackie Adderson and rhythm guitarist Graham Ringham were soon onboard and they spent a few months working the scene before Brian Faulkner entered the ranks in 1959, having stumbled across the band during a rehearsal at The Coronation Hall in Bletchley.

"We went by as they were sounding out a singer, and I said to my cousin 'I could do better than that!'" Brian said.

He tried out a Cliff Richard number and sealed his position.

Jackie and Graham were soon replaced by David Hale and Conrad Winchcombe (later replaced by Richard Eales on keys) and the band swelled further with Robert 'Whizz' Wise on bass.

In demand for gigs, they now called themselves Brian and the Daleks, but when Tony Bryant joined, Brian switched from vocals to tenor sax and Tony assumed mic duty.

"We became Unit Six and did gigs across the circuit," Brian said.

The band would hire a ford van to take them from A to B: "Half the money went on hiring transport.

"Once, one of the band asked some girls to write nice things on the van in lipstick. They covered it and I had to get up at 5am the next morning to clean it off before taking it back!" said Nigel.

From The Craufurd Arms and The Top Club in Wolverton to Caesar's Palace in Dunstable and the American air bases, the band plugged in anywhere and everywhere.

"We thought we were going to be the

NOW AVAILABLE
YOUR FAVOURITE
LOCAL BAND
ON RECORD
CONTACT
NIGEL DEACON ON M.K. 641682
TO PURCHASE YOUR DISC

UNIT SIX

...unds local

...ix went into studios
...record their first
...ord.
...n Keynes Mirror-
...s representative
...the group as a

...als, Dougie, keyboards
...Gordon, bass and
...d guitar — remain, and
...ve quite a following.
In addition to Laurie,
the group now features
Peter Lockwood on
drums and second guitar
man Phil Burrell. The
group is managed by

Nigel Deacon and han-
dled exclusively by local
agent Don Pearson.
Unit Six are in great
demand locally and
farther afield, seldom appearing less than once or
twice a week, and are
well booked up into the
new year.
The 12 songs on the
album, which will retail at
£2.75, are Lucky Stars, I
will survive, Boogie
nights, Only yesterday,
Long train running, Sylvia,
When will I see you again,
Night Fever, Rivers of
Babylon, SOS, Candle in
the wind, and What a
difference a day makes.

Laurie Stevens — from
the age of 10, she was
a professional singer.

Dougie Hart   Gordon Hart   Tony Bryant   Pete Lockwood

best in the world," Brian admits, "You do when you are younger.

"We did all the local barn hops and people would come from as far as Leighton Buzzard, and at the time that was quite a journey. We had our own following, and every night of the week somewhere in the area there would be a dance of some description.

"It was a free time, there were no restrictions, and the kids who came to listen to us came for fun. They didn't expect us to be equal to The Stones or The Beatles."

Brian even met his future wife on a night out at Wilton Hall.

Swapping the sax for the boys in blue, he joined the police in 1970 and bid farewell to Unit Six, but Peter Roberts filled the sax-vacancy, and the band continued to

flourish. After a few years hitting the skins, Nigel stepped aside too, but stayed on to lead the band as its manager.

It was an association that lasted for three decades.

"It was the best time I ever had," Nigel said, "I would do it all over again if I could."

As one band member left, another would step in and the cycle, and the music-making, continued.

On 26 September, 2003, Unit Six celebrated its 40th anniversary by inviting all its previous members to play a special reunion date at The Sanctuary.

While none of the original members are still with the band today, the name survives and Unit Six is now a septet offering soul, pop and funk covers in the area.

The Tremeloes

*Brian Poole turned a schoolboy dream into a reality - and
his band famously beat The Fab Four to a record deal.*

Like countless youngsters before and after them, Brian Poole and Alan Blakley dreamt of fame as musicians. But unlike most others, these schoolboys turned their dreams into reality, with a story dating back to 1956, when they decided to form a band.

Their families holidayed together back then, and so sure of stardom were they that the two teenagers would tell their Devon pals that they were already famous!

Soon the duo and their pair of Hofner guitars were hitting the party scene where they would bust out well-prepared covers of Buddy Holly and Everly Brothers songs.

They enlisted bassist Alan Howard, and at one of those aforementioned parties made acquaintance with Dave Munden who took up position behind a rather small drum kit housed at Alan's house.

The Tremeloes were born: "We opted for that name after the sound on the new amplifiers which we couldn't yet afford!" recalled Brian.

Graham Scott, an older lad from the same school, swelled the unit, and they began playing at venues in their local area of Essex.

Cinemas asked the young ensemble to play during film intervals, and they found themselves on the American camp circuit working alongside fellow newcomers like Geno Washington, although Buddy Holly tracks were still the staple of their set.

"As word spread, almost before we realised it, we had become one of the top dance hall attractions in Great Britain," Brian remembers.

"With this semi-fame we knew we had to buy better equipment, and frequented Jim Marshall's drum shop in Uxbridge Road.

"Along with other bands, we encouraged him to build amplifiers for our needs.

"Later, Jim would ask us to try his 'Number One' amp at gigs, and we did, with much success. Our first PA system was made by Jim, and was the first that could cope with drums, guitars and even bass going through it.

"We were the loudest band in England,

Chart darlings: The Tremeloes

at least for a while!"

Graham Scott was replaced by Rick Westwood on lead guitar and in 1960 the young band turned professional - accepting a five-month engagement at Butlins in Ayr.

"Dave, Alan and I were also being used as a backing session group by Decca Records on many hit records of the time; by Tommy Steele, Delbert McClinton, Jet Harris and The Vernons Girls.

"This all happened just before our Decca audition and was fully instrumental in our signing to the label."

Famously, Decca auditioned both The Trems and new Liverpool beat-combo The Beatles on the same day.

They rejected the latter in favour of Poole and his pals, saying 'The Beatles have no future in show business.'

The deal signed, The Tremeloes became

chart darlings, with Top 10 hits aplenty:

Do You Love Me? hit the top spot, Twist and Shout made number three, and the band followed those with Candy Man, Someone Someone, I Want Candy, and Three Bells, to name but a few.

Chip Hawkes joined Alan, Brian, Dave and Ricky for a manic touring schedule before Brian left in the late 1960s, followed eventually by Chip, and both explored solo careers.

The Tremeloes were both the first and the last band to appear on the legendary Ready, Steady, Go! show, and shifted millions of records during their time. In the '60s they were also the first band to tour Australia, blazing a trail for their peers.

Alan Blakley passed away in 1996, but Dave and Rick kept The Tremeloes name rolling through the decades, and it continues today.

Brian moved his family to Milton Keynes in the late 1980s and continued performing, both as a solo artist, and with his band Electrix.

But there was a new, second generation of Poole musos at work by now - daughters Karen and Shelly.

"They used to tell their teachers that they were going to be famous songwriters when they left school," Brian said.

"When they were about 14 years old they began coming home late.

With friends: Brian (far right) with Bert Weedon, Jess Conrad, Joe Brown, Jim Marshall and Chas McDevitt

"When we questioned them, they said they'd been writing songs with their boyfriends.

"The next night they arrived with their boyfriends and a tape - on it were four songs played roughly on a Casio Keyboard.

"They weren't great songs but you have to start somewhere.

"They said they would call themselves Alisha's Attic...when they were six or seven years old, they had an imaginary friend called Alisha - if something had been broken, spilt or someone had painted on the walls, it was usually Alisha!"

Echoing their father's dream-to-reality trail, Alisha's Attic would eventually find fame with the album Alisha Rules The World, which spawned the hit I Am, I Feel.

Critical acclaim followed the pop hits, and the girls were nominated for Best Newcomer at the 1997 Brit Awards as well as being shortlisted for an Ivor Novello.

Two more albums followed before the sisters called time on Alisha's Attic, but they carried on putting pen to paper for others - Karen's many credits include Kylie Minogue hits, while Shelly's name has been associated with Janet Jackson, Jack Savoretti, Mark Ronson, Paloma Faith and

> **"We were the loudest band in England, at least for a while!"**

Gary Barlow - just the surface of a hugely successful career.

"Someone asked me what my proudest moment in rock 'n' roll was and I had to think - being named Top of the NME polls in 1963? Appearing at the Albert Hall in the Poll Winners concert for three consecutive years? Getting to Number One with Do You Love Me?

"There are many," Brian realises, "But the moment that gave me total satisfaction was looking into the window of HMV in Milton Keynes and seeing my daughters staring back as 6ft cut-out advertisements!

"After that occasion, our daughters gave us many more reasons to be really proud."

Back in 2005 it became too hard to ignore the need to scratch the musical itch once more, and so Brian reunited with The Tremeloes for the first time in almost 40 years. They played a Tsunami Appeal show at The Stables, organised by The Barron Knights and also featuring fellow industry stalwarts Chas & Dave, Jess Conrad and Joe Brown.

And the music continued; in the summer of 2017, the band were back out on the circuit, with Brian at the microphone, playing to full houses.

Solstice

"I thought we'd never get out alive but, to our surprise, once we started playing, the bikers seemed to like us and eventually adopted us."

Prog-rockers Solstice first surfaced in 1980, founded by guitarist Andy Glass and Mark Elton on violin and keys.

Over the years there have been splits, periods of inactivity and many musicians passing through the ranks, but they are going strong today.

Rated highly on the national platform, the band is also a prolific part of the local scene, and Andy has played music, taught it, and encouraged numerous budding players to stick with it and find their sounds.

With Solstice he has played Reading and Leeds festivals, Glastonbury, and at Stonehenge.

When Solstice went on hiatus, Andy toured the UK and Europe with Bill Withers, and enjoyed an extensive USA and European trek with Jethro Tull.

But Solstice has always been his musical main-squeeze.

Andy looks back at the early Solstice days, and the early days of new city music.

"The music scene began for me at The Starting Gate in the heart of the city.

"When we arrived, as youngsters, to find a pub full of huge Hells Angels, we were bloody terrified!

"I thought we'd never get out alive but, to our surprise, once we started playing, the bikers seemed to like us and eventually adopted us. We would play for their wild, spontaneous festivals on the still-to-be-developed land, where they would set up a makeshift stage and 'borrow' a generator from one of the numerous building sites.

"They even came on tour with us around the UK to 'protect and provide.'

"Our spiritual home became The Peartree Centre. We played there all the time, all the MK bands did.

"There were touring bands too, and I remember watching Jason Bonham play."

As Solstice toured the UK they built a following thanks to numerous shows at venues like the London Marquee, before time was called on the band.

"When Solstice split in 1985, my involvement in the MK scene took a different direction. Saxophonist Boysey

Battrum, bassist Craig Sunderland and I put a band together called Backstreet, specifically to support John Martyn at one of Mike Paton's Woughton Centre gigs.

"We were joined by Graham Dee and Pete Hemsley, and spent the rest of the '80s and beyond playing residencies at Dukes in the Winter Gardens, Directors at the train station, at The Point, and a thousand other gigs that welcomed us – because we were a good band that played covers!

"My passion for music led me to put a studio together, while also working as a session player for a variety of acts and labels, and one thing led to another…the Bill Withers gig dropped out of the blue, and Jethro Tull came about from working in the studio with the main man, Ian Anderson.

"The studio also kept me in touch with some of the great dance and techno music that was being made in the city and ironically a remix album of Solstice music by The Lord's Garden (Pete Hemsley and Craig Sunderland) would be far more successful worldwide than any of the originals.

"The album was signed to Sony, and one of the tracks was used by syndicated television show Heartbreak High…it's a strange old world.

"Music has given me so much, and never more so than when creating with Solstice"

"Solstice reformed in 1996, but the only Milton Keynes gig we did was at the Open University.

"Running the Milton Keynes Rock School, I watched Acle Kahney (Fell Silent and TesseracT), Noddy Mansbridge (Heart Of A Coward) and many others mature from kids into incredible musicians. Running the Riot Competition over the years, I've watched some of the bands shaping the MK scene.

"I remember being totally amazed by the whole vibe at our first gig, and that generosity of spirit from the audience has been there, sustaining us and drawing us back, ever since. Great chemistry is a wonderful and rare thing. Music has given me so much and never more so than when creating and performing with Solstice."

In 2010 Solstice delivered Spirit, and chose to launch their first studio album in 13 years with a date at The Pitz.

Unknown to them, Steven Wilson, founder of prog-rock masters Porcupine Tree, was among the audience.

Solstice later discovered Steven had been a fan for aeons.

He first clapped eyes on them in 1982 in Hemel Hempstead: "I had heard Marillion on the Friday Rock Show, and, at the age of 14, went along to see them," Steven told

*Jethro Tull's Ian Anderson
in musical flow with Solstice*

Festival Music, "Support on that night was Solstice. I bought a copy of their Pathways demo tape which I have to this day.

"Many of the new prog bands were playing live in and around Hertfordshire and Buckinghamshire, local to where I was living. But Solstice were the best.

"Musicianship-wise, they really stood out and were very accomplished in what they were doing. And with the violin player adding a folk aspect to their music, they stood above the 'rough and ready' approach of many of the other bands.

"The live shows were always fun, another thing that stood them out from the crowd. I would stand in awe at the magical music being created.

"I remember the guys in Solstice looked 100 years old at that time, with all the hair and beards, as if they had just pulled up with the cosmic caravan in tow...but they looked authentic.

"Seeing them at the Spirit launch gig almost 28 years later, I couldn't believe how much younger Andy looked!"

The Spirit release was followed up in 2011 with the album and DVD, Kindred Spirits.

Not long before the release was set to be pressed, an email popped into Andy's inbox from acclaimed Marvel artist and fan of the band Barry Kitson, who had picked up a copy of Spirit and was quite taken with it.

The result of that email is the stunning artwork that runs through the live album package.

In 2013, the union continued on Solstice's fifth studio album, Prophecy, a conceptual collaboration with Kitson. It also included remixes by Steven Wilson.

"As a fan of our debut Silent Dance, he asked if the multi-track tapes still existed as he fancied remixing a couple of his favourite tracks.

"Bearing in mind he's remixed classic albums by Jethro Tull, Yes, King Crimson and more, I made sure I found them," remembers Andy.

"The result is three beautifully-realised Steven Wilson mixes that make up the bonus tracks on Prophecy."

Critics declared it to be 'arguably one of the finest albums to come out of prog-rock Britain in the last 20 years,' and yet their debut release refuses to go quietly either, with Prog Rock magazine calling it an 'album that saved prog.'

The sixth Solstice studio album, Sia, with new vocalist Jess Holland, is released November 2020.

Del Bromham

Del Bromham/Stray

He has been managed Charlie Kray, influenced Iron Maiden and played with Black Sabbath. Del doesn't just play rock 'n' roll, he is rock 'n' roll!

Del Bromham formed Stray in 1966, while still at school in Shepherds Bush, London.

The band became familiar on the live circuit, and gradually moved from R'n'B covers to original psychedelic rock.

"We called ourselves Stray because it was a short name and sounded good," Del says.

The young player had kitted himself out a little while earlier: "I bought my first solid electric guitar around 1965 in a small shop in Hanwell, West London, called Jim Marshall music.

"Nobody knew then that he would become a legend in the business."

Stray supported artists including The Groundhogs, and hopped onto the Weeley Festival billing in Essex, joining T.Rex, The Faces and Status Quo on the bill.

When a pyro went off during their set, it was mistaken for distress flares in nearby Clacton-on-Sea – lifeboats were scrambled!

The band sent a donation by way of apology.

They toured Europe with Ten Years After, racked up dates with Deep Purple, Free and Genesis, and played the Reading Festival in 1972, sandwiched between Status Quo and Wizzard.

Del performed in a suit made of mirrors. Not the most practical of attire, but it certainly made an impression: "I'm told that it looked amazing."

One year later, and Slade frontman Noddy Holder's reflective top-hat materialized.

In July 1973, the hard-gigging quartet supported a young Black Sabbath at Alexandra Palace.

Live shows aside, and the band sated fans by releasing one album a year during their first few years together.

When vocalist Steve Gadd bowed out in 1974, vocal duties were taken by Pete Dyer.

A trip Stateside followed in 1975 for dates with Spirit and Canned Heat.

Ozzy Osbourne checked in for one show in Hollywood.

He told the band he'd like to produce

them. That didn't happen, but they did give Sabbath's frontman a lift back to his hotel on the Sunset Strip after the gig.

"In the same car the following day, we found this elk horn full of dubious-looking white powder hidden down the back of the seat," Del recounted years later.

"I'm not saying that Ozzy left it there, but make up your own mind."

Stray were also managed, for a short time, by Charlie Kray, sibling of the infamous Ronnie and Reggie twins.

"It was all a publicity stunt, and we made all the daily papers, but it backfired -

other bands were terrified of us."

In 1976 they were added to the debut British tour by Kiss (promoters were concerned that the US rockers wouldn't shift enough tickets on their own), which was followed by a supporting stint with Rush.

Stray went on to headline London's Lyceum Ballroom with Motörhead in support, but things were coming to a head.

Wrong choices and bad luck meant the band never achieved the commercial success that was expected of them, and which they so deserved.

Before 1977 came to a close, having tucked away well in excess of 2,000 shows, the band that many industry folks thought could be the next Led Zeppelin had called time on the music. Stray was done - at least temporarily.

But while the remaining members stepped away from music, The Del Bromham Band became the focus of its founder.

A year or so later, and a move to the new city beckoned: "Back then, Milton Keynes, as we now know it, was virtually non-existent.

"There was certainly no city centre, but I found there was a lot of good local music going on, and pubs which seemed to encourage live music.

"One band was Teaza. They were due to go into the recording studio and asked if I would come up and produce the tracks.

"While I was here I found a house and it's almost like I never went home. I've been here ever since!"

In the decades that have followed, various incarnations of Stray have appeared, with Del as the almost constant driving force of the hard rock troupe,

"I'm not saying Ozzy left it there, but make up your own mind"

which has put 11 studio albums in the racks. Whether with Stray or stage-stepping in a solo capacity, Del has accumulated a keen audience for his sounds, and his influence is far-reaching.

When Del was working those London clubs in the early days, a young Steve Harris would regularly be in the audience, lapping up the live encounters and harbouring dreams of a successful career in sound.

He has gone on to accumulate record sales in excess of 100 million as bassist and leader of Iron Maiden.

Del and Steve first met at the Woughton Centre in Milton Keynes when Maiden played a now-legendary warm-up date at the venue. They now regularly swap rock 'n' roll tales over a beer or two.

The two bands have toured together, and Maiden gave a favourable nod to Del when they covered Stray's track All In Your Mind on the B-Side of the Holy Smoke single in 1990.

Stray celebrated their half century in 2016, and late in 2018 Del released the solo album, White Feather.

The music continues.

Del at Stony Stratford watering hole The Fox & Hounds (2004)

Eddie Stanton

"I had picked up how to play a bit of guitar and piano, and I wrote to amuse friends and annoy the adult world."

It was the 1970s, and at Stantonbury Theatre a songwriting workshop being hosted for students from around Milton Keynes was about to make a big impact on one in particular.

It would seem that the art of music-making was something to be encouraged in education back then; and the workshop was led by husband and wife folk aces Peggy Seeger and Ewan MacColl.

One of the pupils was a young Eddie Stanton. He was already attuned to the power of music, and the course inspired him some more: "I had picked up how to play a bit of guitar and piano, and I wrote to amuse friends and annoy the adult world," he recalled.

He remembers watching The Sex Pistols deliver their debut TV appearance on the So It Goes show. It had a huge impact: "By the next week, I'd gotten Melody Maker and began rehearsing with a young band called Eater."

After a couple of rehearsals, Eddie started making contacts of his own, and with London calling, he moved to the big smoke: "I have the claim to fame of being the last person to play The Roxy venue. It was an audition night, and I was the last one to perform..."

Eddie joined The Piece of Crecy: "We were sort of post-punk, like grunge but 15 years too early..."

Word on TPOC spread using the network of fanzines, and the band picked up a following.

And then Eddie went solo. After too much liquid refreshment during a gig at Northampton's Racecourse, Eddie said he could do better on his own; grabbed some gear and played some stuff – before being carried out of the haunt!

Nonetheless, that night he was offered a gig on a bill also featuring Bauhaus, with John Peel down to MC the show.

Eddie was now out on his own.

Eddie hotfoot it to Iceland

New city druid and singer Eddie Stanton, on a new venture.

With his new band, which played Craufurd Arms in Wolverton last week, planning a tour of Iceland in May or June. dates in England, he will play two concerts in Iceland's capital, Reykjavik.

Being rather off the beaten track, the country does not have many pop concerts from foreign musicians, so it seems Eddie may have a chance of becoming big in Iceland.

As a spokesman for his record company put it: "Nobody else seems to want to go there."

DELAY OVER SINGLE

THE RELEASE of Milton Keynes druid Eddie Stanton's single Tales from the Raj has been put back.

It is now scheduled for release by Polydor in mid-January.

Meanwhile Eddie, pictured above, has written the title track of a new album for DJM's Luna Label.

It's called The Young and the Free, and is performed by Vietnamese Rose, who is married to local rock eccentric Wild Willy Barrett.

Released as a single this week, it was recorded at Pace Recording in Neath Hill.

When in the country Rose and Willy live in a mobile coach which is often seen in the area.

DRUID: Eddie Stanton praying for Iceland success

Now he needed a demo, and he was encouraged to make contact with a studio at Gawcott, a village outside of Buckingham.

That studio was owned by experimental muso Wild Willy Barrett.

Willy and John Otway had already experienced widespread fame with the track Really Free.

"They were living the lifestyle," Eddie recalled, "I remember Willy had a room dedicated to pinball machines at that point!"

Willy was impressed by Eddie's delivery, and suggested he put down an album worth of material.

The LP, Don't Throw Me to the Christians, was pieced together.

Singles were issued through Barrett's Black Eye Records label – Lucifer Wants Me For A Sunbeam was first in 1980, and then Milton Keynes We Love You (featuring MK's famous concrete bovine on the cover) followed a year later.

"That was decided upon much against my wishes," Eddie admits, "I thought it was a novelty song and too early in my career to be released!"

How better to promote Stanton's sounds than to put him on the road with Barrett and Otway?

Things were cooking nicely. And the odd bit of silly PR would ensure his name was regularly taking up column inches in the press. Contrary to popular belief, Eddie's father wasn't a druid, and a news story about Eddie sacrificing his hamster was just that – a story.

"It was complete fabrication!" he promises.

Plans were afoot to re-record that aforementioned album which had never seen the light of day, but the sessions were shelved when a deal was inked with Polydor Records.

The fruits of that union delivered two singles in 1982, The Young and The Free, and Tales From The Raj.

Eddie waved ta-ta to Milton Keynes in 1984, and he has, as he says, 'pottered in and out of music ever since.'

He formed a retro punk band called God's Willy, eventually swapping that moniker for God's Tools, "A play on the earlier name, and also on The T-Rex song (Beltane Walk)," before arriving in Wales where he trained as a nurse.

But Eddie's alliance with Barrett and Otway continues and life only serves to fuel his musicality.

In 2019 Stanton, at the time based in Devon, launched a new label with hopes of delivering new music, and there was talk of a relocation to New Zealand.

Claire

"Milton Keynes felt like a blank page and Claire wanted to make their mark on it. We had to invent our own reality."

A chance meeting between Ian Wilson (frontman) and Peter Devine (guitar) in 1984 resulted in a new band for Milton Keynes.

The two were united by their shared taste in metal-bashing noise and pop music, and decided on the name Claire after the planet - not a girl!

"Milton Keynes felt like a blank page and Claire wanted to make their mark on it," Peter recalled, "We had to invent our own reality and did so with an attitude of our own."

Ian and Peter hit the live trail as a duo, but the line-up soon swelled with drummer Andy Williams, bassist Ian Williams and metal bashing courtesy of Iain Wilkie.

Studio time delivered demos and the band were interviewed on local radio, choosing to talk about their fictitious tour of Berlin. It added to the mystique...

When The Point complex opened its doors in 1985, Claire scored use of its nightclub space to rehearse in twice a week, and seized the opportunity to find their sound, stepping away from the earlier improvised sets. They soon became regular players at The Countapoint in Bletchley.

Claire sent a demo to John Peel in early 1987 and were invited in to record a Peel Session at the Maida Vale studios.

Good stuff.

The band were on a roll, but things took an unsavoury turn when they performed as part of an all-night party in Brickhill Woods – a shooting happened during their live set.

The band consequently found themselves on the front page of the local newspaper for all the wrong reasons.

Undeterred, the music continued, and subsequent gigs were swelled in number, thanks to that Peel Session and their newspaper dalliance. Proof that any publicity is good publicity.

But then where? Milton Keynes had given them all it could, so the band upped

"Life was tough and we had to resort to raiding supermarket bins for food"

and offed to South East London, where a rude awakening was in store.

"The area was depressed and it was difficult to get a gig," Peter remembered, "Life was tough and we had to resort to raiding supermarket bins for food."

With inter-band relationships strained, Iain Wilkie bowed out, and Chris Edwards came in.

Using donated cash, Claire recorded the LP Maxi Power Bulge, which provided the band with an authentic document of their sound, but wasn't strong enough to prevent them from splitting up before the release saw the light of day. The tapes remained in an attic collecting dust.

Fast forward 25 years, and in 2014 Peter was finally persuaded to revisit the LP. It meant making contact with his former band members after decades.

To his surprise, it was suggested that the band reform. The dust was cleared from the tapes, and gigs were booked.

Ian ditched the microphone and began taking care of samples, effects and keyboards. Ben Suttey was brought in to deal with the vocals, and live shows became a thing once more.

Until drummer Andy cut loose, that is, and the band again went into hibernation. But the remaining members still had the buzz, and wanted to make music.

Ian, Peter and Ben invited bassist Gerald White and drummer Darren Capp to join them, and Exploding Ear Ensemble was born in 2017.

Currently, their 'post noise mutated malevolent punk jazz with a pinch of disco disaster' is causing trouble for ears everywhere.

Claire in cuttings (above)

Exploding Ear Ensemble (left): Bringing the punk jazz in 2020

The Blues Collective

"The Blues Collective were a rock 'n' roll riot on stage and off and the members formed lifelong friendships that are as strong today as they were then."

A musical comedy set in Chicago was a smash hit far and wide, and in Milton Keynes The Blues Brothers was the catalyst that stirred a group of creatives into musical action. Things would never be quite the same again...

"A load of us MK music lot were hugely into the film around 1985 or 1986," recalled Caz Tricks, "Scribbo invited me to be part of a new band with that vibe, and I jumped at the chance."

Caz would take the microphone alongside Lorna Scriven as the feisty, sassy backing singers in The Blues Collective.

"That was the beginning of my adventure in one of the best things I have ever done. The Blues Collective were a rock 'n' roll riot on stage and off, and the members formed lifelong friendships that are as strong today as they were then."

The line-up had its core members, but it was a fluid operation and 'membership' varied from around 12 players to 22 – with

"We had so many laughs and a few punch ups!"

occasional guests popping in to take over a song or two.

"We had our own on-stage barman, Desmond Reid, who did so much more than ensure we stayed topped up with our favourite tipple during the gig – he was our on coach and backstage entertainment too."

The Blues Collective made their stage debut in November 1986 at The Woughton Centre, "I could be wrong about that date, though," admits Caz, "There was a lot of booze involved!"

But whatever the calendar date, the band played the gig doing their bit for sales of sunglasses in the new city, and giving music fans something warm and upbeat to feast on.

Not surprisingly, the band struck a chord with many, and a Collective gig became a hot ticket.

The band spread their musical love all over the place with similar success – their feel-good fun was lapped up; from London hot-spots including Dingwalls

and The Mean Fiddler, to The Fringe Festival in Edinburgh, and the Tic Toc in Coventry: "We gigged with some great acts like Bad Manners, Desmond Dekker and Wilko Johnson. We had so many laughs, television appearances, an album of original songs produced by the much-missed Big George, and a few punch ups!

"Some of us had children during those times, some of us now have grandchildren who are musicians.

"There was, and is, lots of love.

"It was great music with wonderful people.

"Whenever you are part of a group of people who undertake a creative endeavour, you take risks together, work hard, and you just know instinctively when it works, and when it rocks.

"You are involved in something with great depth, even if to those outside, it looks like it is just a bit of a lark. An incredible bond is created and despite ups and downs creatively and personally, there is something really special that adds another level to the relationships," Caz realises, "It's magic.

"I am just relieved that social media wasn't around then for so very many reasons!"

Blues and boozy: The Collective at work and play

Monster In The Closet

"Kate drove like a loon through a rather weak police cordon to get us onto the site and the mayhem continued from there."

Monster In The Closet (or Monsters In The Closet, as they were christened by their faithful fans) were a real buzz band for a time.

An unnamed incarnation of the noise-bringers can be traced back to the summer of 1988, but that line-up was changed (early bassist Tim Smith left, and was replaced by Michelle Durrant) and expanded (Julian Pentz and Kate Westell were brought in on electro acoustic viola and drums and percussion), before settling down in the autumn of the same year.

Kate's arrival gave the band its second drummer, joining with frontman Keith Vippond in hitting the hard things.

Alex Limburg Bond was on guitar.

The beats served to give them a more 'tribal' sound, and the name Monster In The Closet was suggested.

The Bob Hope Brothers Radio DJ from Community Radio Milton Keynes (CRMK) came up with the moniker, after the mid-80s spoof flick by the same name.

The first release proper by the Monsters was Living In Shadows (Again), which appeared on a Back Beat Records compilation.

The Monsters didn't stay a secret for long, and the trickle of fans soon turned into a fervent following.

Where Monsters played, disciples turned out en masse: In March of 1990 they gigged at The Cuba in New Bradwell, and the place was so crowded it became physically impossible to cram any more bodies into the building once the band hit the stage.

The landlord was onto a winner and the bar smashed its record for sales of liquid refreshments that night.

Monsters also entertained an audience of more than a thousand when they cut loose in the Big Top at the Maydaze Festival in Campbell Park a year later.

They were scene familiars, and scene favourites who attracted "big enthusiastic crowds at The Countapoint and Madcap, venues that were part of a vibrant counterculture scene in MK at the time.

site and the mayhem continued from there!

"Hawkwind decided it was time to have a punch-up on stage, which was the highlight of their set. Oh, how we laughed!

"Playing gigs with Keith in soundchecks when he was sober and very tight with his rhythm on the drums," was a great thing, remembers Julian.

"When we started it was a bunch of mates jamming the same riff for ages which mutated into Monsters. There was always a sense of humour, a good vibe between us and we all learned as we went along," reflected Julian.

The journey allowed the Monsters to share in some weird and wonderful adventures.

Playing a free gig in Brighton supporting Hawkwind, for one: "Getting onto the site was a laugh, as the farmer who owned the land had covered the place in slurry!

"He was chased away by a rabid bunch of travellers in a souped-up mutant 4x4.

"Kate drove like a loon through a rather weak police cordon to get us onto the

"The gigs were always more nerve-racking though, and you never knew what he would or wouldn't say when he was in the 'Red Zone', with more than six pints in his system!"

The band called time in 1992, but they left some truly great memories behind.

"The Milton Keynes music scene was vibrant because all kinds of musical styles got mixed up with each other; reggae, punk, pop, dance, indie, ska punk, alternative and good hard-rocking rock 'n' roll," said Julian.

"In Monsters we combined them all and got away with it, and that for me was very exciting."

Harlequin

"We told them about one of our tracks called 'Fucking Amazing,' which
was about taking cocaine. We never heard from them again."

With their trippy guitars, banging beats and a rough-edge, Harlequin were a fairly unique proposition in Milton Keynes during the early '90s, appealing as much to the festival-loving fraternity as they did to the rock-heads.

They had the look, the tunes and the attitude.

But perhaps they were too edgy for the men with the cheque books, because Harlequin scared off those in control.

They never won the fame game, but they won a legion of fans in the new town.

Frontman Bitz recalls a band every bit as colourful as its name...

"It started with the Squelchfoot Blues Experiment in the late '80s.

"We were just a bunch of hippies, learning our instruments and writing music we could play while we were tripped off our faces.

"It was more jamming than playing actual songs. This morphed into Illumini, which became more structured in both songwriting and performance.

"Illumini had quite a few line-up changes. We lost a few to the rave scene that was kicking off.

"Let's just say they wanted to be ravers rather than rockers!

"The final line-up for Illumini was Bob Milthorpe on drums, Stuart Thomson on bass, Storm Fisher on guitar and vocals, Rick and me on vocals.

"Some names of note who came and went in the band were Heidi Kemp on vocals, Tony Delahaye on guitar, and Gary Mac on bass.

"We were a festival party band, spending two, maybe three years playing locally in Milton Keynes and hitting the festival scene up and down the country.

"Due to a series of unfortunate events we ended up going our separate ways, and after a short break in the wilderness, myself, Stuart and Bob got together with Adam Monroe and formed Harlequin.

"Lila Higgins and Sue Milthorpe joined us as backing vocalists.

"Games Workshop were starting a record company called Warhammer

Fantasy Records. One of their products was a Harlequin figure, so we decided to call ourselves Harlequin to see if we could get noticed by the record company.

"We got hold of some old leather jackets, trench coats and trousers and painted them in harlequin colours to match the figures.

"We went off to Nottingham to a Games Workshop convention and when we got to the venue, wearing our Harlequin colours, we walked through the hall, up to the bar, bought a beer, casually walked out on to the balcony and waited.

"Sure enough, the CEO of Warhammer Fantasy records came to see us and asked if we were a band.

"Obviously, we said, 'Yes, called Harlequin.'

"He asked us for a demo tape and we said we'd get one to him in a couple of weeks. At the time, we'd only just started writing songs, had three rehearsals, and had done no gigs.

"We left Nottingham, booked a weekend at Pace Studios, recorded the four songs we had, sent them the demo and got signed.

"From this point on, we wrote and rehearsed eight to 10 hours a day, seven days a week.

"We were still a party band though, and it was still sex, drugs and rock 'n' roll.

"Three months in with Warhammer Fantasy Records, and after recording in Newcastle with Tony Platt (who engineered AC/DC's Back in Black album) we went back to our record company to discuss a tour with some big named metal band of the time.

"We talked about songs and told them about one of our latest tracks called 'Fucking Amazing', which was about taking cocaine. This may have been a bit much for them as we never heard from them again.

"There seemed to be a trend appearing; we were about to be booked for a university tour, everything was confirmed, they just wanted to see us live.

"We did a gig in Fishermead which the promoter came to. After watching the gig he decided that we probably weren't what they were looking for.

"He said he didn't think the crowd bringing lines of cocaine on the backs of cigarette packets to the band on stage, and the band snorting said lines whilst playing, was really the impression they wanted to portray.

"The band had become such a catalyst for partying and fun that at one gig hardly anyone turned up, which was unusual as we were selling out venues at the time.

"We packed the gig down, drove back to Giffard Park and realised why no-one was at the gig. There were more than 100 people in the car park waiting for us to get back for the after gig party.

"There are many tales I could tell of our rock 'n' roll lifestyle. It was a tremendous time in my life and I hope it was for everyone else in the band.

"To all the fans who came to watch us, I hope you enjoyed the ride."

Rock 'n' Roll shenanigans:Bitz

Ablemesh

In a pre-internet world, Ablemesh came up with a smart idea to get their sounds heard, declaring it 'a pre-emptive strike on music industry lethargy.'

In this era of streaming music, getting your hands on new sounds is easy. But as a teenager in the late '80s or early '90s, you'd visit the local indie-record stores to get your necessary ear-fix.

And of course, mixtapes were king among pals.

Pre-internet, local bands had to work hard to get their music noticed, too – and needed to be as creative out of the studio, as they were in it.

Some did it better than others. Ablemesh, which operated around the nucleus of songwriters Gordon Glass and Sean Walmsley, were a fine example of music-makers with a great artistic streak.

Although for them, the need to deliver music capable of standing the test of time was always more important than chasing quick success. They called it 'creativity without compromise.'

They knew that without securing decent distribution, unsigned bands faced an enormous struggle to have their sounds heard - and came up with Shareware.

It was, says singer Gordon, "a relatively small run of CDs with the potential to reach a disproportionately huge self-targeting audience."

Recipients would play the CD, tape the four tracks (should they choose to) sign it and pass to a friend.

It was a tidy idea that the band declared was 'a pre-emptive strike on music industry lethargy in general.'

Just three CDs were let loose. One went to the local library. And quite where the other two are today, no-one knows. Their journey mightn't be over yet though.

"One of the tunes on the CD was heard on the radio by a friend of the band as he was driving through Yorkshire," Gordon said.

The 1990s delivered other releases in glorious forms (flexi discs and cassettes) but fans expecting an album had longer to wait. Present Imperfect was recorded in 1995, and found its way onto the band's website more than a decade later.

But it wasn't until 2017, after being remastered, that it was made available for download.

Jon Poole (The Dowling Poole/Cardiacs) and Bob Leith (Cardiacs) both played on the opus. A second album, Sunshine to Mist, was also released in 2017.

Still with Gordon at the helm, this time around Charlie Barbara and Ella Rae joined for the ride, with guitar duties once again picked up by Jon Poole.

In the true spirit of Milton Keynes, the town didn't wait for the industry to come here, MK did things its own way – even holding its own 'Brit' Awards in 1992.
Ablemesh bagged two gongs then – for best band and best 12" of 1991

Togmor

*"Togmor? It sounded sort of 'rootsy' but also quite short and snappy.
Just the thing for a folk/rock band."*

2018 marked 30 years since Togmor came into being, and though there have been inevitable line-up changes during that time, founding member, guitarist Ian Rowe is still steering the folky ship.

Ian and John Gibbons put down the band foundations when a friend asked the pair if they would fill in with a few songs during the interval at a live music night in Bedford.

The show was a success and the landlord asked to book them for a whole evening.

Thinking it would be hard work as a duo, Ian set about recruiting some more friends to make up the numbers and create a bigger sound. Gavin Bunker (drums), Julian Williams (keyboards), Kevin Cranfield (bass) and Jonathan Ginn (fiddle) agreed to do the gig.

After a single practice together and

drawing from each members' back catalogue of songs and tunes, the newly named Togmor did their first paid gig at the Kent Arms in Bedford in autumn 1988.

It worked well, and they all liked the positive reactions their music-making was receiving.

"Gav suggested the name Togmor, which came from a book he was reading about the lifting of the Mary Rose from the seabed.

"It sounded sort of 'rootsy' but also quite short and snappy. Just the thing for a folk/rock band.

"So we called ourselves Togmor and went out to try and get a few pub gigs."

There was no big plan for the band, just the obvious enjoyment they took from getting out and playing.

"I think everyone in the band had their own ideas about where it could go but there never was a collective vision.

"I guess it would now be called 'organic growth,'" Ian said.

That so-called 'organic growth' took them from pubs and private parties to festival shows across the UK, and tours in France.

Plenty of support slots with major artists were enjoyed too, as the band stage-shared with the likes of Fairport Convention, Lindisfarne, Labi Siffre, and Rock Salt & Nails.

Naturally, their time on the road led to an accumulation of nice, naughty and nightmarish memories...

"I remember standing on a stage when we were about to play the festival finale in the medieval village of Bonnieux in France, and looking out over the audience at an incredible sunset. Then 'for refreshment' we had a bottle of chilled wine, supplied by the local vintner, placed in front of each of us.

"I remember thinking, 'It doesn't really get any better than this,'" Ian said.

"At another French festival the night after we had headlined, our then drummer Chris Davy, fuelled by some more excellent hospitality, thought it would be a good idea to jump over a wall.

"Misjudging everything, he fell 15ft fracturing his leg in two places. Travelling back to the UK as a 'special needs' customer of Ryanair, Chris saved our booked gigs by learning to play the kick drum with his left foot."

And there was a memorable Glastonbury weekend.

The festival had wanted Togmor for Saturday night viewing, but they were already committed to headlining their own Togfest event in Milton Keynes.

After a bit of negotiation, they were booked to open the Green Stage at Glastonbury the following morning, hopping straight onto the band bus after their Togfest show and making tracks to Somerset.

"I remember thinking 'this is proper rock 'n' roll,'" Ian said.

Supporting the Oyster Band at the Northampton Roadmender was another wow moment: "The gig was great but by far the best buzz was when, after we

> **"Fuelled by excellent hospitality, our drummer fell 15ft fracturing his leg in two places"**

played, there was a huge queue in the foyer at the merchandise stand but it was actually the Togmor CD they were queuing to buy."

The aforementioned Togfest was born when someone suggested the band should mark its 10-year anniversary, and they booked a show at Bradwell Abbey.

A few other bands joined the bill and the gig was a big success.

"The following year was a small free event held in the Cruck Barn at Bradwell Abbey. We asked for donations and all proceeds were given to Willen Hospice. It went down so well that we felt that we had to do it again. So we did..."

In 2018, the festival celebrated its 20th anniversary, and things have grown magnificently– it is now licensed for 2000, and is a highlight on the calendar of music fans near and far.

Around 200 people donate their time to create what has now become a 'weekend away.'

It runs over two days with 30 acts on three stages and will return in 2021.

Togmor is a unique collective in the new city soundscape, and one of the longest reigning.

"Bringing together the differing musical backgrounds of the band members creates a sound that is both steeped in the roots of folk and celtic music but played with an electric classical twist and some very rocky drums," Ian says.

"Without the band so many people from such diverse backgrounds would not have come together to form friendships and memories that will last a lifetime."

Sadly some Togmor players are no longer here, but in November 2018, 11 previous members came together from as far afield as Canada to play at the 'Togmor 30' concert to mark that three decade anniversary.

And with that milestone reached, Togmor are eyeing up the future.

"There will be more adventures," Ian promised.

"We're not done yet."

Getting fizzy with it: Togmor at the GO! Awards in Milton Keynes

Nicky Prince

A Eurovision encounter, chart success, and a private plane journey with the Godfather of Soul. Nicky Prince has been there and done that.

Nicky Prince 'souled out' at a young age. Raised on a diet of soul and funk in all its forms, her ears were held hostage by artists like Sly & the Family Stone, Parliament, Funkadelic and Stevie Wonder.

In the early 1990s she began letting her own voice loose, working first as a backing singer on the local scene.

Nicky has given her vocals to many new city bands over the years, including jazz-funkers United People and RPM.

And, as part of Gloucestershire-based drum 'n' bass meets dub-rap authority Flipside, she played Glastonbury for three consecutive years to 1999.

Magical moments?

There have been more than a few.

Supporting James Brown in Lebanon with the Cheryl Lucas Band was pretty swell, and she enjoyed a slice of the high life, travelling on a private plane with the Godfather of Soul himself, and flamenco band Gipsy Kings.

In 1998 Nicky enjoyed the Eurovision Song Contest experience, giving backing vocals to Imaani, with her track Where Are You?

"It involved weeks of rehearsals and promotion of the record on Top of The Pops, GMTV, Fully Booked and radio roadshows," she recalled.

And they very nearly took the coveted crown too – falling just seven points short.

With friends: Nicky (below) with Zed Bias and James Brown

In 2000, Nicky tasted chart success of her own when she was the featured vocalist on the Zed Bias garage hit Neighbourhood, which reached No. 25 in the UK singles chart.

In 2004 Nicky delivered her debut album, 'The Many Moods Of' which bagged the Best Album gong at the Citizen Go! Awards, and she has swelled her discography with a couple of EPs in more recent times.

Nicky has stage-shared with names including Roy Ayers, Courtney Pine, Martha Reeves & the Vandellas and Craig Charles, and it has been said that her voice evokes the kind of 'down home gravitas' that you might expect to encounter in Chicago, Detroit or New York.

Frigid Vinegar

Quirky and intelligent lyrics set to a splendid array of samples made
FV radio darlings for a while - but that's only part of the story.

It was a massive airwaves hit; a smart indie-alt hip-hop delivery, waving goodbye to the millennium and bringing in the new one. Within a month of the recording session that delivered Dogmanaut 2000, the quirky track, with its brassy sample of It's Not Unusual, was doing splendidly; John Peel was spinning it on his Radio 1 show, and Steve Lamacq followed suit, championing Frigid Vinegar fabulously well.

"The song went on to be the most requested of the year on Lamacq's show," says Alex Lusty, the man responsible.

A session at Maida Vale studios followed, and the buzz kept building.

"The song transferred to daytime with Chris Moyles and Jo Whiley among those playing it, and I was asked to perform on the poptastic Radio 1 roadshow for a full week, and again two weeks later. I was the only act to do two full weeks and rubbed

shoulders with legends like S Club 7!" he remembers.

The man who began his career as a 14-year-old rapping jingles for Chiltern Radio DJs was on the up and up.

Frigid Vinegar, whose moniker had been inspired by a Reeves and Mortimer sketch ("It sounded punk"), released five singles in all.

The second, How Cheap Is Your Love? landed at number five in Lamacq's end-of-year chart, and bagged single of the week in Melody Maker and The Daily Mirror.

"When we played Revolver at Bar Central it was at the height of Dogmanaut being all over the radio.

"The venue was heaving, people were queuing to get in, and many got turned away. It was a great night, exciting and humbling at the same time..."

But Alex kept things moving, giving up Vinegar for the four-legged 'hoolie rap'

Alex with Radio 1's Mark & Lard (left) and Boz Boorer (top)

players Acarine. A deal was inked with Roadrunner Records offshoot CNR and the album Call It On cut loose. The band were asked to record a song on the soundtrack for the Elijah Wood film Green Street, and obliged with Stand Your Ground.

As a self-confessed Morrissey fan, Alex made the most of it when an opportunity to natter with Moz's guitarist presented itself.

That chat turned into a musical match, and Alex and Boz Boorer recorded the album Life Goes On, as TheOneThree.

Two more albums followed, as the Happy Martyr.

Alex bowed out of Milton Keynes in 2006, but the musical juices still flow - there have been two solo albums taking things back to his roots in an 'old skool boom bap hip-hop vein' and he is currently stirring the pot with the rap/punk concoction Rats From A Sinking Ship who have gathered comparisons to Rage Against the Machine.

A prolific mob, they have put down their politically charged rants on five albums since 2015.

Another Happy Martyr release is on the cards, and back in 2017, Mr Lusty finally got around to issuing that Frigid Vinegar long-player: "Seventeen years late, and called Viva Lou Ferrigno, the original working title for the album back in 2000," Alex explained.

The album comprises the five original singles, and eight new numbers; "...in inevitable irreverent FV style," naturally.

Capdown

"John Peel got a demo and passed it to Steve Lamacq who started coming to shows..."

Capdown are one of the most popular bands to come out of the new city. And they are one of the groups whose music spread the farthest - before they called time on their first stint together they had literally rocked Japan.

The story started when a bunch of 14-year-old mates clubbed resources, musicality and influences and began making a noise together, back in 1997.

They called themselves Soap.

"I lived in the same street as Tim from around the age of eight," recalled bassist Boob.

"He got a drum kit one Christmas and I used to jump around in front of him with a tennis racket. That didn't last long before I was after a guitar.

"I'd known Keith since I moved to Milton Keynes, and he could play guitar really well.

"We started messing about, playing with other friends doing Nirvana covers...then Jake started hanging out.

"Anyway, Kurt had died, we heard Green Day, The Clash and The Sex Pistols, then Rancid, Minor Threat and NOFX, and along came an interest in the world and politics.

"After a while playing with Keith I realised he didn't need another guitar player, and I picked up a bass."

The Olney-based band recorded a demo, and people started getting interested.

Soon the name Soap was washed away in preference of Capitalist Downfall - Capdown had officially arrived.

They quickly became known as a ferocious, no-messing live band with a formidable presence.

Boob said: "We had the bug for some time, but I guess the first time I thought 'Shit, we're actually a band,' was when we supported Link 80 in Islington."

They signed with Household Name Records after delivering a typically perfect performance.

"The show was run by Lil and Kafren who own Household Name Records and they became our punk rock aunt and uncle.

"We were stoked. Tim ran outside and dented the roof of his car by jumping up and down on it so much!

"Shortly after, we were getting reviews in the national press, which was strange.

"Then John Peel got a demo and passed it to Steve Lamacq who started to come to shows, and supported us loads in the beginning."

In early 1999, the Time For Change EP became the band's first formal release.

Fans and critics alike loved it: 'The kind of music you can bop to all night long and not hate yourself in the morning,' one reviewer decided.

"We never had a big record deal with advances and tour support, so everything we achieved came from people liking the band and supporting us, as opposed to a company paying for radio playlists and favourable reviews in the press.

"We sacrificed education, relationships, and everything that resembled a normal life. Even health at times."

The band continued chasing the spit and sweat of live shows, playing numerous supports with artists including Pennywise, The Slackers and Knuckledust, and they rattled the cages of authority on occasion too – political fundraisers that the band were involved with were closed down by the boys in blue in the early days.

After two years of hauling equipment in

> **"We sacrificed everything that resembled a normal life"**

and out of venues with an almost constant tirade of gigs, the debut album Civil Disobedients arrived in 2000 and cemented their position as hot prospects on the UK punk scene.

NME reviewed it and declared that Capdown were 'the best ragga thrash radicals since Bad Brains – FACT!'

Although they put Milton Keynes on the map, they were too busy converting venues full of sweaty punters and laying down releases to figure too much on the local scene at the time.

"We were always a little disconnected from it, but that's not to say it wasn't great," Boob says.

"But at the time when things started to get really good in MK, we were off touring. "We worked so hard on the road – I think in one year we played in the region of 250 shows and wrote and recorded an album.

"The year after, it was 220 shows and an album. The scene wouldn't have happened if it hadn't been for The Pitz. It wasn't built around a band or a type of musical clique; it was built around a building and a shared experience...the smell of chlorine on the way in, and the bright lights and sports club feel."

Capdown's relentless approach to live shows meant their reputation began to precede them. Gigs got bigger, and the live net got cast much wider.

Hard-working: Capdown

Capdown: (clockwise from top left) Keith, Boob, Jake and Tim

"Going to Japan was a dream come true.

"I remember getting off the plane and the heat and humidity hitting us.

"I looked at my three best friends thinking, 'No way, someone has actually flown us around the world to do what we love.'

"It was an amazing feeling, almost indescribable.

"It's a very privileged experience being in a band and one we are all grateful for.

"There are low points too, though, and when things hit rock bottom it's amplified because you live in each others pockets all the time.

"Relationships got strained, but we were always close enough to get through and stay together."

Like any band on their travels, Capdown accumulated their fair share of 'on the road' tales too: "Tim had this really bad photo in his first passport, so we would always put his at the bottom of the pile.

"Whenever we got pulled over at customs, we would give them the pile of passports and they would slowly flick through them. When they would reach Tim's they would piss themselves laughing, get their mates over, demand to see Tim, point and laugh, laugh some more and send us on our way...usually without getting searched, which was helpful!"

Then there was the time Keith showed a record company executive the middle finger: "In the early days we sold out The Underworld on our first headline show – press, labels, agents, they were all there, and a guy from a big corporate label said to Keith: 'I'm from *****, you'd better play well tonight,' to which Keith said: 'I'm Keith from Capdown, you'd better fuck off!'

"Needless to say he did, and we were happy with that. The band was always for us and not to impress others.

"We were happy to make money if it was on our terms and fair to those who supported us.

"I think we achieved that and didn't need faceless multinationals to validate us."

Capdown led the charge until they pulled the plug in 2007. But that wasn't to be the end of the story.

In 2009 Capdown's Civil Disobedients album appeared in NMEs Top 100 Greatest Albums of the Decade, while Kerrang! magazine rated it as one of the five genre-defining 'must-hear' moments.

In 2010, an impromptu get-together re-ignited the spark: "The first gig back was actually a birthday party for me that my wife arranged.

"Some friends' bands were playing and someone turned up with a sax, so we

played a couple of tunes and really enjoyed it.

"When we split in 2007 I think we thought it was some sacred thing that couldn't be touched for fear of destroying it.

"After that night we all realised it was something we loved and something that was important to us, so why should we deny ourselves the enjoyment of doing it?"

Following a couple of unplanned live dalliances, Capdown announced they would be returning for two shows on the Vans Stage at the Slam Dunk Festival in London and Leeds.

Free of the industry hassles, Capdown just wanted to do what they were known for - and rock out.

"There was no bullshit to deal with," Boob said, "...just good friends playing punk rock together again."

The shows were a success, and in 2011 the band took to the road with a UK tour and a return to the Reading and Leeds Festivals.

In 2018 Slam Dunk hosted Capdown across its sites once more.

Dan Stock/Cusp

"As much as I'm a control freak, I don't like to be in control by default. It's good to have people to kick against..."

Dan Stock's name has been around for ages, and he's still only in his early 20s. He first came to attentions as a lad of 13, playing solo, before making a noise as one half of indie-rock duo Reporters.

They caused a few ripples before their brief musical trail ended, and Dan found himself alone once more.

He took time out to write new material before courting fans and labels, and came back blazing.

He was soon found showcasing his style at Reading and Leeds Festivals.

Hot-spot London gigs brought record companies sniffing. They liked the flashes of brilliance and a deal was signed with Heavenly Records in the same year, where his label-mates included Mark Lanegan.

A debut EP was issued in March 2018, but things aren't always as heavenly as they seem, and Dan began building a new music-making unit away from the label: "Sometimes being a solo artist can be a bit one dimensional, but having a band dynamic mixes it up and the outcome is much more exciting."

"The solo period with Heavenly was a massive learning curve"

He utilised the talents of people close by (drummer Jake Gooderham and bassist Adam Webster) and Cusp was born.

"It's still built around my songs, you can hear my love of Bruce Springsteen and The Smiths, but with a modern edge brought in by the other guys," Dan says.

He did still manage to break loose in 2019 briefly though; for a tour with Stereophonics. "They were the biggest and best gigs I've ever done. It was such a crazy experience to play to that many people with just a guitar.

"The solo period with Heavenly was a massive learning curve. It taught me what I want - and importantly what I don't!

"More than anything I want to make the best music I can and share that with like-minded people.

"As much as I'm a control freak, I don't like to be in control by default. It's good to have people to kick against and collaborate with. I feel refreshed, recharged and excited for the future."

Graveltrap

They were schoolboys with a collective dream who inked a record deal and trounced Metallica on more than one occasion.

G raveltrap rode the punk rock machine hard in the early noughties.

Frontman Dan Gibling looks back at the highs - and occasional lows - encountered along the way.

"All four of us attended Kingsbrook School in Deanshanger, where we used to spend lunchtimes learning to play our guitars, jamming out Nirvana and Therapy? covers.

We followed in the footsteps of two other successful Kingsbrook bands - Blindside (later called Phema) and Lupa, with whom we would become great friends.

Our first performance was at the end of year assembly, knocking out a cover of Nirvana demo Opinion, with me, John and Muzz all playing guitars, and a drum machine for the beat.

We played in front of the whole school then my pedal unplugged itself and the drum machine played up. It ended with a mixture of polite applause and mockery from the older kids.

Muzz took drum lessons and we recruited classmate Alex on bass.

Our first gig was in November 1999 supporting Off Target at the Madcap Theatre. Before, we had been the kids in the audience hiding around the back of the Main Arena venue, downing bottles of vodka and moshing around like possessed idiots to Blindside.

Now we were on stage, making our own noise.

John and I were writing songs and singing respectively, but it was after discovering Blink 182 with their dual approach that we found our forte; two frontmen singing melodies and harmonies over fast, hard, four-chord punk rhythms.

As other bands started to texturise their sounds with dynamics and guitar effects, we moved the other way - distilling our music down, concentrating our efforts on big choruses and catchy guitar riffs.

It was the music we liked most and we seemed to be getting quite good at it.

Our first Pitz gig was in 2000, again with Off Target, playing on the big stage with lights, smoke, and a proper PA and monitors.

More shows at The Pitz followed to bigger and bigger audiences, often in support of our friends and mentors Blindside and their friends and mentors Lupa.

The Blindside/Graveltrap double bill became a favourite at The Pitz in 2000 and 2001.

We appeared on the cover of the Citizen's music supplement GO! and my mum pasted our clippings in a scrapbook. I still have it to this day.

Around the same time we cut our first real pop-punk song, Oblivious, recorded for the Madcap release, Music from Legoland.

Our first EP Dilated came out in 2001. We copied it onto CDs at home, printed off the covers and stamped on the CD stickers ourselves - even my mum got involved!

Tracks appeared on various compilations and national radio stations.

In 2002, we made our first visit to Iain Wetherell at Premier Studios who used his know-how to work our rough sound into a rich sounding pop-punk band for our second EP, Write-Off.

It was the first recording I was really blown away with. We were starting to play with a better grasp of the dynamics of song structure, accents and fill-ins.

Blinding Music studios in Newport Pagnell became our home. I can't stress the importance of the studio in the development of the bands that practiced there, and its central part in the cohesion of the MK rock music scene.

Having a place to hang out, smoke weed, play backgammon, party and listen to each other's music was for me the catalyst that drove the scene forward.

It was in Blinding where mistakes were ironed out, promotional plans made and the fat well and truly chewed.

I'd sit there skinning up while listening to Phema knocking out their latest epic tune next door and think 'Crikey, that's HUGE! Listen to that riff, we need to up our game!'

Then I'd be fully motivated to write the best song I could.

It was this mutual appreciation and friendly competition that made the scene special for me. Like one big family of Milton Keynes misfits.

When odd-man-out formed from the ashes of Off Target, Graham from Phema

Punk rock players: Muzz, Dan, Alex and John

and I came up with a collective name for Phema, Lupa, Graveltrap and OMO.

The four MK rock bands spitting out the best stuff at the time would be known as 'The Four Horsebands of the Apocalypse.'

Our second EP Write-Off received positive reviews in the national press including Big Cheese, Metal Hammer and Rock Sound magazines, and slots on bills supporting the likes of King Prawn and Capdown around the country followed.

A promoter passed Write-Off to Moon Ska Records, who came to see us at The Pitz, offered us a record deal and put us in the studio to cut an album.

Concrete and Udder Chaos, a homage to our hometown and its infamous concrete cows, was issued in 2003.

That November we shared the stage with Capdown in the large hall at The Pitz, playing to around 1,000 people. A classy showcase of just how successful MK punk bands had become.

As our album did the promotional rounds, we picked up great reviews and a fair bit of radio play, both in the UK and internationally. We cut a video for our feelgood bounce-along pop-punk track SRJ.

The video landed on TV just in time for our first big Moon Ska tour. CD sales shot up and the video reached Scuzz TV. Thanks to a voting playlist system and our loyal fans, we topped their chart for three weeks.

I remember turning on the TV and seeing us sitting there at Number One,

"We were four suburban kids from MK, out on the road, living the dream"

ahead of Metallica and Less Than Jake - things were really hotting up!

In 2004 we invested in our own van and went out on a series of back-to-back tours.

It was our first real glimpse into the world of sex, drugs and rock 'n' roll and we learned the hard way you have to pace yourself and not be an absolute wreck.

Kids were singing along to our choruses and asking for our autographs. It was a bit weird, and I found it all a little bit fake.

Nonetheless, when we arrived at a venue, we'd jump out of the van as Graveltrap and indulge in the hedonism that came with it.

Our album was in all the High Street shops just above Green Day (a perk of having a name that started Gr...!) and our video on high circulation on rock TV.

We were four suburban kids from MK out on the road, living the dream.

I recall the buzz of returning to play a hometown show at The Pitz and seeing a sign on the front door saying 'Graveltrap - sold out' and having a line of kids outside begging us to sneak them in.

The biggest highlight of the band for me, was the feeling you get on stage when you know you are really hitting it on the button; everything bang in time, all the harmonies in tune and fully shredding your instrument.

You peel yourself away from the energy of the audience and exchange smiles with your best mates on stage and know you are creating something special for that moment in time. That's what made being in Graveltrap so special.

Although alcohol was always on our rider, we also started to become known as the punk band that asked for tea upon arrival. It confused promoters, but we had begun to learn how to tour properly. We would arrive at a venue, have a cup of tea and head out to see the sights and take in a bit of culture.

By the end of 2004, we had notched up big shows supporting Bowling For Soup, Lars Frederiksen & The Bastards, and our childhood idols Therapy?

We embarked on our first headline tour in 2005 and cut a new EP with Neema from Fell Silent producing. It was recorded at the new 4D Studios that had replaced Blinding Music.

Moon Ska wanted to pursue a more ska-based direction, but we were turning rockier by the day, so we parted ways and put the CD out ourselves on our own label, New City Noise.

Our new material showcased a more mature and darker sound with songs about alienation, paranoia and loss.

Due to balancing work and life commitments we cut back on the touring.

In 2006, despite being socially and personally at odds with the lifestyle of the band, we were writing our best songs and re-approached the four chord melodic punk rock with a better understanding of what worked, and what didn't.

We recorded what turned out to be our last EP, Self Adhesive Revelations, which contains the songs I'm most proud of.

By now, emo had gotten popular and more money could be made by putting on a rock disco where the kids could compare hairstyles and belt buckles, rather than support live music.

We called it a day in 2007.

The MK scene provided me with a family of like-minded individuals who were passionate about their music and about carving out an alternative lifestyle in a city where they didn't fit the mould.

The organic nature of how the scene held together, grew and fed itself is testament to the people involved and the passion everyone, musicians and fans alike, put in.

The cornerstones of The Pitz, Blinding Studio and the Citizen newspaper's GO! section gave solid foundations and spawned a mutually supportive and friendly scene.

Without promoters, journalists, photographers and of course the fans, there is no music scene, just a collection of bands who happen to be from the same geographical location. But we had a proper scene that grew organically and sprouted through the cracks in the concrete.

"I am proud to have been a part of it."

Graveltrap with Sammy Jones

285

Fono

"Our meeting was brief, but we took Jon Bon Jovi's advice to heart and lived by it in the coming years."

When Bon Jovi decided to open their stage up to a local, unsigned band for their 1996 shows at The National Bowl, they enlisted the help of the Milton Keynes Citizen newspaper to find a group with the necessary power and confidence to stand before 65,000 fans and rock out.

The competition was a major success, and in the days before digital deliveries, the Citizen office was swamped by jiffy bags stuffed with demo tapes, some arriving with accompanying bribes.

The new city never knew it had so many bands, with more than 100 local collectives mailing off their music, all hoping to grab the gig of a lifetime.

A panel of judges assembled at Great Linford Manor and began the task of ploughing through the sounds. Renowned producer GGGarth Richardson was working in the studio with Skunk Anansie at the time, and lent his ears to the elimination process, along with Linford Manor boss Pete Winkelman and various newsroom hounds.

A long session of interesting music later, and we had our winner.

New rock trio Seven won us over and were tasked with opening the bill.

"I can't begin to describe the excitement, but it was probably very similar to winning the lottery, and the next couple of months were a whirlwind for us," said frontman Del Currie.

"We met Jim Marshall and had a tour of the Marshall Amplification factory, and the company agreed to loan me Angus Young's guitar amps for the show.

"The week of the gig, I had an idea for a new song. We jammed it at one of the rehearsals and it felt really good.

"We decided to play it at The Bowl. I had a few opening line ideas and a chorus, so I knew I would have to ad-lib the majority of the song. It was called Burn Me Up.

"The same week, my father had hit his head in an accident and suffered a brain haemorrhage. It had been doubtful I was even going to be able to play, as I might have to go back to Northern Ireland to be

Fono during the early days: Ian, Andy and Del

with him. But my mum convinced me that dad wouldn't want me to come home and miss the opportunity – he would want me to play the show.

"It was a difficult decision, but I can't imagine how different my life would be if I hadn't played that day.

"We wanted to look professional for the gig – especially playing with Angus' amps, so we got a friend with a big red Parcel Force truck to take our gear to the Bowl.

"It was exciting pulling up to the gates and being directed to the load in area and dressing room. We took a few mates with us who were supposed to be our crew, but I don't think they fooled anyone.

"We were opening the show before Gun and Joan Osborne, and Jon from the Citizen was going to introduce us.

"I got my four Angus Young Marshall stacks set up, all of which had Angus's setting on, written in Sharpie – every knob was marked at 10, of course.

"It had started drizzling and I remember telling the crowd, 'We're just little guys up here playing the big guy's game. You're wet, we're wet, so let's just have a good time together,' and I think that won them over.

"After a couple more songs, I decided to have a little fun, and asked the crowd if they would be kind enough to cheer and make us feel good. They obliged.

"I decided to take it one step further and

> **"Marshall agreed to lend me Angus Young's guitar amps!"**

asked the crowd to jump up and down for me, and believe it or not, they did.

"The rest of the set is a blur, but we played with all our hearts and soaked up every minute of it.

"We finished off with our new song and I managed to ad-lib the lyrics without missing a word.

"We were informed by Jon Bon Jovi's PR person that he would see us at 6pm for 10 minutes. We were very excited to meet the man himself and were escorted in, CD in hand, which we asked him to check out.

"He said he would and even asked for my phone number, which he wrote on the disc with a Sharpie. Would he call?

"We hoped and believed that he would, and I think that's the reason my wife rushed to answer the phone for the next month, every time it rang. He never called. Our meeting was brief, but when I asked Jon if he had any advice for us, he imparted his wisdom: 'Never do a deal with anyone or give anyone a percentage of your work if you can borrow the money from your mum or charge it to a credit card instead,' he said.

"We took his advice to heart and lived by it in the coming years."

Seven went on to ink a US deal, changed their name to Fono and recorded their debut album at Linford Manor.

Del also set up Blinding Music studios in Newport Pagnell, giving the music scene a professional rehearsal space, which grew

Fono

to incorporate a new recording studio.

Fono went from strength to strength too – bagging a slot on tour with Goo Goo Dolls in the US, which saw the guys from Milton Keynes playing before an audience of 10,000-plus each night.

They swiftly shifted 100,000 albums, made good use of Janet Jackson's tour bus on the road, and racked up heaps of radio play.

"We were in Billboard Magazine as a new artist to watch out for, and hit the Top 10 in the new release airplay charts, between Bowie and Oasis," Del said.

Things were going so well Stateside that the band swapped Milton Keynes living for San Diego.

"It was close enough to Los Angeles for all of the music business stuff without us having to become an L.A. band."

Line-up changes occured, but the nucleus of Del and drummer Andy Ridley continued to drive the band forward.

Thoughts eventually turned to album number two, and the band found an old studio in a beautiful location, on the edge of a canyon.

They wrote and recorded daily for months, and by the autumn of 2003 were ready to mix the release.

When the master copies were left overnight in the studio, the band didn't give it a second thought.

But a devastating event would rob Fono of their hard work; Southern California had been hit by wildfires and when the band were allowed back to the area that had housed their studio, the vision that greeted them was crushing (left).

"Everything was gone. All of our recording gear, amps, drums, guitars and memorabilia," Del said, "All of the backstage passes I had kept in my pedal board from our tours, and even my pass for our Bon Jovi show. "Worst of all, we had lost the masters for our album.

"Months of writing and recording had gone down the drain. It was a devastating blow and one that we would never really recover from..."

The band released its last album, Too Broken To Break, in 2007.

odd-man-out

"That was the beginning of a halcyon few years of genuine community that burned with a spirit of cooperation, respect and chaos."

Formed from the ashes of post-rock mob Off Target, odd-man-out was the same band, minus frontman Paul Rivers. His job as promoter at The Pitz meant he couldn't be off playing his own gigs at the same time as running shows for others. Something had to give.

"There was no way it could have ended without a little splattering of blood across a bar room floor," says guitarist Pete Bagnall, "but we got over it and remain close to this day."

The slimline new band, with Pete and fellow OT members bassist Matt Gannon, drummer Dave Lloyd and guitarist Justin Hodges, took their name from a magazine headline and set about getting new material together.

During their formative months, the band made a connection with Blinding Music, and friendships blossomed with Blindside, Lupa and Graveltrap.

"There was something in the air that year," Pete remembered.

"We were all discovering our own individuality and music at the same time.

"It brought a level of camaraderie someone is lucky to experience even once in a lifetime.

"That was the beginning of a halcyon few years of genuine community around the MK scene that burned with a spirit of cooperation, respect and chaos.

"And it's where legendary late-night stitch-ups really developed into an art form - from gaffer-taping pallets to people, setting them on fire, or sabotaging their cars.

"Everyone was scared to fall asleep," Pete said, "Once, I woke up with a PA speaker on my head, blaring out The Final Countdown.

"Justin had poured poppers into my philtrum, Matt had gaffer-taped kitchen roll tubing to me, and several people were diving onto my stomach."

odd-man-out announced their noise for the first time on The Landfill EP.

"Justin and I tried to execute our artistic vision for the EP cover, which was a car driving the wrong way up a one-way street, which actually ended up

odd-man-out at Maida Vale Studios

looking like what it was; my shitty Astra Estate parked in the wrong direction on a Newport Pagnell school road with a very middle-class, yet polite gentleman, pointing out we were going the wrong way.

"The fact it wasn't perfectly executed didn't mean there wasn't thought and artistic desire behind it."

The scene in general was fertile with cool creators.

"As misguided as it sounds, at times it felt like our own little Washington or Seattle forming," Pete said.

In 2002 scores of shows were tucked under belts, and the band revealed an acoustic side for the Citizen newspaper's GO! Awards before winning a Radio 1 competition to support Jimmy Eat World at Nottingham Rock City.

"I wish I could tell you we won it entirely on merit, but the truth is, we'll never know.

"Our friend Scotty transformed into the best plugger the world has ever seen and hacked the planet!

"The end result? A combined few hundred votes for the other two bands and nearly 10,000 for odd-man-out."

In 2002 the band won a Radio 1 competition to support Jimmy Eat World at Rock City

OMO also got to record an Evening Session set in Maida Vale Studios for Steve Lamacq's Radio 1 show.

"The same studio The Beatles had used was now where we snapped ourselves defiling The Fab Four photo opposite the studio entrance door.

"The room consisted of individually acoustic-engineered wood cladding that cost more than £2million to install.

"It contained equipment we didn't know existed.

"We played like demons and the end recording was incredible."

2003 brought The Betty Ford Tour with Lupa and Phema.

"It was carnage, and the memories are hazy; Ecstasy parties in Leeds, Justin firing paintballs up his nose with a mini automatic paintball gun, flyers being stapled to arseholes and some of the most cramped sleeping conditions since trenches during the war come to mind.

"It did little to change the profile of any of the bands, but was one of the most fun tours I've been on," Pete admitted.

Following EPs, singles, tours, gigs galore, festivals, videos, charity shows, radio sessions and consistently good press

291

from the magazines and fanzines, it was time for an album to materialise.

But tragedy followed soon after.

"Not long after recording was completed, on May 23, 2004, a very dear friend of ours, Brendan Read was found dead. His passing signified the beginning of the end."

The party was over.

"We had lost one of the funniest people

we'd ever had the pleasure of knowing.

"If our early sold-out Pitz shows signified the beginning of the noise, celebration and chaos of our scene, then Brendan's passing was the bitter comedown the next morning."

The album's title summed up the state of the band; 'It All Ends Here...'

Bassist Matt left first and the playability never really recovered.

The album got great reviews, but an ill-advised decision to license the record didn't buoy the band.

odd-man-out was over, but with friendships still intact, the band members hold dear plenty of memories.

Pete said: "We buried odd-man-out knowing we had built an engine, fed it fuel and used it to get us exactly where we wanted.

"We mapped out our own definition of success and achieved it.

"Though we were never short of confidence, we didn't ever expect, or want to be, anything more than we were; one of the handful of flames that burned brightly and briefly out of a small town darkness."

TesseracT

*"Never did I imagine that I would see the TesseracT name
in lights in New York's Times Square."*

Many a youngster has plugged into an amp, or badgered those that pay the bills for a guitar or drum kit before convincing their suffering parents to turn over the garage for use as an ill-equipped rehearsal room.

Usually, it causes neighbour upset and headaches, before the majority of players discover girls and alcohol, and swap thoughts of stadium-filling for something a little less ambitious.

But some, like Acle Kahney, get the musical bit between their teeth and refuse to let it go...

Guitarist Acle first showed himself on the Milton Keynes scene in 2001, as part of Mikaw Barish.

The young rock quartet originated at the MK Rock School, a hub for rising musicians in the area.

If you showed a spark, they would nurture it.

"The rock school did a lot for the generation of bands at the time," Acle recalls, "I don't think I'd be where I am now musically if it wasn't for the school.

"One of our most memorable songs was Melodica. It was a hot, summer's day, and we had crammed into my garage with crappy drums and amps to jam.

"Our singer Aria found a toy melodica which was rotting in a box.

"We wrote the song on the spot - the first time I had ever done anything like that.

"We played it at all our shows until eventually the Fisher Price melodica couldn't hack it and Aria smashed it on stage."

When fellow MK players Temperamental floundered, Acle was invited into the ranks.

With a slight line-up reshuffle and a new name, Fell Silent was born.

The band also featured Joe Garrett, who has since turned his hand to songwriting for artists including ex-One Direction singer Zayn Malik, and drummer Chris Mansbridge, now keeping things in check with Heart Of A Coward.

"Fell Silent felt like my first proper

Acle with Mikaw Barish and (below) Fell Silent

Postones, Amos Williams, James Monteith and Abisola Obasanya, the people who would turn TesseracT from a solo affair to a full-blown band.

Acle stretched his time between the two bands for a while, bowing out of Fell Silent in 2009 to concentrate on TesseracT, which was turning into an impressively taut prog-metal unit.

The first album, One, with Acle showing his prowess in the production chair, had taken seven years to reach fruition.

It came out on the Century Media label in 2011. Sophomore release, Altered State, followed two years later.

It was divided into four movements: Of Matter, Of Mind, Of Reality and Of Energy. "It represents the transformations the band has gone through over the past few years," Acle said.

A live DVD and album compilation sated the appetites of fans, before album number three, Polaris, hit stores in 2015.

The band has racked up an impressive CV too – touring all over the world in their own right, and with artists including Devin Townsend, Meshuggah, Gojira, Megadeth and Karnivool. They've wowed on festival stages far and wide, including here in the UK; at Download at Donington Park, at Bloodstock, and Sonisphere on the

band," Acle remembers.

"We had a good following around Milton Keynes, and Enter Shikari took us on tour around the UK and Ireland playing some great venues."

Fell Silent also produced the album The Hidden Words, issued through Basick Records.

At the same time Acle was also tinkering away on material for his solo project, TesseracT, and through gigging with Fell Silent, struck up friendships with Jay

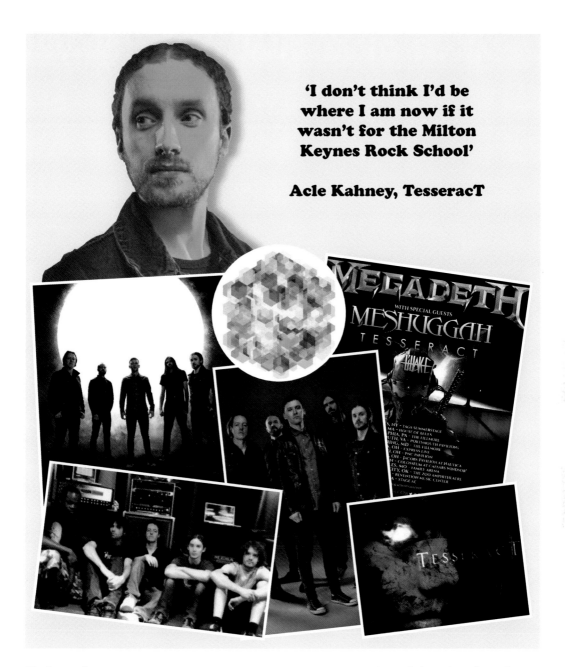

'I don't think I'd be where I am now if it wasn't for the Milton Keynes Rock School'

Acle Kahney, TesseracT

Knebworth estate.

"Sonisphere was great, we packed out the tent and had people queuing up outside to try and watch us."

The band has twice been nominated for a Golden Gods Award, for Best New Band and Album Of The Year respectively, and they grabbed the Prog Music Awards New Blood gong in 2012.

Singers? They've had a few, but after leaving in 2011, Dan Tompkins returned to the fold in 2014 and the band continues to go from strength to strength.

TesseracT released their fourth studio album, Sonder, in the spring of 2018 and number five is coming soon.

Despite the many award nominations and plaudits, for Acle, one night in NYC during the early days of the band still holds special memories.

He said: "Never did I imagine when TesseracT was a solo project in my bedroom in Milton Keynes, that I would see the name in lights in New York's Times Square."

Phema

"We knocked out a few EPs, including Milk & Beans, a pun on Milton Keynes that no-one seemed to get!"

During the mid-1990s, little by little and riff by riff, the seeds of a new scene were being sown.

Hungry kids with big guitars, Marshall Amps, and a desire to make a noise with their mates, were springing up everywhere.

These were the kids who had heard Kurt Cobain, Chris Cornell, Layne Staley, and the dozens who played and sang in their grunge-y shadows, and now they wanted to cut their teen angst loose too.

Over a couple of years, and totally organically, the alternative scene in the new city really started to shine.

At one time, you could barely move for the new breed of bands gigging around town.

Some were appalling, some were good to soak up a beer to, and others had glimmers of greatness, but when the pretenders and the part-time players called time on their dalliances, those serious about the sounds upped their game, matured and started to deliver on those early promises.

Venues were still plentiful then, and bands like Phema, Lupa, odd-man-out, and Graveltrap never struggled to find a gig, thanks to venues including The Pitz, Bar Central, The Main Arena and Zaks catering for the alternative crowd.

When The Pitz offered these bands the chance to cut their teeth alongside seasoned artists, audiences stopped using the support band set as an opportunity to nip to the bar, and started pricking their ears.

Blindside were one of the first out of the blocks to let that teenage inspiration loose: "Our first song together was Reprieve, a heavily Nirvana-influenced number that touched on the subject of suicide," recalled frontman Graham Hulbert.

"I was persuaded to change the lyrics to something a bit more accessible…

"Our first proper gig was at The Main Arena in 1998, and we continued as Blindside for three years or so, knocking out a few EPs, including the seminal Milk & Beans – a pun on Milton Keynes that no-one seemed to get!

"We managed to build a bit of a following around town and slowly clambered our way up the bill at The Pitz, and eventually headlined a couple of gigs there…"

In 2001, Blindside called it a day – in name only.

Guitarist Chris Bowman left the band, leaving Graham, bassist Adam Davison, guitarist Pete Joy and drummer Lee Harrington. A new moniker, Phema, was chosen.

Adam said: "We went to Russia in September of 2001 and headlined a gig for 4,000 people. That was pretty much the time when we decided to drop out of uni.

"In the December, we recorded seven tracks at Premier Studios and used three of them for the Blindside EP, which got a really good review in Rock Sound magazine and earned us a load of gigs around the country."

And that network of bands working together and supporting each other helped when Phema worked on their debut album in 2002, with Tom Platt handling production duties. It was issued in 2003.

"We scored a KKKK Kerrang! review, as well as getting great reviews in Rock Sound and Big Cheese for the self-produced album Oom-noom-shi'bi,"

"Biffy Clyro said we could tour with them, but their management didn't share the band's enthusiasm!"

Graham recalled.

"The title was taken from a line in the film Indiana Jones and The Temple of Doom, and the album included future crowd favourites The Answer and Unbound. It spurred us on to get some touring under our belts, and we spent the next couple of years trying to get noticed - as much as our crummy data entry salaries would allow."

Before too long, the sounds of MK were bouncing across the country, as The Betty Ford Tour, which also featured odd-man-out and Lupa, took to the road.

Phema recorded two EPs, using up all their imagination in the studio, and settling on the titles EP1 and EP2.

"Over the years we were fortunate enough to share a stage with Biffy Clyro, Clutch, Reuben and many others. Biffy actually said we could go on tour with them, but their management didn't share the band's enthusiasm!"

Phema reached the end in 2008.

"We'd all moved on in our personal and musical lives," Graham admits, although a couple of reunion dates were played.

"With hindsight I realise I was really fortunate to be part of that scene. It let someone like me fulfill my bedroom

Phema: Lee, Adam, Pete and Graham

ambitions of playing guitar in a band which is definitely something to be thankful for!

"If being in a band taught me anything, it's to always do what makes you happy, and not try and do things to please others.

"A lot of my friends went down the usual job route and have been successful, and occasionally I used to envy their financial comfort. But I chose to play in a band and feel I made the right choice.

"I have a lot of good memories from that time, and above all, no regrets – there is a lot of stuff I learned that I don't think I would have figured out any other way…"

In 2017, Adam Davison tragically passed away. The scene lost one of its best players, and everyone involved in that same scene lost a friend.

He was a special man.

Today, his bandmates are back in play, making music Adam would approve of in the band Athens.

Lupa

"I fondly remember the time Justin from odd-man-out staple-gunned a gig flyer to his bare ass cheeks in the middle of a service station."

Lupa, a group of Kingsbrook school-leavers had pooled their talents in late '95.

They slimmed from quintet to quartet a couple of years later and issued the Immerse EP on the eve of the Millennium.

In 2000, they travelled to Belgium for showcase dates with Universal subsidiary label Les Enfant Terribles.

"We spent the next few years hanging out at Blinding Music studios, partying and forming bonds with all the other bands on the scene at the time," frontman Tom Platt remembered.

And then they hit the studio and put down an album's worth of material: "It was the first time we had done anything even remotely good.

"My personal highlight of the band was the time when we were writing and recording The Sound Of Repair at Blinding.

"It was us carving out songs and finding our actual voices, rather than those of pseudo-American emulation that we, and particularly I, had been performing up

until then. We had some wild and beautiful days and nights at that place – and they usually had Blinding manager Lee Carter sitting in the corner, just as engulfed in the music as we were."

Lupa started work on the release in 2001.

The scene in Milton Keynes at that time was fluid, fun and supportive - and so when Phema began working on their debut album, it was Tom that handled production duties for them too.

The Betty Ford Tour, which featured Lupa, Phema and odd-man-out, followed.

"It was a riot," Tom admits, "I fondly remember the time Justin from odd-man-out staple-gunned a gig flyer to his bare ass cheeks in the middle of a motorway service station somewhere.

"The shop worker hadn't been trained to deal with that!"

Back home, the bands continued to ply their wares successfully.

Lupa's sound moved on, as did their name.

The Vatican Giftshop in 2004

In 2004, they became The Vatican Giftshop, and enjoyed tasty dates alongside Reef, Mark Lanegan and The Blockheads.

And when they eventually called time on the band, it wasn't the end of their affair with music; Tom maintained his skills by setting up a home studio, and now exercises his vocals and drumming skills in Our Man in the Bronze Age.

Guitarist Matt Clark stayed with music, but switched to working behind the scenes, at labels and publishers including V2 Records, Universal, EMI and Roadrunner.

His company also undertakes forensic royalty audits for high profile artists and supports the buying and selling of leading music catalogues.

When he's not doing that, he is busy overseeing the affairs of hard rock pioneers Deep Purple, who he now manages.

One time Lupa drummer Ben Hallett shifted Stateside, setting up home in Los Angeles where he worked on a number of musical projects including Queen Kwong, which led to an introduction to Joe Cardamone, frontman and instigator with post-hardcore noise makers The Icarus Line.

Before long, Ben was seated at the drum stool.

The uncompromising rabble then toured the UK and Europe with Killing Joke.

Ben's fourth show with the band was a packed out date at Camden's Roundhouse: "It was an exciting, but daunting experience," Ben remembers, "I was playing venues way bigger than I'd

The Icarus Line: Ben (second left), Alvin DeGuzman (centre) and Joe Cardamone (second right)

ever played before, with a bunch of guys I barely knew, so it was a pressure."

Back in his adopted home the live work continued at a pace, including a huge stint on the road with The Cult.

The studio beckoned soon after and The Icarus Line re-emerged with the critically acclaimed fifth album, Slave Vows, in 2013.

The band pushed the material to live audiences again, jumping on more shows with The Cult, A Place To Bury Strangers, and Primal Scream.

Keeping pace, work began on another studio opus, but the band were dealt a devastating blow when bassist Alvin DeGuzman was diagnosed with cancer.

A makeshift line-up was pulled together, and a tour with former Stone Temple Pilots frontman Scott Weiland went ahead.

But that was to end in tragedy, when, just a week into the tour, Weiland passed away.

An accidental overdose had silenced one of the voices of a generation.

"I'd only met him briefly. He was courteous, but clearly struggling," Ben said.

"He was a shadow of the man I saw at Reading Festival as a young fan. I don't think anyone in our band was that surprised by his passing because of what they had already seen.

"It was tragic and awful for his family, friends and fans."

Sadly, Alvin lost his battle with cancer, and with a realisation that things weren't going to work without Alvin as a part of the musical puzzle, The Icarus Line dissolved: "My time in the band gave me the missing string to my bow in terms of playing, which was punk/post punk," Ben said, "I needed that and feel way better for it."

Today, Ben lives with his wife and three kids in L.A and they own a successful vegan restaurant.

But he still has the passion for sounds: "I like the idea of making an album with different singers," he realises, "I'm working out my next move, and have a lot of ideas and music."

Heart Of A Coward

*They've toured with Trivium and Machine Head and issued
four albums - HOAC are one of our hottest musical exports.*

Set up simply as a vehicle for mates to jam together, Heart Of A Coward can't have imagined how far the band would develop when they first started out. The almost inevitable early line-up changes were swift, before the band settled down (Jamie Graham – vocals, Carl Ayres – guitar, Steve Haycock – guitar, Vishal Khetia – bass, and Chris Mansbridge, drums) and quickly began making an impact for their crushing noise.

Their debut EP, Dead Sea helped swell interest and they were swiftly signed to management and pushed out on the road, racking up serious mileage for shows across the UK.

In 2012, album number one, Hope and Hindrance, spawned video singles Shade and We Stand As One, which were soon on small-screen rotation.

A trip to Russia followed, and then they inked a deal with Century Media in time for the release of Severance, which hit stores at the back end of 2013. It debuted at No1 on the iTunes metal chart, and made it into the Top 100 album chart.

A special edition carried a live DVD of their Download Festival debut in 2014, when the band packed out the Pepsi Max stage with more than 7,000 cramming inside to investigate.

In 2014 the tyre treads were worn down some more as they toured with tech-metallers SikTh, before jumping on board a sold-out road-trip with Machine Head, bringing down the curtain on the Severance campaign in epic style.

A burst of songwriting followed in 2015 for album number three.

It took six months to shape up, and Deliverance was produced by the band and former SikTh member Justin Hill.

Chris said: "He has a supreme ear for melody and Deliverance, as dark as it is, definitely takes the crown in terms of 'most melodic HOAC album.' There are a few huge curve balls on there."

Ahead of their epic Download Festival main stage appearance, the band issued the video for the album's first single, Hollow, which caused a commotion.

They then made tracks to Spain swelling

HOAC with former frontman Jamie Graham (centre) and (facing page) with Kaan Tasan in 2019

● **Download Festival**

COMPILED BY SAMMY JONES x @sammyjonesxx

'Playing Download? It's unreal'

By SAMMY JONES

Following their triumphant Download Festival on the Pepsi Max stage in 2013, organisers have invited MK's metallers Heart of a Coward back to wow the masses all over.

Not in the Pepsi Max tent this time, mind – they've been given the task of opening the Main Stage on Saturday.

Our quintet will warm the stage up for headliners Faith No More and Muse.

"It's a completely unreal prospect for us," drummer Noddy told me.

"2013 was absolutely electric, but to be asked back this year to open the main stage is a big tick on the life achievement list for all of us, and unbelievable as a band."

"I've been attending Download Festival as a punter since I was 16, and always had dreams of performing there, when it actually becomes a reality, it is just unreal."

Noddy promises that those turning out for their set will be well rewarded.

"Basically, it's going to kick off," he promised.

"We're going to cram as much into 30 minutes as possible, which means making some tough decisions about what songs to play, but we're definitely getting all the crowd pleasers in there

"We've expect large amounts of adrenaline and energy,

will happen ..."

And when the bags hang up their guitars, the buzz will still be a buzz. Things will be fizzing, if all goes to plan.

"There will be the obligatory fountain of champagne consumed immediately after the show, followed by many rounds of whiskey," he promises.

"You don't get to the backstage at Download Festival too often, so no doubt we will be on the lookout for our assorted heroes and other friends playing, and will hopefully share a drink or two!

"If the after party is anything like last time, things will get very messy."

better time than one wet and dreary experience.

"I have horrible memories of one year when there was a huge rainstorm and I was soaked, ankle deep in mud, trying to set up my tent whilst trying to step it blowing away in the wind. I'm hoping however that again in my life"

And if you are reading this while trying to decide what essentials to pack for your weekend of the heart, heart, worry not. You can travel light.

"Whiskey, baby wipes and sun glasses," Noddy advises. "You need to be drunk, smell good and look cool."

To book for this weekend's festival visit www.down-

OUR BLOCK ROCKIN' PICKS...

Download: HOAC aside, done plenty for mak... here's our pick of t...

Heart of a Coward on this weekend's Download: 'Things will get very messy.'

THE CRAUFORD ARMS PRESENTS

HEART OF A COWARD

HOME TOWN SHOW

THE CRAUFURD ARMS
TICKETS AVAILABLE FROM WWW.THECRAUFURDARMS.COM

TONIGHT
HEART OF
A COWARD
SOLD OUT

At the heart of the matter

ALBUM RELEASE

By SAMMY JONES

The wait is almost over – Heart of a Coward will issue their third album Deliverance, tomorrow.

"It's a massive hurdle and one that a lot of bands fail to make," drummer Noddy told me.

"It's quite overwhelming looking back on everything we have achieved so far and the fact we've reached this point, I release my third studio journey we've had as a band.

"It's something we're all really proud of."

The Milton Keynes metal quintet recorded the album in February and March.

Justin Hill, who also spends time on the stage as frontman with Sikth, handled production duties.

"We've really found our sound with this new record," Noddy said.

"It's got all the elements of the previous two albums, but has been developed.

"We really worked on our songwriting and experimented with some new sounds and layers.

"The third album is always hard because you can't write

the same album twice, but you also can't stray too far outside of the box."

Noddy takes us through Deliverance track by track...

Hollow: Mainly about predetermined destiny, or the illusion of it - so many thousand options but we tend to go for the easiest way. The idea is a future based on that decision, until 'the world is ash and dust.'

Miscreation: About how human beings are essentially an unfinished creative signature that ties, in terms of our potential and rain for thousands of years.

Sounds bleak, but this song is about the aftermath once we realise the damage is too severe to repair.

Turmoil I: A null it on a track relating to our inner strength and versatility when it comes to adapting and surviving - we are amidst the wolves and we won't back down.

Turmoil II: The aftermath of the showdown in Part 1, this song is about what is left for us to use and build upon as society.

It is slightly Biblical in the 'Meek inherit the earth' reference, but changed to 'weak' of course

Heart of a Coward: 'We've really found our sound with this new album...'

Anti-Life: Generally about the pursuit of futile existence – chasing fame or celebrity, celebration of mediocrity – basically all that is rife in our time nowadays. It's an 'Anti' life, hence the title.

A Grain of Sand: We have a tendency to ignore our problems until they are facing us direct...over the realisation kicks in we only have so much time to fix them before they are unfixable – that time passes like a grain of sand in

an hourglass.

Mouth of Madness: About physical and mental exhaustion from our cumulative stress that becomes second nature, and can know personally and you can see the physical signs if you look close enough.

The chorus is through the perspective of the person who's on the receiving end of the anger, asking 'is this what you want? To remain in your prison? Where you won't see the

light any more?'

Deliverance: Mainly about human nature on an emotional level - the way we all deal with that absolute joy or pain in our interactions about dysfunctional relationships and friendships where emotional warfare takes place - then an outsider looking in at it all, wishing they could see what the outsiders sees

Skeletal I & II: The entire album so far has what some may interpret as a pretty negative outlook, however it all sort of comes to a conclusion on this track.

Conceptually, the record is about the difficulties we face in life, much like our last record, Severance - that record is more about the downward spiral, this is more about addressing the things we seperate ourselves from, or embrace, and then dealing with the subsequent events that follow.

So, to cut a long story short, these two songs are about stripping ourselves back to our bare bones and living for the best reason possible, to walk in our own fire that we create and to leave a legacy behind us.

Deliverance will be issued through Century Media Records.

303

the Resurrection Festival bill alongside Mötorhead and Korn. They wrapped up 2015 in support of the new release, with an intimate headlining British tour.

A new year didn't slow them any, and 2016 took HOAC across the UK with Trivium, before a return to Europe, this time with Decapitated.

In August they caused some serious neck-aches with a blistering appearance at Bloodstock Open Air Festival in Derby – playing on a bill alongside Slayer and Anthrax.

Album number four is in their sights though, and the band sees out the year with two sold-out hometown dates playing for the faithful at The Craufurd Arms.

But change was coming, and Heart of a Coward announced the departure of frontman Jamie.

An open advert posted on the band's Facebook page asking for potential replacements to step forward, received close to 200 applicants in just 24 hours!

In the spring of 2018, Kaan Tasan officially filled the gap, and the HOAC machine was back to being roar-some; album number four The Disconnect was issued in the summer of 2019 and the band celebrated with more live dates - including a return to the Download Festival.

"It was one of the most challenging and rewarding writing processes I've ever been involved with," Kaan said of the album.

"Some tracks just clicked and fell into place, whilst others really pushed us all creatively. It was important to get the best out of each other – we really did all go in on this together."

Discussing the more conceptual aspects of the record, Chris said: "The Disconnect refers to the feeling of a complete lack of control over your surroundings and the powers that control your life.

"It's the feeling of hopelessness, anger and an inability to relate to the world you live in. It's a record we are all extremely proud of and this marks the next chapter of Heart Of A Coward."

The early years

HOAC drummer Chris started out in Temperamental (1999-2002), a school band who progressed from cover versions to a metal-led catalogue.

When the quartet split, Chris and frontman Neema Askari formed Fell Silent (2003-2010), with Joe Garrett (vocals), Acle Kahney (guitar), John Browne (guitar) and Max Robinson (bass) and were lauded as pioneers of the experimental metal genre Djent.

Debut album, The Hidden Words, was released in 2008 and the band inked a deal with US label Sumerian Records, and further increased their fan base on tours with Enter Shikari and Devil Sold His Soul. But time was called on the band in 2010: "We've simply all moved on and are taking our musical creativity into new and exciting projects," they said in a statement.

They weren't lying – while Chris took up the drum stool with Heart Of a Coward, Monuments became the musical vehicle of choice for John and Neema.

Joe is now a music-maker with writing credits for artists including former One Direction member Zayn Malik. And Acle? He turned his side-project into his 'day job' with prog metal quintet TesseracT...

Hacktivist

"Seeing people have our lyrics or logo tattooed on them helps to validate the blood, sweat and tears we've poured into the band."

When Timfy James stepped away from MK heavies Heart Of A Coward during their early days, he kept his creativity flowing, churning out riff after seriously heavy riff. But it wasn't to be a one-man project for long.

Timfy made the acquaintance of grime artist J Hurley and a fierce union was formed: "When J heard the stuff Timfy was writing, he jumped in the booth and they recorded our self-titled track, Hacktivist," says bassist Josh Gurner, who was struck by the sounds immediately.

"Hacktivist felt special right from day one," Josh says. "I heard that track before joining the band and was instantly infatuated with this unique new hybrid of genres."

Rich Hawking (drums) and Ben Marvin (vocals) swelled the unit and exciting things started happening, at a pace. They posted their first video online at the start of 2012.

Within a month Cold Shoulders had accumulated more than 50,000 views.

"We'd produced a no-budget studio play through, hoping a few hundred people might take notice, but it was mind-blowing. It put us in the unique position that people were approaching us with tours, management representation and record deals off the back of two songs – and they were the only two songs we'd written at the time!"

The band fused the groove, attitude and brutality of metal and grime. Their foundation of intelligent beats, abrasive guitar tones and duel vocal attack set them apart from the pack – and a rabid fanbase was soon in pursuit.

There wasn't so much a buzz around the boys as a mega roar, and their second video, for Unlike Us, gained support from Radio 1 and Kerrang! Radio when it was released.

Seizing the moment, Hacktivist

Hacktivist and (inset) J Hurley

announced a debut headline tour of the UK, hitting the road before the year end, tidily tying in with the release of their debut EP.

The media got excited – from rock rags Metal Hammer and Rock Sound to broadsheet The Guardian, the band were given a universal thumbs up.

Mini-album EP+ followed in 2013, and Hacktivist stuck a collective toe into Europe with their first German headline dates, plus shows alongside Enter Shikari.

They hopped on the Warped Tour Europe, and the summer shone brightly with gigs at Download, Reading and Leeds Festivals, T in the Park, Sonisphere France and Rock Am Ring.

Australia got to sample Hacktivist's huge, devastating grooves firsthand in 2014 too. Then they hit the road as guests of Korn in the UK and Europe, and joined Limp Bizkit in France.

"The band constantly makes me proud," Josh said, "Seeing people have our lyrics or logo tattooed on them, or having bands we love giving us shout-outs, helps to validate the blood, sweat and tears we've all poured into this. Every goal we've set ourselves we have managed to surpass so far..."

Hacktivist issued their debut album Outside the Box in 2016, and at the start of 2017 Ben Marvin hung up his mic, paving the way for new rap-vox man Jot Maxi to pick up the pace.

Hacktivist spent the year working on new material, taking time out to hit up the Download Festival, this time making their main stage debut – opening a bill headlined by Biffy Clyro.

In the spring of 2018 founding member Timfy announced his departure from the group, replacing a life on the road with one nurturing new talent, producing material and overseeing Old School Studios in MK.

"I have every confidence the band will continue to inspire and push the boundaries of modern music," he said.

His place at the fret has been filled by James Hewitt, and it's business as usual.

And no matter where they roam they take the name of Milton Keynes with them – although some are already familiar with the town, thanks to its musical movers.

Josh said: "There's been a whole bunch of occasions where you might be talking to someone, in Moscow for example, and they say 'Milton Keynes?! Awesome! Heart Of A Coward! TesseracT! Monuments! Fell Silent! MILTON CLEANS!' It refers to the sparkly clean guitar tone that is a staple to almost all 'Djent' bands and was made popular by our own Acle Kahney."

A new Hacktivist album is set for release imminently.

RavenEye

Kiss took them on tour, and Guns N'Roses legend Slash is a fan.
But RavenEye's rock 'n' roll is branded in Milton Keynes.

A solo artist since a young age, Oli Brown was already a name in the field of blues by the time he decided to make a stride into rock music. He was a seasoned pro who had played with artists including Jeff Beck and Joe Satriani.

Nice work if you can get it, and he got it by being awesome at fret-feeling.

While taking a hiatus from the touring world, Oli set to work on tracks for another solo album, but they weren't doing what he wanted them to.

"As much as I enjoyed being a solo artist, I wanted to be part of a band.

"I wanted to put something together that was more than just being about me. It's about a band, a branding, an identity that people beyond the music can share. That felt more moving to me.

"I wanted to start my whole career again from the ground up."

He began putting out feelers for fellow players and soon found drummer Kev Hickman online.

Oli came to Milton Keynes, the connection was made, and RavenEye was born in 2014.

Utilising session bassists they toured Europe as support to the aforementioned Satriani, before bassist Aaron Spiers joined permanently. In 2015, a debut EP, Breaking Out was released and a European tour with Guns N' Roses guitarist Slash was soon in the bag, which was a dream come true.

"Someone from Slash's crew sent him the single and they got in touch to offer us the dates. It was quite surreal. I have no idea who got hold of the track, but would love to buy them a drink!" said Oli.

"When I started learning the guitar I vividly remember watching the music video to November Rain, seeing Slash rip up a solo in the desert, and thinking 'I want to do that!' He is the epitome of rock 'n' roll," he said.

"Our first show was in Oslo and the crowd was nuts," remembered Aaron. "The further we went on the tour, the more people seemed to know who we were. "Our last show was in Nice in France and we got an ovation when we walked out on stage, let alone the roar we got when we finished our set!"

The tour went so well the trio were

Home and away: RavenEye making new friends (below) and a hometown gig at The Craufurd Arms (above)

invited back on the road with Slash – this time on a Stateside tour.

A line-up change was nigh too – drummer Kev Hickman vacated the drum stool in the second half of 2016, and was replaced by Adam Breeze.

"When the slot opened up we lined up a bunch of drummers to audition, but as we had played with Adam before we gave him first shot and it was one of those amazing moments where everything just gelled perfectly. Changing line-ups is never an easy thing, but it invites a whole different energy into your life."

In the autumn of 2016 RavenEye released their debut album Nova. Making good on all their promises, the release was heralded by the media and fans.

RavenEye continued to eat up road miles, playing dates with Deep Purple and Aerosmith, and touring with artists including The Darkness.

While having dinner in a Woburn restaurant Oli received a call that would propel the hotly-tipped trio to the next level – the band had lucked out and bagged the support slot on Kiss' European tour for the spring of 2017, and for a while there, life on the road with the American legends, playing to audiences of 25,000 a

Kiss and make-up with RavenEye: Adam, Oli and Aaron

night became standard.

Keen to snap up the opportunities put their way, the band spent plenty of 2017 playing live, hitting up the festival circuit, grabbing other support slots and they completed their own headline tour of the US.

"We were playing in dirty bars and clubs...we have grown so much as a band," Oli said.

He sees their music-making as 'a love child between Soundgarden, Queens of the Stone Age and Led Zeppelin,' and says there is still much work to be done.

"We've spent a fair bit of time running around as a support band,

and we want to plant our feet more firmly throughout Europe and the USA as a headline band as well," Oli says.

Album number two is coming soon.

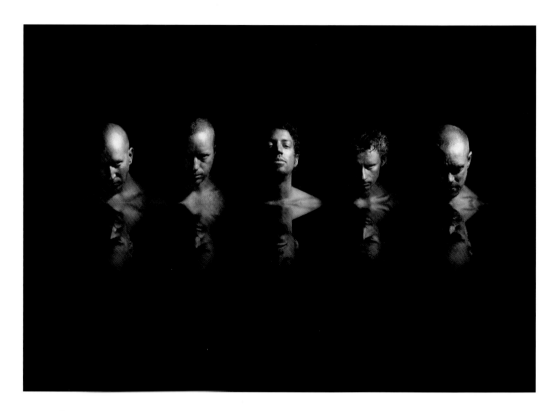

Our Man In The Bronze Age

*"We created an anti-band...with no other intention but to
please ourselves and maybe annoy everyone else."*

Originally a faceless, art-rock, doom-heavy side project, Our Man In The Bronze Age was conceived and nurtured by bassist Adam Davison and guitarist Justin Hodges in the mid-noughties.

The two were pals and touring buddies thanks to time well spent in their respective bands Phema and odd-man-out.

"Jonathan 'Muzz' Muston (Graveltrap), Matt Gannon (odd-man-out) and Pete Joy (Phema) were enlisted and the playing started.

"We wanted to try something a little different," Justin recalls, "We wrote soundscapes, pieces of music, not songs. "No more verse and chorus, no more vocals. We created an anti-band.

"It was such a refreshing experience to write endless flows of music with no other intention but to please ourselves, and maybe annoy everyone else."

OMITBA developed one piece of music,

which clocked in at more than half an hour in length, and debuted it at The Pitz in 2007.

The band made for quite the spectacle – playing in long black robes and gold masks, delivering a doom-laden soundscape while old black and white movies played behind them.

"People didn't have a clue who we were," Justin said, "It totally changed playing live for me."

Audiences were struck, and promoters came running.

Former Graveltrap frontman Daniel Gibling was employed to direct the band's first video, a not-so-cheery visual that was shot in and around church ruins at Clophill.

It was the perfect eerie accompaniement. A revolving door of musicians kept on turning too, and various players robed-up and smashed it live.

At one point the band swelled to a

septet. But at the start of 2010 was down to a nucleus of four.

A new musical direction was settled on, which meant the robes would be ditched too.

Eventually, the new sounds were put to disc, on the 2012 album The Gallows Tree.

Since then, the band has settled on a line-up delivering two drummers, and a theatrical edge capable of stripping down to show a stark beauty, or layer up with a four-part harmony.

Justin and Muzz are now joined in play by Tom Platt (drums), Graham Hulbert (strings and vocals) and Andi Jackson (bass).

Musically, it is an open pit of playability, graciously affording all members their chance to shine, experiment and commit.

A second video, a marvellously realised reel for the Eyebags track was put together, confidently piddling over many a big budget promo reel you might think of.

In 2015 the band made good use of studio time with Tony Platt (whose extensive career in production has seen him engineer or knob-twiddle for AC/DC, Bob Marley and Motörhead - as you'll have read elsewhere in these pages), and they emerged with the Habanero EP.

More recently the band have been working on release number three, which they think occupies the sound space somewhere between their two previous deliveries: "With the rock edge of the last EP being fused to the more atmospheric moments of The Gallows Tree," Graham said.

"People didn't have a clue who we were - it totally changed playing live for me"

"We think we've taken the best elements from over the years and applied them to something that really represents what we're about."

Today, OMITBA is a versatile melting pot of perfection, free of constraints. The band can offer its listener a relentless amount of heavy with a fiery riffage, just as easily as it can deliver with a piano and one voice.

In 2019 the band returned to the stage, but there is more to come, with that new album in the can and set for release in 2021.

"We may have been quiet for the past couple of years, unless you've been within a mile of our rehearsal room, but that will soon be coming to an end!" Graham promised.

Our Man In The Bronze Age (2019): Andi, Justin, Graham, Muzz and Tom

Hope in High Water

*"Stagnation and settling are the death of the soul," say MKs Americana
duo, who use their music to show that 'anything is possible.'*

It's a musical fairytale with an Americana ending, but it might not have been. Josh and Carly originally crossed paths in 2010, but it wasn't until they met again a few years later that both shelved their respective politically-charged punk playing in preference of a united acoustic dalliance.

In 2014, they began living and playing together in quick succession and found a creative force in each other.

They settled on the name Hope In High Water.

"The name is a fairly accurate representation of our music. At times it can seem dark and it deals with some challenging subject matter...but overall we always try to find the light in any situation and the wisdom that can be taken from those experiences; finding hope in the hardest of times.

"We just try to be as honest as we can, to the point that sometimes it can be uncomfortable to share certain songs," Josh said.

"Sincerity is what allows you to connect with people."

They began teasing folk, blues and country into their work and arrived at a brand as intense as it is authentic.

Live shows were rewarded with the thumbs up from fans, fellow artists and industry scribes and in the autumn of 2016, Josh and Carly spent time in the studio, swelled by drums and fiddle, piecing together the debut album Never Settle, which was issued in the spring of 2017.

They said: "The sentiment is that of never settling for anything less than your wildest dreams. Stagnation and settling are the death of the soul. We should never be made to feel that we are destined to forever tread the mediocre treadmill of life. Anything is possible..."

As 2019 drew to a close a new album, Bonfire & Pine, 'a story of healing, joy, freedom, progression and truth' was issued. Josh and Carly, and their 'mountain music from the flatlands of Milton Keynes' continues to push forward.

forest of fools

From medieval English courtyards to effects-laden trance-melodeon, forest of fools promise the listener 'a true musical odyssey for the 21st century.'

forest of fools first pooled their talents in 2013.

"In those days we didn't have much of an idea what we really wanted to do," they admit.

"We'd all encountered each other in and around the place, playing in bands together, watching each other play gigs, or seeing bands," explains Greg Mahon, who takes care of vocals.

"We soon realised that we shared an interest in the idea of making music for music's sake; something that we all enjoyed hearing, that was free of rules and stereotypes, and was like nothing we'd heard before."

forest of fools worked to the rule that 'anything goes, so long as it's good fun,' allowing the band to bring in influences drawn from all over the world.

"We developed what we were doing to a point where we had to make up a genre

> **"We had to make up a genre to explain ourselves to prospective bookers"**

to explain ourselves to prospective bookers and fans, and so the genre Jump-up Folk was born!" said bassist Jam O'Malley.

An EP by the same name did a swell job, putting the band on the radars of those promoters, and fof made the most of it – with introductions at some grand venues and festivals, from the backs of lorries and a wrestling ring, to massive stages with flames shooting out of the top!

A debut album, All Good in the Wood, was issued, and the band enjoyed some magnificent live sets at Boomtown Fair, at the last-ever Secret Garden Party plus multiple sets at Glastonbury.

In 2017, fof released their second album, Forsooth.

The band made use of online facilities to clock up financial support and recorded the LP in London over a period of six months.

"Fun to write, record and design, it's something we're incredibly proud of," resident sousaphone and didgeridoo ace Parkie said, and certainly the band packed it tight with aural delight; how many other releases do you know that take you from medieval English courtyards to an underground party, stopping off en route to engage in 180 BPM D&B masterfully interlaced with African percussion?

And even if you do have a response, we bet your band won't also serve up effects-laden trance-melodeon and psychedelic lead guitar, and nor will it deliver brilliant bass that reacts with didge-inspired, multiphonic sousaphone brass.

The band calls it "a true musical odyssey for the 21st century."

Billy Nomad

"Performing my music is the closest I can get to having a real world conversation with someone about all the complicated thoughts that go on in my head."

The man known on the MK circuit as Billy Nomad is one of our most colourful characters – and one of the most prolific.

In the past 15 years he has released seven albums and a stack of singles, which flit from one genre to another.

In 2019 he issued a single every month: "To keep myself creative and give my community something fresh to listen to more regularly," he explained.

If you like pigeonholing your musicians, Craig Hudson, the man behind the sounds, will give you one almighty headache.

What about the origins of Billy Nomad? Initially, it was all a bit of a giggle.

"When I first started dressing up to perform and messing around with my name, it was a joke – a stab at all the cookie-cutter commercial music babies in town. I'd just stopped working with a punk band," he explains, "I was essentially crap, and being just me on a guitar lacked the right vibe.

"I would get bored watching 'singer-songwriters' performing and would feel uninspired at the thought of giving any audience the same experience," Craig said.

"The face paint and fashion made it more fun for me, and way more fun for the audience."

And that is an important part of the plan for Craig: "I'm not a wannabe celebrity," he promises, "I'm a working class entertainer. As for the name? I assume others think about it way more than I do.

"Billy isn't some kind of cartoon character. He's just another version of myself."

In the past, if he was feeling bad, our entertainer would put his problems down in a letter.

Nowadays, Billy uses his music to share his innermost thoughts.

"When I write music it stems from that same inability to properly express, and the need to have my feelings acknowledged – to know that I'm not alone in the world.

"Performing my music is just about the closest I can get to having a real world conversation with someone about all the complicated thoughts and feelings that go on inside my head.

"Having someone approach me to talk about the feelings they've had listening to my lyrics is just about the best thing in the world.

"The great thing about the music I make is that it tends to flip-flop between styles, ending up appealing to a surprisingly wide audience."

Craig first began gigging in Milton Keynes back in 2004.

He has seen plenty of change in the years since: "Growing up working in music in Milton Keynes, I've met a lot of fantasists and a lot of chancers.

> **"Billy isn't some kind of cartoon character. He's just another version of myself"**

"I like to think I've been both at one time or another," he admits.

"The music scene in MK happens in waves. The problem is there is no serious money sitting here for people who want to take performing on as a career."

When he first started, it was easy to bag a gig and take his sounds to the music fan.

Now? It's not such a lively beast. Venues are fewer, for a start: "... and most places can't be bothered with the stress of booking bands or promoting gigs," he says.

"That upsets me a lot. The thought, 'this place used to be fun' often crosses my mind.

"I want to help bring a little fun back to the world, one party at a time."

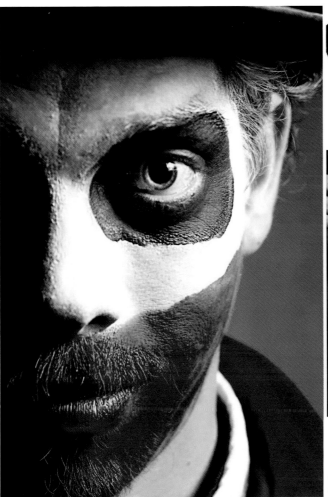

Billy Nomad: 'I'm not a wannabe celebrity. I'm a working class entertainer'

S.G. Wolfgang

*Roll-up, roll-up for a brilliant brand of tightly wound rock 'n' roll
with beards, blazers and blisteringly rowdy tune-smithery.*

Sean Grant had been fostering thoughts of the musical beast he wanted to create for some time in the back of his mind, before finally landing on his real style and calling, and beginning the journey proper, in 2014.

As Sean Grant & The Wolfgang, the band announced their arrival with the EP We The Working Class that same year, followed by War Machines (2015) and 7 Deadly 7 (2016).

The project evolved into a real unit, and a name tweak saw the arrival of S.G. Wolfgang.

They inked a deal with ultra cool Fierce Panda Records too – spending time on the same label who have been responsible for putting out material by artists including Coldplay, Supergrass and Placebo.

"Being on the label was incredible. It was truly rewarding and we had complete control," Sean said.

"At times it proved harder as we didn't get the huge budgets that majors have, but we got to work with people who truly cared about the music, and they wouldn't sign anyone they didn't like."

"It was an honour to be on a label with such a vast and rich history and the same values today that they've always had."

The 'rabble-rousing brand of tightly wound rock 'n' roll armed with beards, blazers and blisteringly rowdy tune-smithery,' set about taking their noise to the next level with the 2018 release of their debut album, which saw Sean at his most honest, and vulnerable: "It's a self-indulgent, narcissistic, nihilistic diary of my struggles with mental health and dealing with inner demons.

"During it's creation I had various internal battles, and if you listen to the lyrical content you'll hear the confessions of my inner self," he admits.

"It's the first time I've written in that way.

"Our music has a vastness to it and traverses the age barrier"

"I normally liked to tell stories, and write about a subject or a person.

"I've realised I was doing that so I didn't have to delve really deep and turn the pen on myself."

And its creator thinks that the band has enough of that aforementioned rowdy tune-smithery to entice anyone.

"I think our music has a vastness to it. It has a little something for everyone and traverses the age barrier."

Wolfgang has been on a little hiatus, but the music-makers are gathering themselves for a return. The new music will be pushed out through their own label. Exciting times are beckoning.

Adrian Stranik

"When they realised Europolis was a violent Futuristic Western and not Bend It Like Beckham, they nearly choked on their croissants!"

Musicians are a fickle lot; there one minute; gallivanting somewhere else the next, and as happens with alarming regularity, a great many of them discover that actually 'music was fun, but you can't do it forever.'

Adrian Stranik sticks two fingers up at that; he's been making MK audiences feel good for more than three decades, and variety? It's the spice of Adrian's playability.

It was 1984, a year that gave us chart toppers by Stevie Wonder, George Michael and Chaka Khan when Adrian first struck out on a 'proper' music tip, with Milk Plus.

In 1987 they began making annual trips across the channel to play at Le Gibus Club in Paris: "That is where we realised we were actually a good band and that it was Milton Keynes that needed to catch up," Adrian recalled.

"I didn't go to school in MK so we didn't have a big network of friends that would come and see us. We went from playing in front of a few girlfriends in the Bletchley Arms to 300 people packed into a hot sweaty underground club in Le Republique..."

In the early part of the new decade, Adrian was back with Jonathan E, who had a penchant for the burgeoning dance scene: "That was my next trick and involved merging rock 'n'roll with electronica with DJ/producer Magic Alec and guitarist Mark Reardon."

Their debut 12" kickstarted the Capital Heaven record label and time in the studio delivered 'an hour of electro-rock-cinematic-psychedelia.' Three singles were cut loose, but the double album, Glock Opera, never saw the light of day in its entirety, although a click to that modern beast YouTube will yield fruits.

Jonathan E rolled through to the end of the '90s, and for the last part of that tenure, Adrian was also in the ranks of

Environmental Science as guitarist and songwriter: "ES emerged from the dying embers of producer Ian 'Spatts' Allen's hip-hop outfit Criminal Minds,"Adrian said.

With the hip-hop aces quietened, science took over: "The next few years were a blur of trains, planes and automobiles as we travelled all over Europe, promoting a string of Big Beat hit singles.

"The band finally imploded and exploded simultaneously in a field in Shepton Mallet."

But you can't stop the ticking mind of a creative, and Adrian changed tack, and tried his hand at getting the film project Europolis into prime position.

Pitching for funds didn't go well: "We quickly realised the only reason most of them would even give us the time of day was because our producer was Indian and female.

"When they realised Europolis was a violent Futuristic Western and not Bend it Like Beckham, they nearly choked on their croissants!"

Europolis was shelved in '07 and The Silver Brazilians took over.

It was the era of MySpace and spoof band members Mo Slim Fatwahwah, Deaf Melon Jellyspoon, Ted D Rocker and Kirk 'The Turk' Terkenstein found an eager audience for their cracking tunes.

In reality this project was a two-part slice of brilliance with Tony Delahaye, and things went very nicely, ta.

A support slot with The Charlatans? Aye, they could do that, they said, safe in the knowledge that someone was taking the piddle. And then the ads started appearing in the music press. The laughter stopped, the music started and things went swimmingly. The following year, the Brazilians went on stage in Hollywood and enjoyed having their tunes spun by Springsteen's E-Street Band guitarist Little Steven on his radio show in New York.

Tasty times for sure.

And there were more to come.

In 2012, Adrian went back to his roots and started a rockabilly project with Stony Stratford double-bassist Bill Mann.

The Broadway Twisters attacked some nice venues together and bagged some decent support slots; Muse's end of Drones Tour party among them. The plan now is to cut loose their long-awaited debut album South by South West 2.

There is still plenty of solo seduction to be had too, though: "A never-ending series of unreliable drummers has got me doing more solo acoustic shows these days, giving me a chance to completely reinterpret old material and explore new ways of writing," Adrian said.

"I'm currently inspired by a lot of 'Americana/Country' acts, such as Noel McKay, Brennen Leigh, Gillian Welch, Dave Rawlings and Sierra Ferrell.

"I've always been kind of halfway there anyway – being as that Rockabilly is basically Country turned up to 11.

"Not sure whether the new material is suitable for The Broadway Twisters, but I've got about three new albums screaming to go!"

Environmental Science and (right) Jonathan E

Naked Next Door

They've got tunes in their pocket, a top producer on side, and a yearning to take their sounds beyond the new town. Meet Naked Next Door...

After so many false starts and should-have-beens for MK music-makers, in 2019 a new breed picked up the baton and have teased the industry to take a chance on the Keynes.

And London-based Honest Records was won over by the cheekily named Naked Next Door, and promptly signed the indie-rockers. The quartet are armed with a raw emotive style just ripe for a big audience: "We want to stay as organic and raw as possible because that's our sound," says vocalist and guitarist Euan Emerton.

"We've never been very technical and never wanted to be, we've always pictured our music sounding the same live as it does on the record. We are heavily influenced by the likes of Oasis, Kings of Leon, Stereophonics and Catfish and the Bottlemen.

"Oasis with their hard hitting attitude always had us hooked, and Stereophonics have a way of telling a story through their lyrics much like Bruce Springsteen.

"Catfish are our modern day Oasis and are one of the reasons we became a band."

Naked Next Door delivered their debut single Tired Eyes early in 2019. The lush-sounding 'scape was one of five jostling for position on the EP which was produced by Milton Keynes' in-demand producer Joe Garrett.

In 2020, second EP, Swerving Out Wide has served them well, and the plan now is to wear out stages far and wide, to further increase that burgeoning fan base.

But no matter where they play, they'll always carry a little bit of new city love with them: "Having venues like The Craufurd Arms made it easy for us to fuel our imaginations," Euan added, "Being able to see live bands from a young age has definitely played a big part in why we are who we are today."

Tuskar

*There may be just the two of them, but the noise they make is gargantuan -
and Tuskar's gnarly nuclear sludge is setting them apart from the pack.*

Having got their teenage kicks playing with a number of ill-fated new town bands ("which more often than not never made it out of the studio"), drummer Tyler Hodges and guitarist Tom Dimmock made a musical connection at the tail end of 2016.

The duo quickly found their niche, and together they boiled up a sick but sexy sounding mash of stoner rock, doom, sludge and black metal elements, pulling it all together under the banner of nuclear sludge.

Moving quickly they hit the road, and have been racking up miles and fans ever since, with a relentless live schedule. And they delivered a couple of EP releases (2017s Arianrhod, and The Tide, Beneath, The Wall issued in 2018, both on Riff Rock Records) to sate fans.

Heck, they've even been the subject of Ray Zell's hallowed Pandora column in Kerrang! magazine, which is the stuff that rock 'n' roll dreams are made of.

"We've got a young, refreshing view on an old scene," Tyler says, explaining the formula that has seen them stage share with genre leaders including Red Fang, Crowbar and Conan.

The debut album is set for release in 2021.

Action Beat

"Everyone in Bletchley thought we sucked so bad...no-one could have predicted that we would have a deal with our favourite label."

Indie-label and promotion nucleus Fortissimo is the brainchild of Don McLean. It originated in 2001, and held its first curated show, at The Pitz, the same year. The Fortissimo name?

Don says: "It was found in an old guitar tuition book, and means 'to play a piece of music loud and fast.'"

It was a perfect fit.

The first CD to come from the collective arrived in fast food boxes stolen from Pizza Hut. In 2002/2003 Wednesday nights at Wolverton venue Zaks belonged to Fortissimo, and were promoted by Don. Bands including Ikari, Dark Hadou, The Brave and Riotmen were the initial players. Don was thrilled to book his favourite band, The Ex, in 2003: "It was the first real band I had put on," he recalled. But there would be many more; US artists Neptune, who make their instruments from scrap metal, toured the UK in 2005, with Don responsible for booking the tour.

Don's band Action Beat toured the UK in 2006, and shook Europe a year later. While others around town practiced an unnecessary swagger, the Fortissimo crew got on with the business of creating.

In 2009, the impro-noise bringers inked a deal with Southern Records, and called the resulting album The Noise Band From Bletchley.

The album pulled in solid reviews: "Everyone in Bletchley hated us and thought we sucked so bad," Don remembered, "No-one could have predicted that we would be the band to make it out of Bletchley, play more than 100 shows a year and have a deal with our favourite label."

Long live bouts became the norm, and in 2010 they hit the road for an 11 week stint. That same year, Don swapped Bletchley for a new life in New York.

But Fortissimo, and Action Beat, continued. While plenty of bands were fuelled by the Fortissimo name in those early days, it's safe to say that many of them have since broken up or fallen by the wayside. But Fortissimo is still a thing. And Action Beat are still that noise band from Bletchley.

In the summer of 2019 they hit the road again - with a West Coast tour of America.

Torus

They might be relatively new to the MK fold, but Torus are beginning to cause serious waves for their roar-some riffs.

There was no one moment of musical enlightenment for Alfie Glass - music has always been there; it's what happens when you come from a creatively rich household.

"I grew up in a family of musicians and there was always music in the house.

"For as long as I can remember I have picked up and played whatever instrument is lying around, but it was the guitar and drums that really fired me up," he said.

Alfie started his first band when he was just into double figures, and has never looked back, putting his style down on as many different projects as possible.

He took his chances on the Sky TV programme Guitar Star too.

It was a fantastic chance for serious exposure and Alfie, by this time all of 13 years-old, was mentored by the man responsible for some of rock music's most famous riffs; Black Sabbath's Tony Iommi.

The time spent learning from Tony, together with his blossoming raw talent served Alfie well and paid dividends; he was the overall winner of the Rock Heat and made it through to the Grand Final of the competition.

"I learned loads from that show, but it was jamming with my hero Tony that will always inspire me."

A few years on, and now comes Torus, an unashamed rock beast which gives Alfie the chance to experiment with his love of the hard and the heavy, with a pinch of stoner and even a little psychedelic thrown in.

Bassist Harry Quinn was an obvious catch to assist him on the journey; the two had worked together in previous outfits Flowertoy and Harry Quinn and the Lost Faces.

With the duo now knuckling down and massaging their style, 2020 is going well; the band are on the hunt for a permanent drummer, and they have been flirting with a major label - the industry bigwigs are keen to strike up a working relationship.

Watch this space.

GO! Awards

Milton Keynes didn't need to wait for others to show their appreciation of its talented players - it organised its own annual awards show.

The Milton Keynes Citizen newspaper organised GO! Awards – named after its dedicated music and leisure section – garnered plenty of support during the few years it ran, from the late 1990s to the mid-noughties.

Readers voted in their droves for their most favoured music-makers, and the award nights were a great chance to sink a few drinks with fellow scene players.

It was like a micro Brit Awards, with none of the budget, but with plenty of mess!

Big winners over the years included Fono (who shared the National Bowl stage with Bon Jovi) and Radio 1 Evening Session faves Frigid Vinegar.

Best Band awards were dished out to Phema, Bosomunkee, fidjit, Six.Point.Five and Togmor.

When Radio 1 DJs Mark & Lard and former city dweller Chris Moyles beat the local disc spinners to the DJ of the Year award, they sent acceptance speeches.

The Peartree Bridge Family would routinely bag a gong at every event: "One of our biggest claims to fame was our bottoms making it into the pages of The Citizen, when we were given Best Cover Band in MK, an award we were proud to win every time," said aptly named guitarist Ronnie Bottom.

John Dankworth, Cleo Laine and Marshall Amplification's Jim Marshall were awarded Lifetime Achievement awards.

Jim was in the building to collect his, accompanied by his pal, guitarist ace Bert 'Play In A Day' Weedon.

They received a standing ovation when they took to the stage.

Other faces taking the same award included Pete Winkelman, who headed up Linford Manor recording studio before bringing football to the new city, Song Loft ace Matt Armour, and Del Bromham, founding member of hard rock mob Stray, who was caught unaware.

Iron Maiden's Steve Harris sent a video message: "I grew up being a Stray fan and covered one of your songs in Maiden, as you know. You deserve it and now they know you deserve it," Steve said.

"I was stuck for words!" Del

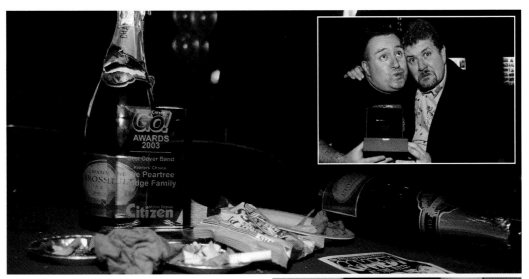

remembered, "I just went down to enjoy the evening and totally didn't expect that – it's the icing on the cake really.

"I just enjoy playing, whether it is to 50 people or 15,000, and that's the reason I did it when I first started playing, not for how much I was going to get paid at the end of the night – the trick is not to lose that."

And he gave a nod to the newspaper too: "I travel all around the country and I've got to say that outside of the music press The Citizen does more for the arts and entertainment than any other paper."

The 'Made it Big' Award went to Adam Ficek after he hopped behind the drum kit and kept Babyshambles in check, at a time when frontman Pete Doherty was splashed across the tabloids almost daily.

The awards were loud, lairy and sometimes messy. And for many, the hangovers were legendary.

328

Winners, players and faces: Graham Hulbert (left) and (above) Sir John Dankworth and Dame Cleo Laine with their Lifetime Achievement Award and (below) Jimi Volcano

Award winners Tarpot

Did you know?

Milton Keynes has lots of 'Did you know?' moments.
We've had a song written about us too…

A long time before keeping check on monstrously marvellous moments like I Feel Free and Strange Brew, Cream drummer **Ginger Baker** was lined up for a job with John Dankworth's band.

Of course it never happened: "The rest of the band were all very keen. I didn't get the gig because I had a drug problem. It was a pretty bad time in my life, because everyone told me I'd get the job.

"Jazz is my only love, really…" he said.

1960s freakbeat combo **The Game** had their single The Addicted Man withdrawn following a less than favourable reaction on Juke Box Jury due to its content. DJs criticised the track and attacked what they assumed was its pro-drugs message.

DJ Peter Murray said: "It was a terrible record. The most disgusting that I have ever heard."

The track was co-authored by Alan Gowing, who later made Milton Keynes his home.

Answering his critics at the time, Alan said: "The whole aim of our song has been distorted. We are firmly against drug addiction, and we would never encourage drug taking."

Original copies of the 7" now swap hands for around £500.

On May 19, 1976 **Keith Richards** crashed his Bentley near Newport Pagnell – he had fallen asleep at the wheel and driven off the M1 – ploughing through a hedge and into a field.

During a search at Newport Pagnell police station, police found traces of cocaine.

DURAN DURAN

PLANET EARTH

ON EMI RECORDS

FIRST SINGLE RELEASED FEB 2nd EMI 5137

Duran Duran striking a pose at centre:mk in 1981, and opposite

The case was heard in January 1977 at Aylesbury Crown Court.

He was found guilty of possessing cocaine, given a £1,000 fine and warned by the judge that if it happened again, he could look forward to being detained at Her Majesty's pleasure.

When **The Police** played in Milton Keynes in 1980, they made a generous donation to the town's Peartree Bridge Centre.

"Before The Police did their concert at the Milton Keynes Bowl they made it clear they would donate cash to any youth organisation in the area that helped young musicians," said the centre's Dick Emmings.

"When I thanked the group's manager Miles Copeland, I asked him if he had any preference as to how we spent it. 'Just get the kids off the street,'" he said.

The money paid for a four-track recording studio, 200-watt PA system and lighting equipment, and financed the release of an MK compilation album.

Duran Duran's first photo session – the cover for their first single Planet Earth – was hosted in Milton Keynes in 1981, at what is now known as centre:mk

Esteemed photographer Andy Earl was the man behind the lens.

The band also dropped in at Milton Keynes' sewage works for another shoot at the time, which Andy says was referred to as 'Duranasty.'

Cliff Richard filmed the Wired For Sound video in Milton Keynes in 1981.

Everyone of a certain age will recall Cliff roller-skating his way along the arcade of centre:mk listening to a newly available Walkman cassette player.

The single went to number four in the UK charts.

More than 3,000 people flocked to Middleton Hall in centre:mk in October 1982 to see country superstar **Glen Campbell** at play.

He thrilled fans with hits including Wichita Lineman, Southern Nights and

Wired for Sound:
Cliff Richard filming in Milton
Keynes in 1981

Left, an advertisement for Glen
Campbell's Middleton Hall show

ONE NIGHT ONLY

Don't miss this golden opportunity to see the superb

LIVE IN CONCERT

GLEN CAMPBELL
AT MIDDLETON HALL
CENTRAL MILTON KEYNES

ON SUNDAY, OCTOBER 17, 1982
AT 8PM. SUPPORTED BY ANGIE GOLD
TICKETS: £12, £8.50, £6.50, £4.50, £4.00

Available now direct from Round Table. Send cheque and SAE to:
19 BENNET CLOSE, STONY STRATFORD, MILTON KEYNES

or tel: (0908) 562370

Or call at: The Box Office, Borough of Milton Keynes Civic Offices, 1 Saxon Gate East, Central Milton Keynes.

Access and Barclaycard welcome

Gentle On My Mind, and even Amazing Grace, complete with bagpipes.

The concert was organised by the Milton Keynes and District Round Table, and raised enough money to provide one premature baby unit at Milton Keynes Hospital.

The Woughton Centre made local headlines in 1985 after trouble erupted during a concert by **Desmond Dekker**.

Violence flared when a youth at the bar was slashed across his ear and face with a knife.

"Fighting skinheads turned an evening of reggae and soul music into a night of violence and bloodshed," reported the Mirror newspaper, "Heads were kicked, broken glass was used as weapons, as well as knives, and casualties were ferried to Milton Keynes Hospital."

The Beastie Boys 'badge theft' episode

hit Milton Keynes in the summer of 1987, causing chaos and thousands of pounds worth of damage to Volkswagen cars in the area.

The company's spares depot in Blakelands said it was issuing 130 per cent more than normal of virtually every kind of VW badge.

A spokesman told the Milton Keynes Mirror: "It is incredible, we are turning out about 250 badges a week and we are putting it down to the Beastie Boys."

Police weren't down with this new OTT fashion though: "It is an offence, it is theft and causes a lot of damage.

"We would ask parents to be more involved with the conduct of their children, if they see them with these badges they should stop them committing these kind of offences," said Inspector John Simonite.

A bit of a Blur: Alex James and Damon Albarn with Kevin Sparks

The Smiths track Is It Really So Strange? features the lyric 'I lost my bag in Newport Pagnell.'

Former **Bloc Party** bassist Gordon Moakes was educated at Ousedale School in Newport Pagnell.

He now works with the band Young Legionnaire and lives Stateside.

In October 1991, the MK Citizen newspaper launched MK's first comprehensive pull-out music and leisure guide, **GO!**

E17 went MK16 for one day only, when the Tony Mortimer-led quartet played for fans at the aforementioned Ousedale School.

Naughty boys **Blur** were banned from The Pitz in 1991, after a fan was hit on the head by a flying bass guitar at the gig in Milton Keynes.

The episode was later immortalised in Alex James' autobiography 'A Bit of a Blur.'

Kevin Sparks was the unfortunate gig-goer struck by the instrument: "All I remember was watching the gig at the end," he told The Citizen.

"There had been a lot of trouble at the

> **"It is incredible, we are turning out about 250 badges a week and are putting it down to the Beastie Boys"**

back with objects like bottles and Coke cans being thrown around.

"When I put my hands on my head, there was blood on them.

"I thought I had been hit by a bottle and my first reaction was to look back. The blood came down faster.

"I pushed myself to the front but the security kept pushing me back because people had been trying to stage dive.

"But when they saw the blood they let me over and I had to get up on stage and walk out the back. I was then taken to the front entrance.

"The first I realised I had been hit on the head by a bass was when Alex James was really apologetic.

"I was only 16 at the time and I was a bit gobsmacked and star struck."

Two weeks later Kevin received a call from EMI saying that Alex and Damon wanted to make a formal apology to him live on Horizon Radio.

At the meeting he received a signed CD, T-shirt, and four backstage passes for a show at London's Astoria.

Kevin said: "Looking back on it I know things now that I didn't know then and I should have sued them!

"It didn't even occur to me then. I was more than happy with four backstage passes."

MKs Tim Searle is now head of animation at Beano Studios, but in 2002 he was responsible for the cutting edge show 2DTV, which was produced in Stony Stratford.

2DTV was a satirical animation series which had a regular sketch featuring George Michael, former Spice Girl Geri Halliwell, and Elton John.

So when a call came in from **George Michael**?

"I assumed it was from Jon Culshaw, one of our voice artists messing around," Tim recalls.

"Eventually it became apparent it wasn't Jon and really was George Michael saying he wanted to meet to discuss a possible project.

"I have to admit I remained fairly skeptical until I was sitting in front of him the next day."

It transpired that George was a huge fan of the show and wanted Tim to come up with a video to illustrate his forthcoming single, Shoot the Dog.

"He explained his concerns about the

Milton Keynes' 2DTV was responsible for George Michael's controversial Shoot the Dog video

way the UK was seen to be cosying up to the USA at the time and wanted to try to do something to bring attention to what he saw as a dangerous policy. He said he had real worries for the safety of his family and friends in London.

"He liked the way we used comedy animation to lampoon events and figures. "He thought a comedic video would get his message to a wide audience, he encouraged us to make him look ridiculous. He was very self-deprecating."

Time was of the essence and the video needed to be completed in three weeks.

"It was an exciting, intensely demanding, fun project. We were so busy and excited that we didn't fully appreciate how brave George was being by getting us to do it.

"He was the first high-profile public figure to voice his concerns, but he understood the risk."

George Michael was a genuine legend in music, and a genuinely nice man, says Tim.

"I'll remember George as a friendly, enthusiastic collaborator with a sharp sense of humour.

"He was genuinely interested in what we were doing and made some really handy, smart notes during the production.

"While the initial reaction was 'mixed'

with some real hostility, it was exciting to see George perform the song with a huge George Bush and dog inflatable and our animation on a huge screen in his later world tour - to great reaction."

Tim added: "He knew he was risking his career with Shoot the Dog but he was more concerned about the safety of his family and friends."

In July 2000, **Zed Bias** hit The Top 30 with Neighbourhood. The track had gathered interest from UK Garage label Locked On who signed it in September 1999 and it shifted 13,000 on the underground.

XL Recordings picked it up, and with vocals from Milton Keynes' Nicky Prince it became a tempting radio proposition. It settled at No.25 in the national singles chart.

Frigid Vinegar recorded a single, Diddleysquat, with comedian Les Dennis!

By 2004, and with a name change to Acarine, Alex Lusty then bagged a slot on the Green Street film soundtrack with Stand Your Ground.

While I Pursue My Way Unharmed is a hidden track on the album Suicide

Pact – You First, by Irish-alternative mob **Therapy?** The album was recorded at Great Linford Manor, and the hidden track is 666 seconds of sound recorded in shopping hub centre:mk

The band utilised other things in close proximity elsewhere on the album too, recording the track God Kicks in a local woods at 2am.

And the noise at the start of the track, Jam Jar Jail? That's the sound of a butterfly trapped in the window of the recording studio. Just so you know.

Therapy? also recorded a 30-minute horror film while working on the album. It remains unreleased, but was titled The Speedo Menace.

Bands notoriously try to wring the most from their riders, but some go that bit further.

Ja Rule apparently requested a Love Chair in advance of his appearance at The Empire, while Finnish folk-metallers **Finntroll** pulled out of their Pitz date when their rider request wasn't granted.

What did they want?

"A £440 buy out for food, full sandwich deli spread, nine cases of lager (24 can packs), bottles of hard liquor, a bottle of champagne and large pizzas for 22 people."

Now-defunct Wolverton venue **Carriages**, formerly **The Main Arena**, was a hive of comedy and music for a wee while in the late 1990s, before the shutters came down in March 1999. It did a swell job of bringing fast rising talent here while it was open for business, though.

Comedy fans were well looked after; in February 1999 the venue presented sets by Noel Fielding, Chris Addison, Dave Gorman and Sean Lock.

So far as music was concerned?

A few decent nights played out there, in the company of national and local bands. Alt-rock quartet **Gene** played the venue on February 24, 1999, with support from a young rock mob. Their debut album had yet to be released and the boys played for the fee of £90 plus a crate of Stella.

They were called **Muse**.

In 2010, they were back. Kind of.

They played for £90 and a crate of Stella...they were called Muse

The band's impressive full-stage production was set up at the National Bowl for a tech-check.

Milton Keynes rocks – and in 2007, the RAC made it official – adding the **National Bowl** to its Road Atlas.

Amy Winehouse clearly forgot the code of pantomime conduct when she attended a performance of Cinderella at Milton Keynes Theatre in December 2009 – that you shout at only the baddies, not heckle the cast in general!

The Back To Black singer attended the show to support her friend, the former pop star Kavanagh, during his stand-in appearance as Prince Charming.

But instead of booing the Ugly Sisters and cheering Cinders, Amy decided to cut loose with abuse, shouting and swearing at stars including Hollywood legend Mickey Rooney and funny man Bobby Davro.

When she left the auditorium, she assaulted Richard Pound who was working as the front of house manager, pulling his hair and kicking him in the groin.

A month later, and with dozens of paparazzi focusing their lenses on that beehive, the star was back in the new city, to face the music at the Magistrates' Court.

She could have been sentenced for up to six months, but pleaded guilty to common assault and a public order offence and was given a two-year conditional discharge. Winehouse – who was charged under her married name Amy Civil - was also ordered to pay £85 costs and £100 compensation.

It was her second visit to the new city. In 2004, Amy was among the hotly-tipped musicians appearing at The Stables in Wavendon for the BBC Radio 2 sessions, that were recorded there annually.

Backed by Sir John Dankworth's band, she let her vocals loose on material including the George Shearing composition, Lullaby of Birdland.

Royalty paid a visit to Bletchley in 2012. Princess Anne came to town to mark **Marshall Amplification's** half-century in business, and was so impressed with

In court: Amy Winehouse at Milton Keynes Magistrates' Court in January 2010

the brand she broke with convention and delivered an impromptu speech.

The Company Band, side project of Clutch singer Neil Fallon wrote a song about the new city, called All's Well In Milton Keynes.

We're not sure that all is actually well in the town, but it's a cracking mention nonetheless.

"The lyrics came about from my first impression of the place," Neil said.

"Maybe it's because I'm a Yank reading too far into the surroundings, but MK seemed like a Pink Floyd song put into the flesh, no pun intended, but I'll take it.

"I think what set me off was the concrete cows in the pristine green fields.

"The cover of Atom Heart Mother came to mind. I've since learned they are an art installation, but initially thought they were there as some engineered pastoral atmosphere.

"Being essentially a tourist, the scenes seemed decidedly 'English countryside' but there remained some sense of mild dystopia.

"I was told at the time that MK was designed after the American town plan style and that many thought it clashed with English sensibilities.

"I don't know if this is true or not, but I was (and still am) intrigued with the idea of a planned town, regardless of its locale."

Princess Anne at the Marshall HQ

Marshall man: Bon Jovi's Richie Sambora

50 Cent

In November 2016, a special guest joined Manchester Storm and Luc Johnson from MK Lightning at Planet Ice in Milton Keynes. **Justin Bieber** visited the ice hockey team before heading to London to perform for a sold-out 02 Arena audience.

As guitarist with post-punk legends Killing Joke, **Kevin 'Geordie' Walker's** music has influenced the likes of Nirvana, Soundgarden and Tool.

But he spent a number of his formative years in Milton Keynes, and was a pupil at Leon School in Bletchley.

Big George Webley's arrangement of the Mike d'Abo track Handbags And Gladrags (the signature tune for Ricky Gervais' smash-hit The Office), features Fin Muir on vocals.

As front man with '80s rockers Waysted, Fin toured the States with Ozzy Osbourne and Motley Crüe in 1984, before going solo and hitting Milton Keynes in the 1990s.

Fin spent 15 years here, for a while as lead singer with 5 Go Jazz, and he headed up Dukes Wine Bar in The Winter Gardens.

The first time **50 Cent** came to town, the New York City rapper was supporting Eminem at the National Bowl. It was 2003, and his In Da Club single, taken from the debut studio album Get Rich or Die Tryin' was making waves.

Fast-forward to 2012 and 50 Cent returned to the new city. This time around it wasn't in a gig capacity - he popped into the head office of Home Retail Group.

He wasn't checking out clothes airers or looking for a new tumble drier, mind you.

Icy meeting: Pop superstar Justin Bieber (centre) with Manchester Storm and Luc Johnson at Planet Ice

Bailey McConnell (left) and Pip Akers

Nope, 50 Cent was in town to promote his SMS Audio headphone range.

When former **Spice Girl Geri Halliwell** tied the knot with Red Bull boss Christian Horner in 2015, they chose to say 'I do' at St Mary's Parish Church in Woburn Village, in front of guests including Emma Bunton, Myleene Klass, Dawn French and Jennifer Saunders and, from the world of motorsport, Niki Lauda, Sir Jackie Stewart, David Coulthard and Kimi Räikkönen.

But it wasn't the only wedding in the area that attracted long-lens snappers and national press interest: In 1984, Aspley Guise made the headlines – when **Kajagoogoo** keyboard player Stuart Neale married his belle and the reception was held at the Holt Hotel.

The local press reported, 'Police were on duty to keep out the fans who still managed to track them down.'

Pip Akers performed in front of will.i.am, Tom Jones, Jennifer Hudson and Olly Murs on The Voice in 2019.

Police were on duty to keep out the fans who still managed to track them down

Pip has spent more than a decade singing professionally, and now teases the best from others working as a voice coach in the area.

When she's not doing that, she can be seen and heard hitting the notes with her own live band.

She's more than a bit good.

Bailey McConnell proved a hit with judges when he appeared on Britain's Got Talent in 2014 while just 14 years old.

Judges David Walliams, Alesha Dixon and Amanda Holden were united in praise for the Milton Keynes lad, who delivered a self-penned tune. Bailey went on to make the semi-finals of the competition.

His debut EP Crystalise followed in the summer of 2015 and the mature sounding five-track single release saw the singer-songwriter open up about his battle with depression.

In 2017, **Sarah Ikumu**'s show-stopping rendition of And I Am Telling You, from the movie Dreamgirls, saw her earn the coveted golden-buzzer from Simon

Cowell - fast-tracking the 16-year-old straight through to the live finals of the ITV1 show.

Kaiser Chiefs stopped by now-defunct dining space and bar The Living Room in Milton Keynes for a gig in front of 100 or so drinkers at the start of 2012. Ricky Wilson and his musical cohorts treated the assembled to a set of five songs, including their anthem I Predict A Riot.

The late, great **David Bowie** famously played Milton Keynes Bowl in 1983 and 1990, and the town made its mark on the global superstar, who used to sign off correspondence to his friend Brian Eno with the pseudonym.

Speaking shortly after Bowie's death in January 2016, Brian spoke of his friendship with the star, which had spanned more than 40 years: "Over the last few years – with him living in New York and me in London – our connection was by email," he said.

"We signed off with invented names: some of his were Mr Showbiz, Milton Keynes, Rhoda Borrocks and The Duke of Ear.

Milton Keynes' famous **concrete cows** are celebrities - you can buy your own miniature versions of the bovines, their faces adorn postcards and calendars, and tourists visit MK Museum to meet the acquaintance of artist Liz Leyh's original creations.

So we really shouldn't be surprised to see them popping up on the odd album or single cover; and they are genre defying moo-sic makers too - the cows have featured on releases by the National Youth Jazz orchestra with John Dankworth, by past MK punk-pop players Graveltrap, folk rockers The Cock and Bull Band and Eddie Stanton took their form for the cover of his single, Milton Keynes We Love You.

When people think of music industry hotspots, it's fair to say that Milton Keynes doesn't rank too highly, but it should

In a spin: The concrete cows take centre stage on releases by local artists

do - it is a hotbed for top brands.

Aside from boasting one of the best-known outdoor music venues in the country in The National Bowl, global brand Marshall Amplification has helped put the town on the map, and MK is also home to the UK headquarters of Yamaha and Korg.

"In all seriousness, if you took its association and what it has done for music of all kinds, from manufacturing through to playing, the music industry quite literally wouldn't be what it is today without it," piano ace Rick Wakeman said of Milton Keynes.

"It can only be done in a new town, you can't slot it into old places."

And there we leave this look at some of the music makers and creatives that have contributed to the rich musical fabric of Milton Keynes so far.

But right now, somewhere in MK, the next big track could be a scribbled line on a fag packet, or a riff yet to be recorded.

And that's exciting, right?

Here's to the next chapter of new city noise.

341

343

★★★★★★★★★★★★★★★★★★
★ **WAVENDON** ★
★ **WAP** **ALLMUSIC PLAN** ★
★ presents ★
★ **ALVIN** ★
★ **STARDUST** ★
★ **THE KING OF ROCK** ★
★ **Saturday, 5** ★
★ at 7.30 p ★

'BOWL' IS NOT
A PRIORITY

I WAS really shocked to read in the Gazette that taxpayers' money should be spent on a project like the "Hollywood Bowl" in Milton Keynes. It is surprising that Labour members in the Borough Council have supported this project. What they fail to realise is that there are other priorities which are to be looked into in this area.

People living near Bletchley shopping centre (Duncombe Street, Osborne Street, etc) have been deprived of car parking facilities in their own streets for the years. A circular, along with a form to sent to all the residents in this Bucks County Council

Bletchley Leisure Centre
Milton Keynes
Saturday, 20th January, at 7.30 p
HARRY SECOMBE and Friends
Supported by the BAND of the ROYAL ARTILLE
Tickets £3.00, £2.50, £2.00, £1.00

Friday, 16th February, at 7.30 pm
TINNERS
£1.50, £1.00

17th February
PHONY ORCHESTRA
for the price of one at 6.30 and 8 pm
Malcolm Williamson
NEL FRIEND
ny No. 1, Liszt Piano Concerto No
T SANDERLING
£2.50, £2.00, £1.50

February, at 7.30 pm
'n' Roll Show on Earth
WADDY
SOUNDS FAMILIAR
£3.00, £2.50, £2.00, £1.50

133 CHURCH STREET
WOLVERTON
ARCHER MUSIC
TEL (0908) 316625
would like to announce
**MILTON KEYNES FIRST
ROCK CONTEST**
For amateur and semi-pro rock bands
apply at shop for application form

T-B
boog
out
THE T-Bone
Band boogied
style in crow
capacity
Woughton on S
day night.
The campus theatre
packed and doorme
hopefuls were turned aw
from the farewell gig of t
city's most popular fami
fun band.
Offers of recording con
tracts and concerts had
begun to hog the band
down as individual mem
hers felt the band had gone
they wanted it to.

BLETCHLE
OCTOBER 24th
d try that instrument you've
play : Special offer Vouche
MISSION FREE with ticket. Tickets availab
MARSHALL'S MUSIC
146 Queensway, Bletchley
OBER 24th   7.30 - 10.
ED BAR

3rd WAP
FOLK FESTIVAL
GREAT LINFORD MANOR
MILTON KEYNES
SAT 14 JULY '79·NOON-MIDNIGHT
PRESENTING THE
DUBLINERS
AND
JOE STEAD ★ KATY HEATH
BOB FOX ★ STU LUCKLEY
PAUL DOWNES ★ EARL OKIN
★ BRANDYWINE BRIDGE ★
PAUL FRANCIS ★ MOULTON
MORRIS ★ GEORGE NORRIS
MITHRAS ★ MATT ARMOUR
JEFF WESLEY
TED & MELISSA WILTSIE
AND OTHERS!
CRAFT STALLS · BAR

LEAD SINGER: Tracey Walters

Summer Serenade
in the Gardens of Great Linford Manor
Milton Keynes

Milton Keynes Chamber Orchestra
Conductor Hilary Davan Wetton
Renaissance Dances - Susato
Wind Serenade - Dvorak
English Marches - Haydn
Music for the Royal Fireworks - Handel

Sunday 16 July 1978
730pm for 74½pm

Champagne and strawberries after the concert
included in the set price

Tickets £3 from Frames' Tours, 13 Wolverton Court
Bletchley; James Line, 10 St. John Street, Newport
Pagnell; Aslan Books, High Street, Stony Stratford
or by telephone reservation Milton Keynes 313714
(10 am till 10 pm) no later than Saturday 15th July
Concert only tickets £1.75 at Theatre

Peaches
DISCOTHEQUE
Every Wednesday
Jazz — pm
9 pm till late
From Soul to Rock DJ
JOHN OSBORNE
Wednesday, August
Personal appearance of
State of Grace
That's when we'll be
from
August 17
Miss Wet T Shirt
Competition
ing your own Bikini
bottoms!
PEACHES

Martines *goes live ...*
LIVE ROCK
JULY 29 introducing "HA"
AUGUST 5   "MARCH"...
Dress as you please ... 50p admissi
... Cheap drinks ... over 20's
ANY BANDS INTERESTED IN APPEA
CONTACT RICHARD MORRIS ON (09

Over 80's Night
Peaches
Brunel Centre
Bletchley, M.K.
Tel: M.K. 71411
on
Monday's
Resident Trio & D.J.
9.30 to 1 am
This advertisement admits one
and a guest to our Opening
Night free of charge on
Monday, 13th
October, 1980

★★★★★★★★★★★★★★★★★★
★ **The Craufurd Arm** ★
★ **Stratford Road, Wolverton** ★
★ MILTON KEYNES ★
★ **Friday, 23rd February** ★
★ **BEDROCK ROADSHOW** ★
★ 8 till 11. Admission 50p ★
★ First 10 Females admitted Free ★
★ **Monday, 26th February** ★
★ **THE ERIC BELL BAND** ★
★ (ex-THIN LIZZY) ★
★ Plus DISCS. Admission £1.50 ★
★★★★★★★★★★★★★★★★★★

thful as Samaritans
dle the worried

Anti-Pope band are barred after
Catholic anger boils over

SWAN
SONG
FOR
WAP

EXPRESS LOANS
£1,000-£50,000
HOPETRUST FINANCE
Wm Younger

CELEBRATE
WITH
US!
at
Peaches
1st ANNIVERSARY
PARTY
MONDAY, FEBRUARY 19
TICKETS NOW AVAILABLE!
LOTS OF PRIZES, COMPETITIONS, GIVEAWAYS AND FUN! FUN! FUN!
Peaches Discotheque
Brewers of Younger's Tartan,
Younger's Scotch Bitter and

Coke
adds life to...

PEACHE
1st ANNIVER

Bletchley Leisure Centre
Milton Keynes
SATURDAY, 14th OCTOBER
7.30 pm
HAWKWIND
IN CONCERT
TICKETS £2
Available from Bletchley and Stantonbury Leisure
Centres and Directorate of Recreation, Market Square,
Stony Stratford, Milton Keynes 562144

STANTON
THEATRE
THURSDAY, 17th APRIL, 7.30 pm
STEPHANE GRAPPELLI
with the
DIZ DISLEY TRIO
TICKETS available from 24th March
£1.75   £1.50   £1.25   80p
From: Bletchley Leisure Centre, Princes Way, Blet
ley; Council Offices, 7 Station Road, Newport Pagn
Pagnell; Council Offices, Market Square, Stony Str
ford; Council Offices, Market Square, Stony Stratf
ford; Harry Lecks, 4 Church Street, Stony Stratfor
Information Unit, Milton Keynes Development C
poration, Wavendon Tower, Wavendon, Milton Keyn
(25p reduction for Senior Citizens)
ENQUIRIES: STONY STRATFORD 2371
Presented by the Borough of Milton Keynes
Development Corporation

sic at
Stables
eatre
venden

Sun. Nov. 15 8 p.m.	**JOHN AMIS** (of TV's My Music)	£3.00 £2.50 £1.00
Sat. SOLD OUT	**JOHN DANKWORTH'S QUINTET** Extra perf. Nov 20	£2.50 in advance £3.00 on door
Wed. Nov. 88 10.30 p.m.	**STILGOE THROUGH MIDNIGHT**	£2.50
Sat. SOLD OUT p.m.	**JOHN AND CLEO'S CHRISTMAS GALA** Extra perf. Dec 14	£7.50 £6.00 £4.00

Wavendon Allmusic Plan, The Stables
Wavendon, Milton Keynes MK17 8LT
Box Office Tel: (0908) 583922

347

Image index